The Way Home

The Way
HOME

A COLLECTIVE MEMOIR OF THE
HAZELDEN EXPERIENCE

WITH A FOREWORD BY JUDY COLLINS

HAZELDEN®

Hazelden
Center City, Minnesota 55012-0176
1-800-328-0094
1-612-257-1331 (FAX)
http://www.hazelden.org

Library of Congress Cataloging-in-Publication Data
Solly, Richard.
    The way home : a collective memoir of the Hazelden
    experience / [written by Richard Solly and Yvonne Pearson] ;
    with a foreword by Judy Collins.
        p.   cm.
    Includes index.
    ISBN 1-56838-159-X
    1. Hazelden Foundation.   2. Alcoholics—Rehabilitation—
Minnesota—Case studies.   3. Narcotic addicts—Rehabilita-
tion—Minnesota—Case studies.   4. Recovering alcoholics—
Minnesota—Case studies.   5. Recovering addicts—Min-
nesota—Case studies.   6. Twelve-step programs—Minnesota
—Case studies.   I. Pearson, Yvonne.   II. Title.
HV5281.H39S65   97-28093
362.29'186'0977661—dc21   CIP

00 99 98 97   6 5 4 3 2 1

Book design by Will H. Powers
Cover design by David Spohn
Typesetting by Stanton Publication Services, Inc.

CONTENTS

Foreword

THE CHARACTERS IN THIS BOOK, Andy, Liz, Nate, and Joanna, are all chemically dependent. That is, they are addicted to alcohol and other drugs. The characters' stories are based on the lives of real people who have gotten clean and sober at Hazelden. They have little in common, except one thing: they each suffer from a very democratic illness, a powerful, cunning, and baffling disease. Each has come to Hazelden's treatment program frightened and suffering, and each in his or her own way is lost. All hope for relief, joy, and peace to be restored in their lives.

Some of us know people like the characters in this book. They have traveled an extraordinary road to freedom, a journey of twists and turns, miracles and dark nights, despair and hope.

Having had an analogous journey through Hazelden's family program, I am honored to write the foreword for this inspiring volume. It is a wonderful book, and I hope it will reach those millions of people who know nothing about the illness of chemical dependency and the social and economic impact that it has on our nation. It is an illness that affects the lives of millions of chemically dependent people and their loved ones.

In March 1984 I found myself at Hazelden's family program. I knew all about the family program from a distance through a dear friend who sobered up, then worked at Hazelden. His story was like a myth from an ancient time when heroes slew dragons and rescued maidens. Hazelden hovered in my imagination, no more than an illusion to me for many years.

When I actually found myself at Hazelden, I was frightened, but I was also beginning to gain a sense of hope. I distinctly remember one morning when I awoke around six thirty. The light outside my window was soft and misty with fog. I had a quick breakfast of coffee, fruit, a bran muffin, and apple juice, and then hurried into my black running suit, white shirt, and pink parka. I wanted to get my blood pumping before another day of meetings and lectures in the family program.

I hit a run as soon as I stepped outside. I was running to shake my anxiety, to retain my sanity. I felt as though I was running for my life. The trees along the path are big pines, probably a hundred years old, their green arms stretching to the sky. Chemically dependent people and their families have been running and walking under those branches for decades, feeling the same hopes, the same confusion I was experiencing. My feet pounded beside the majestic trees, and the wind blew off the frozen lake beyond the pines, singing through the tall branches, sighing with a sound I loved so much. The day before, the lake's still-frozen surface had been spotted with fishermen and brightly colored four-wheel-drive trucks. Parka-clad bodies and boxy fish houses were like primitive paintings, tiny still lives in the Minnesota landscape.

I was running down this path because my son was in his third week of what was a five-week program of treatment for chemical dependency at Hazelden. He had finally surrendered after years of using alcohol and other drugs. He told me that Hazelden was the place where he felt he could find the most help. During the previous days, I had already met and shared with many family members and friends of alcoholics and other drug addicts in treatment. Some of these chemically dependent people would stay in treatment for twenty-eight days; some would stay at Hazelden for several months, depending on the degree to which the illness had progressed.

Under the canopy of pine, in the cold, crisp March air, I remembered the rigid anxiety I had experienced when I first arrived at Hazelden. Like the secondary characters in *The Way Home*, I had been relieved on one level about my son's decision to go into treatment. I was also tied in an emotional knot, needing to control, terrified that my son would not stay sober. In the meeting rooms of the family program, I was to hear once more what I already knew: that I could not control my son's sobriety.

I was panting, running as fast as I could. My breath was coming hard. I could feel the tears on my face, some from the cold, some from relief. I prayed under my breath: "God, grant me the serenity." I checked my watch and hurried back to my room where I showered and dressed for the group meetings. The long nights of darkness were over. The sun was shining, at least for that day. And that day, I knew, was all I had.

In the family program, I learned that chemical dependency is not a moral weakness. I learned that addiction is a mental obsession and a physical allergy of the body, a craving over which the alcoholic has little or no control. I learned that all the family members of an alcoholic or other drug addict are affected by this disease. Chemical dependency is, in fact, a family illness.

I also learned that chemical dependency, unlike cancer, high blood pressure, or other diseases, is a self-diagnosed illness. This means that unless the alcoholic admits his or her disease and the need for help, there is little anyone can do for him or her. The family and friends of someone with this illness may think they have control over their loved one's recovery, but they are doomed to disappointment. The truth is, we are all powerless over the illness and recovery.

I learned, however, that regardless of the alcoholic's success at abstinence, family members can recover. We can recover our sense of humor, our emotional balance, our ability to detach with love, and our sanity. I experienced the fellowship, tears, laughter, and concern of other family members. There was a family who had intervened on their father and husband. The mother, daughter, and son had come to heal. I wrote a letter to my father, long dead, and read it out loud to a man who reminded me of my father. We were both able to weep over the past and experience the healing of the present. I felt the camaraderie of survival, the closeness of fellowship.

The lessons I learned in Hazelden's safe, serene environment have helped me as I witness the pain of addiction in some of my colleagues in the entertainment and other high-profile fields. While they may see no way out of their despair, this book serves as a reminder that it is possible to enjoy the gift of life without chemicals. This book breathes of hope for the hopeless.

The stories of the addiction and recovery process in this book, of course, are not the whole story. These are happy endings, because the characters in this book make it through the dark woods. There are millions of happy endings in recovery. But there are others who are not able to stay sober, who die in relapse, who do not recover.

That is why we need more education about addiction to alcohol and other drugs as a treatable disease. We need more places like Hazelden, more understanding of the physical, emotional, and spiritual aspects of chemical dependency. Hazelden, with its wonderful environment that restores the dignity of each individual who enters there, is a home where the suffering, shaking lost soul can find peace, love, and support. As a result, the world is a brighter place for all alcoholics and their families. There is more peace, more love, more joy in the world today because of the work that occurs at Hazelden.

I have to remind readers that this is not only a book about Hazelden. It is a book about the chemically dependent person's journey, not only during treatment but before and after treatment. This book is about "where they were, what happened, and where they are now." I know that the millions who know nothing about this problem that afflicts our nation will profit from reading it. It is a wonderful book about healing.

Judy Collins
APRIL 1997

ACKNOWLEDGMENTS

THE WRITERS wish to express their gratitude first of all to the many extraordinary staff members of Hazelden who opened their offices to us and spent hours of their time patiently answering our questions and instructing us in the many aspects and nuances of treatment for alcoholism and addiction. We wish also to thank the publications committee and especially Damian McElrath, the project director, whose humor and direction helped us through the complex tasks of translating the powerful experience of recovery, and Rebecca Post, who gave us unfailing support and wise guidance in the writing of this book.

We thank the many patients who generously opened their lives to us and let us live their stories with them as we participated in treatment programs. We thank the former patients who shared with us the details of their suffering and transformations. And finally, and most important, we thank the four chief characters. They trusted us with the intimate and profound experiences portrayed in these pages. The writers, Richard Solly and Yvonne Pearson, also wish to express their gratitude to each other for increasing the satisfaction and pleasure of writing this book.

The Way Home

Introduction

THIS BOOK is about a way home. By home we do not, of course, mean a clapboard farmhouse, or a suburban rambler, or a high-rise condominium, but a place of serenity within one's self as comfortable as a favorite room.

Many of us know at least occasions of serenity in our cloudy skies. But people addicted to alcohol and other drugs don't have the slightest relief. They often describe themselves as being uncomfortable in their own skin. This book is about people like that, people who have lived in the alienating territory of addiction and have made the long journey back, people who finally feel at home within themselves.

Stories of addiction abound. They are horror stories, almost beyond imagining for people who have not visited that frightening territory. We hear the stories of successful executives who end up without a place to live, or mothers who cannot stay off crack while they are pregnant, or affluent young adults who quietly drink themselves to death. And we hear tales of people attending Alcoholics Anonymous, going through treatment, coming into touch with their Higher Power, finding their lives again. We read pamphlets about the Twelve Steps, instruction manuals, how-to books. But how do we understand this miracle?

In *The Way Home,* you will witness the miracle through the stories of four people: Andy Monroe comes from New York, a successful journalist who lost his job and his reputation to cocaine and heroin; Joanna Thomsen is a mother of young children, a midwestern suburban housewife who lost a marriage and a potentially stable life to alcohol; Nathaniel Radcliffe is a California high school student with high expectations who saw his grades and his happy connection with his family disappear behind a fog of marijuana smoke; and Elizabeth Toggen, over the course of a lifetime, watched her legal career eroded by the ravages of alcoholism. Although names and details have been changed to preserve their anonymity, these are real people. They have been through treatment at Hazelden, and they represent the many people whose lives have been changed, people who come from all walks of life, students and teachers, laborers and professionals, mothers and fathers, young and old. As you read this book, you will make the arduous journey with these people. But let us first give you a road map of sorts.

In 1935, in Akron, Ohio, Alcoholics Anonymous was founded. Since then, AA has come to be regarded as one of the most significant American grassroots movements in the twentieth century. Its influence has extended throughout the world. When we ask ourselves what has helped to stop the violence on the streets and in families, what program has put more people back to work, what program keeps drunks from driving, what principles have allowed people to adjust to painful past experiences like incest and rape, what force has continuously exerted influence over criminals and convicts, what method has motivated programs for drug abuse in schools—Alcoholics Anonymous and its principles of honesty, openness, and willingness is an important answer.

In 1949, Hazelden recognized the potential power for healing in Alcoholics Anonymous and created one of the first treatment centers in America based on its principles. Along with the Twelve Step program, Hazelden adopted other supportive measures for patients, including medical and mental health treatment. Because alcohol and drug addiction is a disease that erodes every aspect of a human being—the body, the mind, and the soul—treatment must address each of these dimensions. In other words, treatment must be holistic.

The elements regarded as essential to a successful treatment program are education, therapeutic engagement, and fellowship. In this book you will observe patients go through detoxification, eat good food, play, and heal their bodies. You will watch them receive information through lectures, through meetings with counselors, and through conversations with other patients. You will observe as they learn how the disease grips them at a physiological, cellular level; as they participate in treatment and therapy groups and gain insight into their feelings, their reactions, their behavior; and finally, and perhaps most important, as they experience the transformation of connection, a spiritual healing.

The spiritual dimension is the most difficult aspect of healing to articulate and yet is the agency for everything else. Here the medium is indeed the message—the loving care and dedication of the staff, the respect and regard for each human being, the insistence on each patient's responsibility, and ultimately the recognition that they must, and can, rely on a power greater than themselves. For some this is a traditional conception of God; for some this is the love and support of community; and for others it's the wisdom of the universe.

Thousands of people have begun the journey of healing at Hazelden and taken the tools with them into the rest of their lives where they continue to enjoy the blessings of recovery. The people in this book are only four examples. We invite you to live with Andy and Joanna, Liz and Nate, their stories of struggle for recovery, their stories of hope.

1

Twilight

THE MEN AND WOMEN in the bright December dining room stopped talking and turned their attention to Andy Monroe and his friend Nick. The two had walked to the counter together and Nick had picked up the large brass bell and was shaking it vigorously above his head. It rang and resonated. Andy had rung the same bell two years earlier, and now he had come to celebrate and take the ritual walk with his old friend from New York. It plunged Andy into memories: how the wooden handle had felt solid, reassuring in his hand, and how big his smile had been under his baseball cap as the men and women applauded. Some of them, the ones he had lived with for nearly four months on the Jellinek unit, stood, hooted, and clapped louder.

The bell sounding through the dining halls two years ago had announced Andy's last meal at the Hazelden treatment center in Center City, Minnesota. Later that evening he left for Fellowship Club, a halfway house in St. Paul, still a thousand miles and four more months away from his home in New York. The ringing bell had announced not only his departure but also his arrival into a new life, a life without alcohol or drugs.

Andy accompanied Nick into the other dining room, where the women in primary treatment were eating dinner. Joanna Thomsen heard the bell and grimaced. The rest of the women in the room turned from their food to acknowledge Nick, to clap for him and for their own hopes as well. But Joanna was new to treatment. She had arrived at Hazelden's Lilly unit for primary treatment only yesterday, and all she could think of was her baby and her husband. She shut her eyes and could see Molly lying in the crib in her blue teddy bear pajamas, her auburn hair curled in disarray. She could feel again the sleepy weight of her baby's body when she held her one last time, before saying good-bye.

Her husband, Jeff, had laid out a blanket and pillow in the backseat of the blue Ford so Joanna could sleep while they drove the three hours from La Crosse, Wisconsin, to Center City. They left before sunup, and the cold air had jarred her awake. Now, as she sat at the institutional dining room table among strangers clapping at the sound of an annoying bell, all she could think of was making a plan to get out of this place in time for Molly's first birthday next week. She could not comprehend that in one short month she would be standing in this place, feeling some of the same excitement that Andy and his friend seemed to be feeling.

Years earlier, Andy had felt as hopeless as Joanna felt now. The bell he had rung then had signaled devastation instead of triumph. It was a tiny white doorbell to a Harlem apartment. And once inside, there were other sounds that ravaged his life: the sound of crack cocaine sizzling like bacon in a glass pipe, the scratch of the steel rod that scraped residue from inside the glass, the click of the lighter and hiss of the butane burner. Later, there was the shatter of a breaking lamp, the flat thud when Andy was thrown across the room, the angry shouts, ambulance and police sirens—all sounds of a life being torn apart. During the last week of February 1992, after he had lost his job and was locked out of his house, Andy boarded a plane for Hazelden and began the long journey to recovery that would allow him to be in the dining room this December evening.

Now Andy was watching Nick lower his arm and hold the bell at his side. The applause abated, and everyone resumed eating. He put the large brass bell back on the cafeteria counter, alongside the bins of forks and knives and spoons, where the next graduate would take the reassuring handle in his or her hands. All of the men and women in the dining room would have a chance to ring the bell and announce to everyone listening that they too were coming back to life. Though some would relapse, the current ringing was a celebration. Hope resonated in the room.

The Warnings

Andy knew well before he came to treatment how dangerous alcohol and drugs could be. He'd written an article on addiction as a journalist for a weekly newspaper in Scarsdale, New York, where he lived and worked. "Alcoholism is literally a matter of life and death for the people whose lives it touches," Andy wrote. For another newspaper, he had researched a lengthy front-page article on alcoholism and a treatment center in Rhinebeck, New York, where he himself would spend weeks in rehab two years later. Poring over books, journals, and magazines, Andy learned that alcoholism and drug abuse cause over fifty thousand deaths on the road each year; that at least 45 percent of people charged with violent crimes, robberies, burglaries, and theft tested positive for the use of drugs; and that there were more deaths, illnesses, and disabilities from substance abuse than from any other preventable health condition. Still, none of these statistics and their implied warnings had been convincing enough to keep him off drugs. Not even the death of his own father.

Andy admitted his father to Cleveland Clinic in June 1990. He had returned for the summer to the Cleveland suburb of Beachwood, where he grew up, to help his mother care for his father, who was dying from alcoholism. It was a Tuesday evening when he drove his dad to the hospital. During the next three months, Andy watched as the veins in his father's esophagus erupted and hemorrhaged, his stomach distended when his liver could no longer process salt, and his skin became jaundiced. The coma that followed was a nightmare of unrest and silence. Andy was sleeping on a cot in the hospital room the night his father's breathing became raspy and shallow. As his father took his last breath, Andy said to himself, *If I don't stop drinking and using drugs, I'm going to die like this too.*

Andy was thirty at the time of his father's death. Convinced that he wanted a better life than what his father had, he promised himself, during his dad's last summer, he would never pick up another drink or score drugs. All through the burial arrangements, the wake at the funeral parlor, and the services at St. Timothy's Church, where he once served Mass as an altar boy, he never drank. He hardly thought about it.

After the requiem mass and the procession of cars to the cemetery where his father was buried beside Andy's sister, who had died eight years earlier from cancer, Andy and his mother held a service at their home. Friends, relatives, and his father's business acquaintances came to offer condolences. Andy sat on the front steps with two cousins. He watched them sip wine. He knew he couldn't join them, and he didn't want to. Still, two nights later, he walked over to his father's liquor cabinet, opened the small glass doors, and took out the bottle of vodka. He gripped the bottle tightly, unscrewed the cap.

One wonders how Andy could watch his father convulse in a coma as the result of alcoholism, and still open the vodka, knowing it would put him back on his father's path. For someone who has not experienced it, understanding the power of addiction is like trying to understand a foreign language by watching the speaker's hand gestures and facial expressions. You can only get approximations, brief glimpses, of the reality. Addiction is a disease, an overwhelming compulsion, a language even the addict or alcoholic doesn't comprehend.

When Andy saw the vodka in the cabinet, it was as if his hand worked independently of his brain. He grabbed the bottle before he had a chance to think, looked at it in his hand, felt his stomach tighten with the effort to resist, and thought, *I should put this back*. He could taste it on his tongue, feel its warmth in his chest, feel the lightness it would bring him. *What the hell*, he thought, and poured himself a glass.

Andy couldn't say "no" to the vodka that night. Nor could he say "no" to the crack that he would score months later. No amount of self-discipline, knowledge, or understanding could keep Andy—or fifteen million other people in the United States who are chemically dependent—from alcohol or drugs.

Hiding Ourselves

When Joanna heard the clattering of the bell that Nick was ringing in the dining room, all she could take in was the chaos of a distant world. She didn't see how the wind rippled the snowdrift into a wave outside the window, nor did she notice the dramatic purple earrings Libby wore or the way Cassie fiddled with her blond hair as she talked. The four other women sitting at the table tried to draw her into their conversation, but she barely responded. "I'm from Chicago," she said through a compliant smile. Then she picked up her tray and left the dining room.

Joanna was binge drinking the week before she arrived for treatment—her second treatment. She had two months of sobriety before that decisive week. It was a Wednesday evening, and she was home alone, as usual. About four o'clock she went through the house turning on all the lights so she wouldn't have to walk into any dark rooms later and be surprised. It had been ten years since the man had jumped her from behind the bushes when she was walking to her apartment, but the fear still stalked her. She put her daughter, Molly, to bed about seven, and then called Jeff at his office. When her husband told her he wouldn't be home until later that evening, she sat down in front of the TV to wrap Christmas presents and watch CNN.

A little drink to keep me company while I wrap all these damn presents would be nice, she said to herself. During her last binge, she had hidden a bottle of vodka at the bottom of a box of old rags in the basement. She went down and got it. Later, as she sat sipping her lemonade and vodka and wrapping a green silk blouse for Jeff's mom, she was struck with a brilliant idea. The next morning, she could wrap bottles of vodka as Christmas presents, label them for herself as gifts from friends, and put them under the tree.

Thursday morning Joanna spread dry Cheerios on the high-chair table for Molly and set out a plastic cup with a couple inches of milk in it. She glanced at last night's empty vodka glass sitting by the sink and turned quickly away. She really didn't want to lose control this time. It was almost Christmas. She rinsed the glass and put it in the dish-washer, clasped her arms around her chest, and started pacing. No, she wouldn't pour herself a vodka. She heard a clatter and turned to find that Molly had tipped her plastic cup upside down, and milk dribbled from the high chair to the floor. Joanna glanced again at the sink where the vodka glass had been two minutes before, and then rushed at Molly. She pulled her out of the high chair and scolded. "No! That is not what you do with milk." Molly's screech went through Joanna like electricity. She set Molly on the floor and paced back and forth. She knew how she could calm herself. She went downstairs and returned with the vodka bottle. Joanna poured herself the last glass and sighed with relief.

After Molly was finished eating, Joanna lifted her from the high-chair, dressed her in a snowsuit, and went to the grocery store. It was easy to hide her liquor since she could buy it at the grocery stores in Illinois. She stocked up on one-gallon bottles of vodka and several fifths. By the time Jeff came home, an array of beautiful new packages nestled under the tree. Packages with rocking Santas and cream-colored Madonnas disguised her vodka purchases. Joanna also hid one large bottle behind the laundry detergent in the basement. Her husband wouldn't find it there since he never did the laundry.

Joanna was not only hiding vodka bottles from others, but she was also hiding the bottles—her addiction—from herself. That afternoon, while doing the laundry, Joanna drank heavily from the bottle hidden behind the detergent. By seven, she decided to lie down for a nap. She had planned to wake up in an hour and put her daughter to bed. She wouldn't admit to herself that she had passed out; she simply slept the entire night.

When she awoke Friday morning, the house was quiet. It was late enough that the sun was shining through the bedroom windows. Her head felt swollen, her mouth parched. Even her eyes seemed puffy and dry. She struggled into her bathrobe and shuffled in her slippers to the nursery.

The crib was empty. Joanna stood still for a moment and stared. *Where was Molly? Was she hurt?* She ran to the kitchen and found no one. Joanna's heart was thumping. She ran to the living room, then downstairs to the family room. The house was utterly quiet and empty. *Oh please God, let Molly be safe*, she thought. She rushed back to Molly's room, threw open the closet door, and breathed a sigh of relief. Her diaper bag was gone, and so was her snowsuit and her blanket. That meant Jeff had taken her to Joanna's mom's. Jeff had done this before during Joanna's blackouts. *I should call my mother*, thought Joanna, *but if I do, I'm going to get a lecture. All that really matters is that Molly's safe.* Instead, she walked to the Christmas tree and pulled out one of the gifts to herself.

Jeff called sometime in the afternoon, said yes, of course, he'd taken Molly to her grandmother's. They would pick her up the next morning and drive to his parents' house in La Crosse for Christmas Eve. And by the way, he'd scheduled her to enter Hazelden's treatment center on Christmas Day. Joanna's stomach flip-flopped. She was cornered. She mixed another vodka and lemonade.

The next time she awakened, it was dark again. The digital clock radio sitting next to the bed read ten o'clock. Jeff wasn't beside her. He must have fallen asleep in the family room. She felt sick. Dehydration was like a bad case of the flu. Her eye sockets were dry and her joints ached. Her arms seemed to tremble. Joanna struggled downstairs to the tree to get a vodka pick-me-up. She froze. All the packages were gone. She pushed herself to think clearly, then walked to the kitchen, opened the pantry door, and shoved aside the packages of pasta until she saw the six cans of Campbell's mushroom soup. She quickly lifted the one on the far left. Two months ago she had cut the bottom out of the can, emptied the soup, and washed the inside. Then she had placed it carefully back on the shelf over a baby-food jar filled with vodka. Six of them in a row prepared for just such an emergency as this. But the jar was gone. She lifted the next can and the next. Nothing. She went to the front closet and grabbed her purse; Jeff had taken her keys and her money.

By this time she was feeling panic. Once before, when she'd gone cold turkey, she had experienced a seizure. She was afraid it would happen now. She was damp all over. She saw flashing lights; she couldn't focus. Her head was throbbing, and worst of all, she couldn't seem to connect her brain to her muscles. She began to think through each movement. *Walk to the family room*, she told herself. *Go over to the pullout couch. Now kneel down slowly.* Jeff was snoring. *Slide your right hand into Jeff's pocket. Feel for the keys, for the money*, she told herself. *That's right. Slowly, slowly.*

It took an eternity. Time was as frozen as the December snow.

After she had eased the keys and money out of his pocket, she drove to the convenience store for more vodka. By midnight she was back, mixing a glass of lemonade in the kitchen. But where had she set the bag with the vodka? Oh yes. On the counter. She struggled to the family room again to make sure Jeff was still sleeping, then went back to add the vodka to the lemonade. As she gulped the drink, the vodka burned in her throat. She loved the tingle over her skin. Within minutes she could think again, move again. She was normal. She cleaned up the kitchen, then packed bags for herself, Molly, and Jeff for the Christmas Eve trip the next day. She hid the remaining vodka in the black leather bag she used for magazines and cosmetics when they traveled, the one she kept in the car with her. Finally, she crawled into bed and fell into an exhausted sleep.

The Elevator Down

By the following summer, in Scarsdale, New York, a year after his father's death, Andy had returned to smoking crack, though only once a week, usually on a Saturday night. But he hadn't had a drink since that night after his father's funeral. He was nearly convinced that staying sober for over a year meant not only his alcohol problem but also his drug problem was under control. He reasoned that he was now using crack moderately. Since his treatment two years earlier at the facility in Rhinebeck, Andy was sure that he could control his own use of drugs and alcohol.

In September 1991, Andy started a new job as the associate editor for a travel magazine with a circulation of over eighty thousand readers, primarily travel agents and tour operators. He moved to Little Neck, Queens, a bedroom community, to be closer to work, shortening his subway ride. He rented a beautiful three-bedroom house with two other young men, both brothers, on a street lined with tall elms and gnarly oaks that created a colorful canopy of leaves over the lane during fall.

Now, living in a beautiful home in Queens and with work that would send him on winter trips to the Caribbean, he told himself he had every reason to stay off drugs.

His first assignment was in Montserrat, a small island in the eastern Caribbean, just southwest of Antigua. Three years before, Hurricane Hugo ravaged Montserrat. The government had rebuilt and now hoped to lure tourists back to the picturesque island of lush tropical foliage, rugged landscape, and dramatic views of seascapes from new hillside villas. The government had invited a group of travel writers and tour guides in hopes they would favorably review the island in their magazines. Andy's two roommates patted him on the back when they heard of his dream gig.

The Montserrat government provided Andy and a group of writers from international publications with first-class airfare from New York City. Soon after the plane lifted off, a stewardess asked the passengers in first class what they wanted to drink. All the writers ordered alcoholic drinks. Andy didn't want to drink, but he didn't want to draw attention to his sobriety. He was embarrassed by being an alcoholic. He reassured himself that one drink wouldn't hurt.

The sound of the ice cubes clinking when he lifted the glass to his mouth made him feel almost giddy. He relaxed and started talking with the other writers on board. The flight took nearly three hours, and before the plane landed, Andy was lifting shot glasses of whiskey, one after the other, to toast the government of Montserrat.

For the entire week, while visiting different villas, Andy drank dark beers, rum, cognac, and whiskey. After a few days, what he drank no longer mattered, only that he drank. One morning he woke up with a fierce hangover. The notes he took for the article he was expected to write seemed uninspired to him. He walked down to the villa's narrow black sand beach, dropped into a chair, and shoved his feet in the cool sand. He brought a drink with him, figuring it would help him feel better. After a few minutes, he felt bites on his feet and ankles. He looked down and saw sand fleas. As he scratched and flicked them off, he glanced out to sea, wondering why he felt so uncomfortable on this island where he was meant to relax in comfort.

When the plane landed back at La Guardia Airport, another writer asked Andy if he wanted to share the taxi fare to Manhattan. He lied and told the writer he was going to visit a friend. Instead, he dropped off his luggage and got on the train to Harlem.

After boarding, Andy found a window seat and stared out the window, not wanting to be recognized. He tapped his feet under the seat in front of him. As the miles passed, the landscape outside began deteriorating. The expensive high-rise condominiums began to vanish as simple brick row houses and tenements appeared. He spotted more and more empty lots along the railroad lines. In one lot, a group of men stood around a trash can with flames leaping out of it. Graffiti, written in large bold lettering, appeared on station walls as the train sped past. Andy was still wearing his sport coat, tie, white shirt, and expensive slacks. He took off his tie, rolled it up, and shoved it into his pants pocket.

When Andy got off the train, he took a gypsy cab, an unregistered car operated privately since few commercial cab companies would drive from the upper east side to the upper west side where Andy was headed. The cab driver laughed when Andy told him that he had just returned from a weeklong stay at a Caribbean island. "What the hell you doing here?" the driver asked. Andy couldn't answer.

If addiction to alcohol and other drugs is an elevator, this was Andy's last chance to get off before it snapped from its cables, hurtling him down at an unbelievable speed. When Andy got out of the cab in front of a dilapidated brownstone apartment, he felt light-headed and giddy. The expectation of cocaine often made him dizzy. Trembling and sweaty, he would feel a sudden rush lifting his stomach. He felt distressed. Andy was getting "thirsty," a term crack addicts use to describe the craving for cocaine.

Andy tipped the cab driver and slammed the car door behind him. He stood in front of the brownstone. Next door was an abandoned apartment building, an empty lot stood across the street. He walked up the few broken stone stairs and rang the bell a number of times. "All right, all right!" a young woman hollered over the intercom.

He could see Sally coming down the long hallway. He always called her Sal. Everyone in the neighborhood did too. She was wearing tight, unwashed jeans, a stained, white halter top, and sandals. When she opened the door and let him in, Andy smiled. Her dark brown eyes had circles under them. He wondered who she might have been sleeping with while he was gone.

She knew why he rang the bell impatiently. It was Friday. Andy would spend the weekend with her, and they would smoke crack together. He never paid any rent to Sal, but he always bought her cocaine when he spent the weekends. He followed her down to her apartment. He wouldn't say anything about his fear of contracting HIV or AIDS from her. It troubled him at moments, like now, as he entered the apartment.

He explained to her that he must leave for home Sunday night. He couldn't risk calling in sick on Monday at the magazine as he had done occasionally at other jobs.

Two days later, that Sunday, he did leave Sal's.

The Phone Call: Admitting Defeat

Four months later, on January 27, he once again arrived in Harlem, only this time with $1,500 cash in his pocket.

Shivering, he stood at the steel door of an abandoned brownstone, a few doors down from Sal's. The condemned building, called "the spot," was used for dealing crack. Andy approached a young man who couldn't have been more than fifteen years old, one of the lookouts who worked around the clock, pacing back and forth in front of the building. Andy asked if Glamor was working. Andy knew he was. The young man, who watched for police, wouldn't have been there if Glamor wasn't working.

Andy walked up the steps, pounded once, then stooped down toward the space below the door, hollering, "Gimme four." He slipped a twenty dollar bill under the door. Back in Queens, this purchase would have cost him sixty bucks. He took a strange delight in feeling he somehow beat the system by paying so much less in Harlem than the other middle-class silver-spoon addicts in Connecticut. He was right. Crack costs much less in Harlem, but scoring is much more dangerous.

Four bullet-shaped, purple-capped plastic vials slid out from under the door. Andy picked them up. Each vial was filled with six little rocks of crack cocaine. Later, he would give them, instead of flowers, as a surprise gift to Sal when she answered the buzzer. Before that day would end, Andy and Sal would smoke over three hundred dollars' worth of crack.

He often shared his crack and smoked "blasts," six pebbles of crack in a pipe. His money went fast. Andy never slept, smoking one pipe full of crack after another. The lights in Sal's apartment were kept off because the glare felt so intense and disturbing to him. When another addict rang Sal's bell, Andy covered his ears. Every sensation was magnified on cocaine. Even the crinkling of bedsheets sounded too loud. Only the first inhale of crack, its rush into the lungs, sending what felt like electrical charges radiating through his body, sexualizing every gesture and glance, felt good. It had to be repeated over and over, every hour, day after day. After four days, ninety-six straight hours without sleep, Andy passed out. When he awoke, he ate, showered, and discovered he was broke.

It was now Tuesday, and he had already missed two days of work. He had planned to spend only the weekend in Harlem at Sal's and be back at work Monday morning. Though he hadn't called or notified anyone, he strangely reasoned that it didn't matter. He was an exceptional writer and employee. He would call tomorrow and make some excuse. Then, all would be forgiven. But his elevator was already free-falling, soon to crash.

For Andy, all that mattered now was scoring more cocaine.

The travel magazine had given Andy a corporate American Express credit card with unlimited credit to purchase airline tickets and pay for hotels and villas, taxis, and meals while traveling in the Caribbean. He assumed that he could use the credit card and pay off the bill before the company discovered what he was doing. He took four drug dealers,

members of the Bullet Top Gang, with him to a store where he pur-
chased over five hundred dollars' worth of expensive sneakers for them.
In exchange, the dealers gave him forty vials of crack. As days passed, he
made more purchases in exchange for drugs: leather coats, Timberland
boots, jewelry, and audio equipment.

Then Glamor himself, the leader of the Bullet Top Gang, asked
Andy for two walkie-talkie sets priced at $475 a piece. Each set included
a waist pack, hidden microphone, and earpiece, the kind Secret Service
agents used. Glamor wanted them so his dealers could broadcast pickup and drop-off times to each other. Andy traveled to Times Square to
buy the two sets. However, on his return, he gave Glamor only one set,
keeping the other until he received his payment of drugs.

Two nights passed and Andy still hadn't been paid. He found
Glamor and five of his crew at the local pizza parlor. "You better watch
out," Andy said to the gang leader. "The other walkie-talkie is tuned to
your frequency. You never know who might be listening in."

Glamor shook his head in disbelief. He nodded to his crew, and five
men, all in their late teens and early twenties, muscular and agile, instantly jumped Andy. They knocked him to the floor and kicked him
repeatedly. Any one of the five could have easily pulled out a gun and
shot him.

Days later, the gang members would beat Andy a second time in Sal's
apartment, leaving lamps broken and chairs turned over. Sal wanted
Andy out. He had stayed too long, over two weeks, and wasn't able to
provide Sal with a regular supply of crack, since the magazine had can-
celed his credit card. Back in Long Island, a felony charge was filed
against him, and his roommates had changed the locks to the house.

Outside, he could hardly walk. It had been fifteen days since Andy
had taken the train to Harlem. Fifteen days of bingeing and smoking
crack. Fifteen days and over $6,000 fraudulently charged to a credit
card. Fifteen days that produced numerous phone calls from his employer to his roommates and a formal eviction from his house. After
Andy had been absent for six workdays, his employer sent a registered
letter stating that a nonresponse would be accepted as a resignation. In
effect, Andy was fired. He had lost more than his job, his friends, and
family. He had lost his soul.

After fifteen days, the only hope left on a snowy evening in February was in a phone booth. It was after midnight when he called. He

prayed his father would answer, would return from the dead at this moment to help him. Instead, his mother picked up the line. She had been looking for him, she said. She sounded as if it were a medical emergency. And it was.

The Invisible Line

In northern Illinois in June, the twilight lasts forever. Day deepens so slowly into night that Joanna often wouldn't notice the darkness until lightning bugs started flashing. When she was a girl, her family lived in a big, white clapboard house. Her father, who taught high school social studies, picked up odd jobs in the summer. Often he'd paint houses. When he arrived home, Joanna's mother would have dinner ready—tuna-macaroni salad and lemonade, or maybe meat loaf and mashed potatoes and peas. After dinner, in the summer evenings that seemed to stretch out forever, Joanna and her two sisters would play on the big wraparound porch. It faced west, and her parents would often sit in the porch swing sipping gin and tonics and talking about Aunt Jenny's new Chevrolet or Mayor Kraus' plan to open a new hardware store.

Slowly the sun would lower in the sky, until it reached that point, just above the horizon, when its light turned the cathedral elm in the front yard a golden green and bathed the grass in the same mysterious, beckoning color. It was Joanna's favorite time of day. Until suddenly her mother would say, "Okay girls, time to turn into pumpkins," and Joanna would discover that the sun had disappeared entirely.

It was a long way from that Illinois porch to the vodka concealed under the Christmas tree, and though the experiences of Andy and Joanna may seem extraordinary, even bizarre, they are the experiences of thousands of people who have lived ordinary lives. Andy grew up in a quiet Cleveland suburb and played baseball at Cranwood Park on summer afternoons. His father owned a small tool and die company. His mother worked part-time at a local grocery store and was busy taking care of her children.

Andy was a good student, graduated from Columbia University, and landed a solid journalism job. Joanna and Andy were no different from other chemically dependent people. Addiction strikes people from all walks of life, from the rich to the poor, from the highly educated to the illiterate, all races and a variety of ages. It is a no-fault disease and occurs in all types of families. It sneaks up on people, people who begin to drink or use drugs in settings and patterns consistent with society's habits and values. They are social drinkers, they have a drink once in a while to calm their nerves, they enjoy a few beers on the weekend. For many people, drinking stays at this level, but for a significant group, the frequency and amount of drinking climb slowly. The process of becoming addicted is often subtle, and one day an invisible line has been crossed. Alcohol or drugs have taken control.

Joanna began to drink beer on weekends in high school to ease her shyness. Four or five sips and she'd feel herself loosen up: her shoulders, her hips, her feet, even her smile. A weekend drinker, too, at the University of Wisconsin at Madison, she was part of a crowd that started on Thursdays and didn't stop until Sunday night. Early in her sophomore year, late on a Friday night, she and her two roommates sat at a bar with two seniors they'd just met. Her roommates were charged, giggling, pulling the guys up to the dance floor. But Joanna couldn't get into it. She had drunk five Heinekens, not as much as usual, not enough to slur her words, but enough to give her a bit of bravado. The beers had made her sleepy, and she wanted to walk home despite the late hour.

She grabbed her jacket from the back of her chair, threaded her way through the crowded tables, and pushed the door open. The moon was almost full and bright enough to cast soft shadows on the sidewalk. She walked east, past the two-story stucco houses, most of them filled with Madison students. The maples were just starting to turn yellow. She could hear music coming from houses along the way. It was chilly, and she began to shiver. She picked up her pace.

A block from home the maples were replaced by hedgerows that obscured the bottom half of the duplexes. She began to walk more quickly still, when suddenly she felt rough fingers gripping her neck. "Just keep walking," said a deep voice. A man brought his right arm from behind her and held a knife in front of her chin. The moonlight reflected from the four-inch blade. After an initial burst of panic, Joanna went numb. "Where do you live?" he demanded. She led him to the small apartment on the first floor of a duplex.

After the rape, he warned her not to tell anyone, said he knew where she lived and where her family lived, and ran out the front door.

As soon as the door slammed behind him, the fear she had shut out overpowered her. She shook violently, sweating and crying. She dragged the telephone into the hall, sat down on the floor, and dialed her sister, who lived just a few blocks away. But she didn't tell her. All she told her was that she was spooked. Someone was scratching on the screen window and she was scared. When her roommates walked in and wanted to know why she was crying, she said she'd been assaulted outside but had gotten away. *If I hadn't been drunk*, she thought to herself, *it wouldn't have happened.*

For weeks afterward, she received mail addressed in crayon, the handwriting like that of a child. The first letter said, "Don't go to the police. You will be sorry. I am watching you." One evening the phone rang; Joanna was expecting a friend. When she picked up the phone, her body suddenly stiffened at the sound of the voice. "I'm watching you," it said. She slammed down the receiver.

She continued to drink, perhaps even increased her drinking, but no longer to ease her shyness. Before the rape, drinking let her mingle more comfortably at parties. Now it eased her fear and shame. Eventually, after she married Jeff, who traveled extensively, she would also drink to ease her loneliness. But there was no moment, no week, no month that anyone could put a finger on, when Joanna came to be an alcoholic. Sometime during the next few years, as slowly as summer days move into night, Joanna crossed the thin, slippery line between social drinking and alcoholism, between problem drinking and addiction.

Later, Joanna would come up with reasons why she became alcoholic: shyness, pressure to be popular, a brutal assault, an intense fear of being alone, depression, marriage to a graduate student and then life with a toxicologist who was absent frequently, shame of not being good enough. Joanna had read about possible contributing factors to alcoholism: family dynamics, personality makeup, peer pressure, depression, anxiety, or other emotional problems. They all fit for her in one way or another. In *The New York Times* she had read about growing evidence that some people carry a genetic vulnerability to addiction that may make using alcohol or drugs more dangerous for them. Later she would realize that her father was probably an alcoholic too. But whatever the reasons, alcoholism is often stealthy. Like Andy, Joanna did not set out to be an alcoholic or drug addict, nor did she realize what was happening.

For Joanna the twilight lasted a long time. It was years before she opened her eyes and realized the world around her had turned dark.

Out of Control

Joanna had been through treatment in Chicago shortly before she got pregnant, and it was easy to stay off booze then. Jeff opened his own office and had plenty of work. They were able to buy a house in a Chicago suburb, and Joanna helped organize Jeff's accounts, setting up her own desk in the big sunroom. She spent the rest of her time keeping the house immaculate, cooking perfect meals, and preparing for the baby. For the nursery, she chose elephant-print wallpaper, cream-colored carpet, bright green curtains, and a crib with a matching green canopy.

She put a rocking chair with a green gingham pillow by the east window, and when the morning sun flooded the room, she would sit in the rocker and pore over her collection of baby books: Penelope Leach, Benjamin Spock, T. Berry Brazelton. One afternoon, she sat in the rocking chair and read about the devastation of fetal alcohol syndrome, about how it can cause mental retardation and malformation. There were pictures of babies with small heads, narrow eyes, flat noses, thin upper lips. "Babies with this syndrome may have damaged bones, muscles, skin, eyes, heart, and sex organs, and they tend to be irritable and hyperactive." It made Joanna realize how lucky she was that she had stayed away from alcohol during her pregnancy.

If the nursery lost its pristine beauty after Molly arrived, it acquired a chaotic vitality: stuffed animals and blankets, books, bottles, wails, sighs, and laughter. Joanna was lost in this new life, wandering from diaper pail to kitchen to nursery. Although the dark's unwelcome surprises still haunted her, she would forget to walk through the house in the evening turning on all the lights. Often, at midday, she would nap with Molly. Joanna would lie on the queen-sized bed in her and Jeff's room, nurse Molly, then lay Molly on her own chest, her face nestled sideways into Joanna's neck. She could feel Molly's tiny breaths on her skin. She worried something would happen to Molly, to Jeff, something would happen to take this away from her. Joanna had never been so happy and so sad in her life.

Five weeks after Molly was born, on February 15, Jeff called from the office to tell Joanna his buddies had invited him to go to Arizona on a golfing trip. She tapped her nails on the kitchen counter. How long would they be gone? Four days? Jeff hadn't been gone overnight since she'd gotten out of treatment. If she showed any fear of staying home alone, he would get irritated. She kept her voice soft and even. His golfing was important to him, and he hadn't traveled the entire time she was pregnant. The stress of work was terrible, and he had to get away from time to time, he reminded her. And he'd take her and the baby on a trip in March. Maybe they'd go to Florida. She'd be fine. Yes, she agreed, she'd be fine. Molly was sleeping through some nights now, and Joanna wasn't quite so exhausted. Besides, she could take Molly to Mom's if need be.

Joanna pulled some chicken breasts from the freezer to thaw for dinner. Her throat felt tight. She wondered if all the windows were locked, if she should sleep with the light on while Jeff was gone. She thought, *It's been almost a year since I've had a drink. I know I could have just a couple of vodkas to keep myself together. I know I can stop after that.*

When Molly woke up from her nap, Joanna went to the store for a bottle of vodka and had two drinks while she fixed dinner. She felt the familiar loosening of her shoulders, her hips. It was going to be so much easier now to show Jeff how cool she was about his leaving for a few days. The next morning, she decided to have a couple drinks to get her through the day.

She ran downstairs, grabbed a large crystal water glass, and filled it with some vodka. Then she added lemonade. She tilted it back and downed it quickly, followed by one more. After that, she decided, she would stop. Molly was lying in a bouncer on the floor beside her, and Bill Clinton's voice was coming from the television in the next room, where the morning show was making a steady hum. Life was good, and she was not going to ruin it with alcohol. She reached out and poured one more strong drink. That would be it.

When she and Molly woke up from their morning nap, she nursed the baby, changed her diaper, laid her safely in the middle of the queen-size bed, and went back down to the kitchen for a drink of water. She noticed the vodka bottle sitting on the counter. It was only half full now, and she felt panic. She couldn't think about Molly lying in the middle of her bed upstairs, or Jeff coming home in a few hours; she couldn't think about supper or about a trip to Florida in March. All she could think about was what would happen when the other half of the bottle was gone. She swallowed hard, reached out for the crystal drinking glass, and poured a little more this time.

When Jeff came home from work at five o'clock, Molly would be in her crib and Joanna would be passed out on the living room sofa. Joanna would have no more than six weeks of continuous sobriety during the next year, and by Christmas, she would be bingeing every three weeks. The lightning bugs had begun to flicker again, but Joanna's eyes weren't open to see them.

2

Taming the Storm

JOANNA ARRIVED at the Center City campus of Hazelden on Christmas Day. A fresh snow decorated the pines that edge the long road leading to the treatment center, a sprawling complex of low-slung buildings. Later that night, a full moon would outline a deer pausing on the expanse of lawn that opened onto South Center Lake. A red fox would stop among the pine trees to watch the brick buildings, their sliding glass doors shut against snow-filled patios. Joanna would not be able to see this from her room on the medical unit, nor would it have mattered if she could. Joanna wouldn't notice anything but the shaking caused by withdrawal, the queasy pit in her stomach, and her aching joints.

Jeff shut off the car engine, and Joanna sat up, pushed her hair out of her face; her palm was sweaty against her cheek. The sun was blindingly bright, and the cold air rushed in when Jeff opened the back door for her. She pulled her blue parka closer and climbed out of the car. She almost slipped on the ice, but caught herself. Jeff was already at the trunk pulling out her black overnight case, and the big blue suitcase they had borrowed from his parents a year ago. He walked back toward her, a case in each hand. "You okay?" he asked.

"Umm." Together they walked the fifty feet from the car to the double glass doors. Once inside, the warmth of the building enveloped them.

"Hello," said the woman they met in admissions, an older woman with graying hair. "Can I help you?" Joanna thought to act excited to be there so that Jeff would believe she was serious. She tried to smile when Jeff introduced them. They answered some initial questions, and then a nurse took them through the next door into Ignatia, the medical unit where patients enter Hazelden and spend the first twenty-four hours. The medical unit was, like all the Hazelden treatment units, named after a pioneer of addiction treatment. This particular unit was named after Sister Ignatia, a nun who helped Dr. Bob, cofounder of Alcoholics Anonymous, secure medical treatment for alcoholics in St. Thomas Hospital in Akron, Ohio. In Hazelden's Ignatia unit, a doctor would give Joanna a physical examination to evaluate whether she was medically appropriate for treatment. Then, like so many other entering patients, she would have to go through detoxification.

The nurse asked Jeff to leave Joanna's luggage inside the doorway next to the nurses' station, and led them to room 27, where Joanna would stay, directly across from the station. Next to the room stood an artificial Christmas tree with tiny blinking lights: red, green, yellow, blue, and white. As Joanna followed Jeff into the room, she wanted to pull the plug.

Jeff helped her off with her parka and hung it in the closet in her room.

"Jeff," the nurse said as she turned toward him, "would you like to wait here while I take Joanna's vital signs and ask her a few questions? You could have a cup of coffee in the lounge."

Joanna turned toward Jeff, grabbed his arm. "Don't leave me." Her voice was small, almost a whimper.

"This will only take a few minutes, Joanna." The feeling of competence surrounding the nurse would have been reassuring in most circumstances. Her voice was gentle. "I am so glad you've come. I think you'll like it here very much."

Joanna's face was drawn; the large circles under her eyes looked like charcoal. She nodded her head in agreement. She wanted Jeff to believe that she agreed with the nurse, even though she was thinking, *There's no way. I'm not staying. I just have to get a plan together.*

Looking over her shoulder at Jeff, she obediently followed the nurse to a small room with a desk, a couple of chairs, and a blood pressure gauge. The nurse asked her a few questions about her alcohol use, asked when she last had a drink. "Three days ago," Joanna lied. Though the nurse could smell alcohol on her breath, she wrote Joanna's answer as she gave it. She then took her temperature, which was slightly elevated at 99.6°; her pulse was 120 beats per minute; and her blood pressure was high—140/100. She explained to Joanna that the high blood pressure and fever were normal responses to alcohol withdrawal. "As are your sweaty hands and your shaking," she added. "I'll bet you're feeling pretty queasy and achy, aren't you?" Again Joanna shook her head. "Have you ever had a seizure?" the nurse asked.

The question took Joanna back almost two years. Jeff was driving her to a psychiatrist in Chicago when her body suddenly went rigid and started to jerk. Her head fell back against the seat cushion. Although it looked terrifying to Jeff, Joanna wasn't aware of what was happening. As she came to, in the fleeting moment between consciousness and unconsciousness, she felt the rigidity, the shaking. Her tongue was sore, and when she raised her hand to her mouth, she discovered blood on her lips. Jeff was veering toward an exit ramp, and she was trying to make sense of his words, of the change in direction. He was saying he thought she'd had a seizure, and that he'd used the cellular phone to call the emergency room.

Joanna studied the heather carpet. "Yes. Once," she answered. The nurse handed Joanna a small paper cup of water and four small green-and cream-colored capsules. The nurse repeated what Joanna knew from previous treatment: Librium is part of a drug family called benzodiazepines and is a tranquilizer that helps keep the body calm through withdrawal. Though withdrawing from alcohol is a quick process—two or three days—it is also potentially more dangerous than withdrawal from any other drug. Withdrawal can precipitate grand mal seizures, in which the energy that flows between the brain synapses gets backed up, and the brain, like a computer that needs rebooting, essentially shuts down in order to normalize itself again. Joanna's previous seizure meant that she had a low seizure threshold, but that risk wouldn't really surface for at least another three days. "By that time you will be tapering off the Librium, and we will put you on phenobarbital for a few days to keep your brain calm." Joanna swallowed the Librium capsules quickly.

Like a child, Joanna followed the nurse as they returned to her room. The nurse continued, "The Librium will stop your body from shaking and it will dull that pit in your stomach. In a couple of hours we'll give you another 100 milligrams. But you should know that it will also make you feel quite sleepy and your legs may feel a little rubbery." The nurse stopped to pick up the luggage on the way to the room. Joanna wanted to get back to Jeff, to look at his tall frame, hold on to his long fingers, to let him be her anchor in this swaying world.

Joanna thought about Molly at her in-laws. Molly had probably finished her lunch now, and Joanna's mother-in-law would be rocking her, giving her a bottle, and soon Molly would be drifting off to sleep. She would rest in the port-a-crib they kept for her, with a Winnie the Pooh propped up in the corner. Her chubby fingers would be curled into fists, and her mouth would still be making sucking motions as she fell asleep. For Joanna, this was an ache far worse than the ache in her joints. Though she could locate it somewhere in her chest, she couldn't soothe it, nor would the Librium take it away.

When the nurse left the room, Jeff drew the ivory drapes against the bright sun, and Joanna lay down on the twin bed. He sat next to her, put his large hand next to her face, and she curled into a ball, holding Jeff's hand tightly. They stayed like this for a long time. If he started to move, she held his hand more tightly. Eventually she let him get off the bed and go to the bathroom. When the light that was coming through the drapes began to fade, Jeff stood to put on his jacket.

Joanna grabbed his sleeve. "Please don't leave me." An unwilling cry caught in her voice. "Don't leave me. I promise I'll be good." Jeff covered her small hands with his large ones and gently moved them. For the hundredth time, he tried to reassure her. "This is where you need to be, Jo-Jo. I'll take good care of Molly. Don't worry."

Joanna watched him go through the door. The light in the room was gray now, and the quiet pervasive. Twilight moves fast in the winter. She hugged herself and rocked on the bed. For Joanna, as for many addicts, going through detoxification was a naked plunge into the blizzard, visibility reduced to nothing, the only sound the storm in her ears. Joanna was no different than many of the women as they first enter treatment, ravished by the shame and loneliness of leaving their children, and focused on getting home to fix relationships with husbands or lovers. Though the unit had space for twenty-two people, it was almost empty on Christmas Day. Some of the other patients on the unit that night were also anxious, some angry, some both. Most of them had arrived either very drunk or very high.

Through her open door, Joanna could see the nurses' station, the jovial, dimpled face of Santa that hung on the wall, the foil-wrapped presents piled on the station's counter. She wondered if there was something in a package for her. She wanted to walk, but there was nowhere to go, and she had no energy for it. At about five o'clock the nurse came back into Joanna's room, said dinner would be sent over soon, and suggested she stretch her legs by walking to the lounge. She'd taken her third dose of Librium by now—300 milligrams, enough to make anyone, except those going through alcohol withdrawal, unconscious—and her legs felt a bit unsteady. "Come on," said the nurse. "I'll give you a hand up."

As Joanna passed the nurses' station, she picked up one of the wrapped packages, and noticed it was light as air. Several people were watching television in the lounge and two women sat talking in the corner. Joanna pulled up a chair a few feet away. These women were also very frightened, but they appeared less alone to Joanna, who was hidden at the dull center of a swirling white storm. Would she ever feel the way they looked? After dinner she went to bed and let the storm subside into sleep.

"This Time I Mean It"

Andy arrived at the Minneapolis–St. Paul airport on a February afternoon, two years before Joanna. A half hour before, Andy had been in the lavatory, unfolding a plastic packet in which he kept his last hit of cocaine. He had told his mother, who drove him to the airport, that he was going straight. "This time," he said to her as she hugged him goodbye, "I mean it."

But it seemed pointless to throw the cocaine away, to flush the last packet down the toilet. Andy thought about saving it for later in the week, but he didn't want to be caught with drugs at Hazelden. So he lifted the powder up to his nose, snorted it, and shook his head. He liked the rush. He put away his billfold, glanced in the mirror, and rubbed the residue of coke into his gums, numbing them. He returned to his seat.

After he left the plane and walked into the crowded lobby, Andy looked for somebody to greet him. No one was there. *Christ*, he said to himself. *Now what am I going to do?* Then he recalled his mother saying he should go directly to baggage carousel 14, where a Hazelden driver would find him; his mother had told Hazelden what Andy would be wearing.

When he reached the baggage claim area, a middle-aged man wearing a cowboy hat approached him. "Hi, I'm Tim from Hazelden. I'm your driver," he said, introducing himself, and putting out his hand to

Andy. He shook it, said "hello," then turned away from the driver to search for his bags.

Tim had driven hundreds of people from the airport to the Hazelden rehab center. Sometimes he felt like the mythological boatman who transported people across the river Styx and out of the underworld of Hades. He was responsible for getting patients like Andy safely from one bank of the river to another. If Andy was on a journey from hell to heaven, from the misery of a crack habit to sobriety, Tim would be the person to transport him from one place to the other. Of course, it was up to Andy to do the hard work, but Tim could get him there.

Andy tried to look nonchalant as he leaned against the pillar waiting for his bags to come down the chute. Tim saw in him the pose of a terrified man. It wasn't easy leaving the destructive but familiar world of drugs for the unknown.

"Let me get that for you," Tim said, reaching for the bag that Andy lifted off the carousel. Andy startled when Tim motioned that he would take the bag. "It's okay," Tim said. "I'd be happy to carry your bag, really." Carrying a piece of luggage was nothing compared with the work Andy had ahead of him, Tim thought.

Andy handed the luggage over to him and followed Tim to the exit doors. As they stepped outside, Andy thought about the beating he took at the pizza parlor in Harlem. He felt that if Tim knew how much of a crack addict he had become, he wouldn't have picked up his bag. In fact, he probably would never have showed up to meet him at the airport.

Outside in the lot, Tim found the blue station wagon parked in aisle "E." He opened the hatchback, loaded the bag into the car, and walked around to unlock the passenger's side door for Andy. Andy was standing at the door, shivering. "Jesus," he said. "It's cold."

"You'll need a warmer coat than that one," Tim said. Andy had heard about Minnesota winters, but couldn't imagine the cold that now seemed to grip his shoulders. Andy felt edgy and scooted quickly into the seat, slamming the car door shut. It didn't feel much warmer in the car.

Once on the main highway to Hazelden, Tim talked about the two horses he owned on a small farm outside of Center City. "Beautiful black mares," he said. But Andy was staring blankly out the window. He didn't notice any of the barren trees lining Interstate 35. "What?" he occasionally said, when realizing how little of the conversation he had heard. Tim smiled and repeated himself. He changed the subject to New York sights, like St. Patrick's Cathedral and the Statue of Liberty, places he had visited on a vacation the summer before. "I heard you have a hell of a cathedral here in Minnesota," Andy remarked, trying hard to appear conversational. He pressed his finger against a facial muscle to calm its twitching.

"You bet!" Tim said, laughing to himself about the irony of having one "hell" of a cathedral. "In St. Paul. Next to the one in New York City, it's the largest basilica in the country. You might have seen it when we were closer to downtown, but we're past it now," he added.

Andy was in no mood to talk to the driver. He ignored Tim's remarks about the cathedral. Besides, Andy hadn't even visited the Statue of Liberty himself. What did he know about it? He kept silent for the rest of the way. Tim would glance across the seat at him, and could imagine the cloak Andy had drawn around himself. Once in a while, Tim would see Andy shake his head and flick his cheek, as if a fly had landed on it.

While driving north from St. Paul, Andy heard a faint clicking sound and wondered if it was the odometer, registering mile after mile. He leaned over to look at the gauge, but couldn't see anything from his angle. He considered asking whether the noise was coming from the odometer or from the tires rolling over the highway. But he didn't ask. He rubbed his ear with his thumb and finger, wondering now if the clicking was a variation of the strange sounds he sometimes heard while high on cocaine.

Before turning off Highway 8, the driver pointed out to Andy the large blue and white Hazelden sign they were approaching on the side of the highway. As they turned off the main road, the traffic suddenly vanished. A tall water tower capped with snow loomed over the tops of the pine and fir trees. Tim loved this last mile of the snow-covered road that weaved through thick birches, small hills covered with snow on the sides of the road, paths and cross-country trails. He knew that few patients recalled these minutes in the car, entering the grounds. Tim knew that Andy was so anxious he wouldn't spot any deer in the woods, either. Weeks later, this road, the trails, and deer tracks would become very important to Andy, but for now they hardly existed.

Andy did notice, however, a thin light through the trees. As the road wound around to a clearing, he saw the sliver of the quarter moon. For the first time since he could remember, he enjoyed the moon, its light flickering behind the trees as the road weaved in and out. "What?" Tim asked, hearing Andy whisper.

"Nothin', nothin'," Andy said. "Are we here?"

A Short Stay

Inside, Andy sat down in front of a woman at a desk. Having been in treatment once before, Andy expected the woman to treat him matter-of-factly, emphasizing appropriate behavior now that he was at Hazelden. To avoid confrontation, he would admit to her, if asked, how wrong he had been, and would apologize for using drugs. He wouldn't be surprised if she got up from her seat, took him to another room for a crewcut, then to a shower where he would be told to scrub.

Instead, the woman smiled and asked about his flight from New York. She chatted with him about her nephew who lived in Albany. Had he ever visited the city? she asked. He felt bad lying when asked about the last time he used. "Yesterday," he said, glancing over his shoulder. "Yesterday, I think."

In a short while, she took him to Ignatia.

The woman showed Andy his room, the lounge, the television, and refrigerator. When she opened its door, showing him the juices, fruits, and lunch meat, she encouraged him to help himself. Andy couldn't remember the last time anyone was so welcoming and generous.

A loud protesting voice was heard near the nurses' station. A new admission, an older man in his fifties, had had his Valium confiscated by one of the nurses. His hair was disheveled, his eyes were bloodshot, and he spoke loudly at the nurse. Andy suddenly felt himself superior, a much better looking man than this alcoholic. He watched the man take some pills from the nurse and drink them down with water.

"Aren't you going to kick him out," he asked the woman.

"No," she answered calmly. "These things happen. He'll adjust."

"Are you going to give me any pills?"

"I don't know. The nurse will tell you. People withdrawing from cocaine rarely require medication."

Andy kept nervously running his finger inside his watchband as he toured the unit. When he returned to his room to wait for his suitcase, he tapped his foot on the floor, crossed and uncrossed his legs. Whenever anyone passed by his opened door, he glanced over his shoulder to see who it was. He had heard that many New Yorkers come to rehab in Minnesota, and he worried that someone might recognize him. Perhaps someone from the magazine might show up here. There were a couple of guys at the office who drank a lot, he remembered. As he got up to shut the door, the nurse arrived with his bag.

The cuts on his face from the gang members' beatings were already healing. Still, the nurse inquired about them as she sat down opposite him on the bed. He dismissed her concerns with a wave of his hand. "They're nothing," he said to her. "I got them in a freaky accident. They don't bother me."

"When was the last time you used any drugs or alcohol?" the nurse asked.

"Yesterday. Last night. I'm not sure" he lied. "I told the other woman."

"Do you have any cocaine or other drugs with you?" the nurse asked. After Andy shook his head no, she explained that his bags would need to be inspected. He was expecting this. It was the reason he snorted the cocaine on the plane.

He jumped off his bed and began unzipping his suitcase. "Slow down," she said. "We're in no hurry. Please, let me." She finished unzipping the bag and opened it on the bed. She unrolled his socks, put her hands into the pockets of his trousers, checked the cuffs for any pills or small packets of cocaine, and emptied his shaving bag onto a towel. His mouthwash, Tylenol, and cough drops were put into a paper bag. He was allowed to keep his aftershave lotion.

The nurse could easily imagine how humiliating it was to have your luggage opened on the bed by a stranger, to have your clothes unfolded and handled. It made her uncomfortable as well. As she opened his shaving kit, she tried to engage Andy in conversation about his trip, and the ride from the airport to the center, to put him and herself more at ease.

Afterward, Andy was taken to the lounge, where he was encouraged to relax, watch television, talk with other patients, or rest. He hadn't yet begun to crash, to come down from his cocaine high. Within hours, though, he would begin to tire and lie down in bed. He would sleep all evening, all night, through the next morning, until noon the following day.

When he was awakened for lunch, Andy felt happy. "Good," he snapped when asked by the nurse how he felt. He had no reason to feel well, he thought, but still he did. He didn't realize how close he had come to being beaten to death, to overdosing on crack, to being lost for good. He knew he was warm and comfortable on Ignatia, but he hadn't learned yet that Ignatia was only like a foyer, a kind of corridor between his death and rebirth, his addiction and sobriety, between the apartment in Harlem where he smoked crack and the small room he would share with three others on Shoemaker Hall, a men's unit.

At Ignatia, he was safe. There were no gangs now to beat him up, no woman to kick him out of his room, no cocaine to make him steal money. In Ignatia, he would enjoy twenty-four hours of comfort and caring, things he hadn't experienced for years. But his room at Ignatia was only temporary, a short stay to bracket his life until he was ready to continue. It would not be Ignatia, but the months ahead, that would determine if Andy would prosper.

3

The Open Door

IT WAS THE WINTER OF 1991. Seventy-year-old Elizabeth Toggen and her husband, Jonathan, flew from Des Moines, Iowa, to West Palm Beach, Florida, rented a car, and drove to the Hanley-Hazelden Center at St. Mary's. Though Liz felt extremely anxious, the palm trees on the boulevard, the bright sun shining that February afternoon, and the ocean water seemed like paradise. Liz had endured harsh winds, blinding snows, and subzero temperatures all winter. Despite the warmth, her hands, folded in her lap, quivered. Her stomach was upset. She rummaged in her purse looking for antacids.

When they arrived at the center, they passed four white signs that led to the parking lot. The signs read: One Day at a Time; Live and Let Live; Let Go and Let God; First Things First. Walking toward admissions, Liz looked across the lot and spotted a fountain in the courtyard of the complex that sprayed tiny rainbows into the air. She slipped on her sunglasses and gripped her husband's arm as they walked into the main office.

The nurse who escorted Liz to an interviewing room in the medical unit noted to herself how much older than seventy Liz looked. Liz's forehead wrinkled like rice paper. Her skin, especially under the eyes, seemed loose and ready to peel away. The nurse had to lean forward to listen; Liz's voice was soft and sounded caught in her throat.

Liz, who was forty pounds overweight, moved very slowly. She deliberated each step from the front desk to the unit office. "Do you have any medications with you?" the nurse asked.

Liz opened her purse on the counter. The nurse found medications for hypertension and arthritis, health problems that can be caused by decades of alcohol abuse, poor diet, and lack of exercise. She told Liz that all medications would have to be kept at the desk, including her sleeping pills. "But I can't sleep without them," Liz objected.

"Oh, don't worry," the nurse said reassuringly. "We'll take good care of you." The nurse then put the blood pressure cuff on Liz's arm and pumped it. The gauge read 180/110. Her pulse was 115. The nurse felt Liz's hands; they were sweaty and warm. When asked, Liz stuck out her tongue. The nurse could smell the alcohol from Liz's last drink on the plane.

"I only had one drink," she said to the nurse. "I don't drink that much." The nurse believed her, figuring that Liz's liver probably worked sluggishly and processed toxins slowly. After fifty years of drinking, Liz, like most older women, didn't need large amounts of alcohol to get drunk. In fact, her tests would later show high levels of ammonia in her blood, an indication that she was intoxicated.

The nurse left Liz in the office for a minute to call the staff physician. When older adults arrived in detox, it was standard procedure to notify the physician immediately, because many more medical complications can result during withdrawal. The nurse returned and handed Liz two capsules of Librium, a 50 milligram dose. Liz took the cup of water and swallowed the pills. "They might make you feel tired, but they will get rid of that shaky feeling you have." The nurse glanced down at Liz's trembling hands. In two hours, after the blood test showed that the medication was indeed being metabolized, Liz would receive another 50 milligrams. Had Liz been twenty years younger, she would have received a higher dose, perhaps twice as much, because her liver would process the medication more quickly.

The nurses checked on Liz frequently that night. She complained about her legs feeling weak. Liz was encouraged by the nurse to stay in bed and rest. "Please," she said, "use the call light if you need to get up in the middle of the night." The nurse was worried that Liz might fall and break a hip or shoulder bone weakened by osteoporosis. Later in the evening, Liz would walk to the lounge, holding a nurse's arm as surely as she had held on to her husband when they first arrived.

That night, her blood pressure was taken every three hours. Her door was left open, despite Liz's complaints about the noise in the hall, so the nurses could watch her from the station. They didn't want her to risk getting out of bed without their help.

During Liz's initial interview, a second nurse talked with Jonathan. He had to be forewarned. "Detoxification from alcohol is a very serious matter for anyone, but we are even more concerned when the person is older," she said. Jonathan nodded and listened attentively. He had been told by a psychologist whom he had taken Liz to see how serious a problem her drinking had become. He now understood that her life was in danger. The psychologist had recommended the Hanley-Hazelden Center at St. Mary's, saying it was one of the best treatment centers for older adults in the country.

It had been difficult for Jonathan to push Liz into coming, but he felt he had little choice. For many years, Liz's stepchildren dismissed Jonathan's concerns about her drinking. "She's old and retired now," they said. "Let her enjoy her last years."

"But she's not enjoying herself," Jonathan had remarked to his eldest son. "Can't you see how sick she's been these last two years? It seems we're at the hospital every month for something."

Now the nurse was saying to him, "After fifty years of drinking, we don't know what to expect when she gets sober." He was filling out a health history for Liz. "But we're going to watch over her very closely."

"What do you mean?" Jonathan asked. "Are you worried?"

"Five decades of drinking will make it difficult for your wife's liver to process toxins," explained the nurse. "And detoxification can be traumatic to the body."

It was impossible to tell if the confusion Jonathan often noticed in Liz was from drunkenness, organic brain syndrome, or Alzheimer's disease. No one would really know until she was sober. Although detoxification was less dangerous than continuing to drink, for Liz or any older person, it would also be an incredible shock to her physiology.

Jonathan would spend the next few nights at a Holiday Inn not far from the center. He would stay in Florida until Liz's health was no longer at serious risk. Soon, she was transferred from the medical center to the women's unit. For the entire following week, before every meal, Liz would still check in with a nurse at the medical unit.

Drawing a Dream

Born in 1921 in Ames, Iowa, Liz was raised in a household with parents who valued education and the arts. Though many of her neighbors were descendants of Iowan farmers, both of her parents were college educated, a remarkable achievement for her mother in the early 1900s.

Her father, an architect, loved music and often played duets with his son, who was first violinist in the high school orchestra. Neither parent drank. Prohibition, which had forbidden the manufacture and sale of alcoholic beverages, had begun in 1920 and did not end until the Eighteenth Amendment was repealed in 1933. By then, Liz was twelve.

Before that, she had never seen a bottle of beer or whiskey. The little she knew of alcohol was from stories her parents told about their neighbor, a man who bootlegged whiskey from his house. Often Liz would race to the front window when a car pulled up to the neighbor's at night. Her mother would whisper something to her father. The people buying the booze were always men, and in the dark they seemed dangerous. It was unthinkable that women might buy bootleg whiskey or appear drunk in public. Once, while watching two men open their car doors, Liz was caught peeking at them from behind the curtain. Fear shot through her body.

Liz lived with her family in a simple clapboard house with two bedrooms. "No architect should live in a house like ours," her father often quipped at the dinner table. All of her father's professional friends lived in more beautiful homes with large kitchens and wainscoting, turrets, and front porches with swings suspended from the ceilings. Her father often spoke of moving, but year after year passed without a change in residence. Almost every Sunday morning, Liz watched her father design imaginary homes for their family to live in. "When we can afford to," he'd say. He made hundreds of drawings of their dream home, which were eventually rolled up and stored in the attic. During the week, he worked at the office on elaborate designs for expensive homes in Des Moines.

In 1929, after the stock market crash ushered in the Depression, Liz walked home from elementary school for lunch every day at noon. Her mother, who worked as a teacher before Liz was born, often quizzed Liz on spelling words during lunch. Afterward, Liz might stand on a chair while her mother hemmed her dress, humming "lullaby and goodnight" through a mouthful of pins. Her mother made many of her clothes. Liz would try to stand still, but she wanted to get back to the schoolyard before the afternoon bell rang, and it was hard not to wiggle and squirm on the chair.

After years of dance lessons, Liz began dancing ballet for a civic opera company in Des Moines in the summer of 1936. She was fifteen.

She danced in the Gilbert and Sullivan operas *The Pirates of Penzance* and *The Mikado*. She also began touring at state and county fairs in Wisconsin, Minnesota, and the Dakotas. Liz and all the girls in the troupe were closely supervised by parents and teachers, who warned against dancing like showgirls at nightclubs, bars, or places where people drank, even at Shriners' parties. Liz was told terrible things could happen at such places.

A member of the National Honor Society, Liz enrolled in the University of Iowa when she was seventeen. Tuition was only $36.00 per quarter then, but Liz rarely had spare change for anything other than clothes and school supplies. She still had never tasted wine, beer, or any alcoholic drink. And she still believed with her father that they would soon own a beautiful home constructed from one of his drawings.

What Ladies Drink

By twenty, Liz had entered law school, one of only two women in her entire class. One day she was invited to a fraternity party by a fellow law student, one of the most handsome. She was drawn to his dark brown eyes, thick black hair, and soft-spoken voice. She had heard that there would be beer and whiskey at the party. Afraid of getting drunk and acting foolishly, she asked the only other woman in the class to be her drinking teacher. Liz knew that her friend, Ella, often drank on Fridays after cashing her paycheck from her part-time job at a dress shop.

That Friday, Liz met Ella, and the two went to a bar across the street from the shop. Employees from other stores on the street were already at the bar. "Hey, Ella! Who's your friend?" one of the men called out. Ella introduced Liz to the three men at the table, all from the clothing department. While Liz was talking with them, Ella went to the bar and ordered two Cuba libres—rum and cokes. Liz took the drink from Ella without hesitating, pretending in front of the men that she knew how to drink. Ella didn't have time to instruct Liz to sip the drink slowly, to savor the thick taste and the sting on her tongue. Before the afternoon was over, Liz had her first—and her second—drink, her first dizzy spell, and her first hangover the next morning.

At the fraternity party, Liz had three drinks and danced until after midnight. Two weeks later, Liz took her mother out for lunch at a local restaurant. When the waiter asked what they wanted to drink, Liz ordered sherry for herself and her mother, who was impressed with how much her daughter had learned since attending college. "One glass of sherry," Liz told her mother, "is what ladies drink." It was the only drink that her mother could ever remember having.

In the Mood

As one of the few women law graduates from the University of Iowa, Liz was actively recruited by law firms and companies from all over the country. She had calls from both coasts, and from Texas, Florida, Georgia, Chicago, Cleveland, and even a law firm in Oklahoma City. World War II had broken out, and many of the men Liz graduated with had gone on to military service, so the need for lawyers was high. Liz, lured by the excitement of a large city, moved to New York City to work in the large legal department of a large corporation.

At first, she lived in an apartment with two other women, both legal assistants for the same company. It was difficult to find housing. Later, she rented a place for herself, across the street from Barnard College, only blocks away from Columbia University. Here, among many students and recent graduates, Liz learned not just what to drink, but where, how, when, and why. In the bars all along Broadway, she could gulp down a single shot of whiskey, on any day of the week, for a reason as simple as the weather. She learned to dance the fox-trot to popular tunes like "In the Mood" by Glenn Miller, "I'll Be Seeing You" by Tommy Dorsey, and "These Foolish Things Remind Me of You" by Benny Goodman.

She drank with friends and other young women lawyers. The women in the Wacs often drank scotch or bourbon during the war, but Liz and her friends had to resign themselves to drinking rum. They often made daiquiris, but Liz would get sick from the fruit juices. They took cabs or subways, which allowed them to drink longer and stay later at bars. Often the drinking began early, around five o'clock, when they went for cocktails and hors d'oeuvres at hotels like the Waldorf Astoria or the New Weston. Liz never drank alone. Drinking was fun for her; it made her more comfortable, a better dancer, less self-conscious. Besides, everyone she knew was drinking. Magazines, newspapers, television, and billboards were all advertising the glamor and benefits of alcohol. Prohibition was definitely over.

The Way Home

In 1948, after five years in New York, Liz was increasingly depressed, lonely, and unsure of herself. And she blamed herself. She was twenty-seven years old and unmarried. Sometimes she felt like an old maid. Two men had courted her. One was her boss, a man in his early forties. The other, a recent Fordam Law School graduate, loved to drink and dance with Liz all over New York City. Both men loved bourbon, bridge, and dancing. Both were lawyers with promising incomes. Both had received a 4-F from selective service, excluding them from being drafted into the Army. One had terribly flat feet and the other poor vision. They loved Liz and rode the subways with her to theaters, ball games, libraries, and museums. Both had proposed marriage, and both were rejected.

How could she have rejected these marriage proposals, she wondered. After the war, every attractive and competent woman was married. Why wasn't she? But neither man had been able to convince her. They were respectable and kind, she thought. And they were fun. But marriage? She didn't feel the spark, the unequivocal "yes" in her gut. She liked them immensely, but she didn't think she loved them. Emotionally, she felt locked in place. It made her wonder whether she could love anyone. Perhaps the fault didn't lie within the men but within herself.

At the end of the war, law firms were required to rehire the men who had fought as soldiers. Liz was laid off. This, too, fueled her growing uncertainty about herself. She questioned her competence not only as a woman but as a lawyer. It seemed her personal and professional lives were crashing down around her.

During this time, Liz would stop at bars after shopping to drink by herself. It was the first time she could remember ever sitting in a bar drinking alone. She quickly discovered that only a highball or a martini could relieve the weight of her depression. By the time she had her second drink, the veil would lift a little. She might smile at the bartender. *I don't have to be married to be happy,* she'd say to herself. Each sip brought more relief. But the comfort she felt was short-lived. At her apartment, a telegram arrived from home. Her father had suffered a serious heart attack. That evening she phoned him at the hospital. Liz told him that she had decided a week earlier, before his heart attack, to leave New York City and come home. There was nothing to keep her in New York, she told her father. She packed her things the next day.

Back in Ames, Iowa, she stayed at her parents' house, the same house where she had grown up. One afternoon, up in the attic, she found her father's drawings, the ones of their imaginary home, "the mansion," as he often called it. They were rolled inside a large, strong tube that was covered with a thick layer of dust. She wiped the tube clean with a rag and brought it downstairs. The next afternoon, while sitting on the bed with her father, who was now strong enough to sit up, Liz unrolled the drawings one after another and together they revisited old dreams. Two weeks later, he died. Within a year, Liz's mother would be diagnosed with terminal cancer.

Between that spring day in 1948 when she returned home from New York City and the day she arrived at Hanley-Hazelden, over forty years had passed—forty years of drinking over the deaths of her father and mother, over her own loneliness, over problems at her job as the first woman general counsel for a state university, over her eventual marriage, over a lifetime of joys and sorrows. During her last fifteen years of drinking, she had consumed tall glasses of bourbon every day after work until bedtime.

Finally, in Florida, it looked as if Liz had once again found her way home. Only this time home wasn't a dream on tracing paper stored in an attic; it was a much more substantial one. This time she would learn how to find home in her soul, more palpable and solid than any house she had lived in.

Vital Signs

As the plane flew over Minnesota, nearing the Minneapolis–St. Paul International Airport, Nathaniel Radcliffe, a sixteen-year-old from Los Angeles, looked out the window. It was May 15, 1995, and he should have been flying to Virginia to visit Roanoke College. The college was nestled in the Blue Ridge Mountains, and Nate had heard that kids rolled kegs up the trails after dark. It was the first prospective college visit he had planned. Instead, he was flying to a drug rehabilitation treatment center called the Hazelden Center for Youth and Families.

Nate was dismayed by the flat landscape he saw from the plane. Once the plane landed, he and his father retrieved their baggage and rented a car. Nate had to push back his seat to accommodate his lanky frame. From the airport, his father drove west along Highway 494 and north on 169 to Plymouth, a suburb on the northwest side of Minneapolis. Nate tried not to think about the day a week earlier when he came down to the kitchen to grab some cereal before going to school. He opened the *Los Angeles Times* and saw the headline, "Juveniles picked up for drug paraphernalia," on the front of the Metro section. He was one of those boys. Had his dad read the article? "Aw shit," he said out loud. He folded the paper and tucked it under his arm.

He and his father hardly talked during the short drive to HCYF from the airport. Nate was remembering what one of his buddies had told him. His buddy had gone to treatment in Phoenix, and he was strip-searched for drugs when he went in. "It was humiliating, stripping down to my underwear for that nurse," his buddy had said.

When the Honda made the sharp right into the Hazelden center, Nate was startled. A thick stand of maples covered the land around the center, a building sided with weathered cedar. Big pots with pink and red geraniums stood next to the door, and a garden with white and pink impatiens had been newly planted. Nate felt his shoulders relax as he followed his dad into the building. They were greeted by a short woman with dark, cropped hair. His own hair hung in greasy strands to his shoulders, and he was so skinny his clothes hung on him.

"I'm Theodore Radcliffe," said his dad, extending his hand to the woman. "My son, Nate." His deep voice was grave.

"Welcome," she said. "We're so glad to have you. Have you had lunch?" When Nate's dad told her no, she suggested they get a sandwich from the cafeteria. But first, she wanted Theodore to meet the admissions supervisor, who would introduce him to their program, show him the building, and answer any questions he might have. Meanwhile, she would take Nate to the medical services unit for a brief physical exam.

As they walked toward the MSU, Nate saw other kids his age in the halls, both girls and boys. They were chatting and laughing. A boy in Nike tennis shoes, white tennis shorts, and a navy blue jersey gave a high-five sign to a frail boy whose hair was dyed purple, green, and blue. Several of the kids nodded at Nate and said "Hi." One of them, a short, red-haired girl with a nose ring, said, "Hey, dude, you're gonna like it here."

Nate snorted to himself. *What was this? Were they crazy in Minnesota?* Still, he pursed his lips and wondered. This girl looked pretty happy. He noticed a courtyard with big trees and cedar benches.

As a nurse took his blood pressure, she explained that since he was withdrawing from marijuana, there probably would be no physical symptoms. Still, marijuana is stored in fat cells and stays in the body for a long time, so if he'd been smoking a lot, he would feel its effects for some time. In a while his memory would return to normal and his mind would work with its normal agility. "There's a compound in your brain that transmits nerve impulses. It's called acetylcholine, and marijuana destroys it. That's what causes the memory problems," she said.

"Yeah, yeah, I know all that stuff," he told her.

"Yeah, I know you know all that stuff," she chuckled. "By the way, I heard you're dynamite at soccer. You'll have to tell me about that sometime." She put a thermometer in his mouth and held his wrist to check his pulse. When she finished, she asked Nate about the last time he used and what drug.

"Marijuana," he said, "three days ago. Nothing since."

She told him they would be checking his vital signs every four hours, and if he started shaking or got uncomfortable, hot, muscle cramps, or "crawly skin"—she didn't say that these were symptoms of heroin or alcohol withdrawal—he should tell them. She had no way to know if Nate had told her the truth; scared and angry kids often lie about the drugs they've been using. When she was done with the exam, she asked him to wait in one of the upholstered chairs in front of the windows by the nurses' desk.

The MSU was almost full the day Nate arrived, and two other kids were checking in at the same time. Jenna, who was withdrawing from speed, was in constant motion, pacing or tapping her feet, playing with the long string of beads hanging around her neck, twisting her long, tangled black hair, and pulling at her purple tie-dyed shirt. She twisted her rings, one on every finger of both hands, and fingered the small, green star pasted near her right eye.

Gary, who was short and stocky with disheveled black hair that reached his shoulders, was withdrawing from heroin. Unlike Nate, Gary and Jenna were going through withdrawal from physically addictive drugs. Their young, resilient bodies would not find detoxification as tough as adults did, but it still hurt. Gary's shoulders were hunched, as if the air around him were heavy. The lids of his eyes were half closed, and he was pressing the palms of his hands together, back and forth, back and forth.

The Open Door

Meanwhile, Nate's dad was standing with the admissions supervisor in one of the patient bedrooms on the primary treatment unit. The large room had four twin beds, each separated by a wardrobe and a desk. There were no clothes strewn on the dark carpet or on the oak chairs sitting by the desks. On one bulletin board was a picture of Cindy Crawford, on another a cartoon of "For Better or For Worse" clipped from the Minneapolis *Star Tribune*. Large sliding glass doors opened onto a deck that looked over a stand of maples, poplars, and birch. "Do you keep those doors locked?" asked Ted.

"No, actually, we don't," the admissions supervisor said. His voice took on a pitched quality. Nate's dad could tell that the supervisor was proud of the place. "In fact, this door is the heart of our program. It's about choice and dignity. No one has to stay here. The kids can open the door and walk out anytime they don't want to be here. Of course, if they do, we'll call you right away and tell you, but no one makes them stay." The admissions supervisor told him a bit about the rules, about keeping the floor clean, beds made, and rising at 6:30 A.M.

Ted rolled his eyes. "That'll be the day you get my kid out of bed at 6:30 in the morning."

"Actually, you'd be surprised," said the supervisor. "When all the other peers—we call the kids 'peers'—are getting up, the new kids fall in with the program. Responsibility is key here. We try to set the scene so the kids will carry these things into aftercare. We find that people with long-term recovery have integrated a sense of responsibility into their lives." As they walked back to the MSU, Ted saw a courtyard, this one with a picnic table and chairs, and lots of greenery. The patio was bricked, with tufts of grass growing between the crevices. "Your grounds are really very lovely," he told the supervisor.

"Yes, it's a great place to work. We sincerely believe that pleasant surroundings promote recovery. You've brought Nate to a good place. But I also want to stress that he has to do his part. Kids do get kicked out of here. We don't have a lot of rules—just four—but they are inviolable: no using alcohol and drugs, no sexual contact, no violence, and no stealing."

Dear God, thought Ted, *please let it work.*

Making the News

Nate would sleep on the MSU his first night in rehab, but after dinner he attended a patient government meeting in the large lounge area on the primary treatment unit. Couches, chairs, and end tables lined the circumference of the room. The group leader, Carl, sat at the end of the room in front of a wall of glass that looked out over the woods.

"God . . ." Carl began, in a chanting tone.

The other thirty-two teenagers, squeezed four to a couch, some on folding chairs, some perched on the end tables, a couple on the floor, all forming a large circle around the room, joined him. "Grant me the serenity to accept the things I cannot change, the courage to change the things I can, and the wisdom to know the difference."

Melanie opened a small book of meditations called *One Day at a Time* and read the first part of the entry under May 15. Then she looked up. "Do I read the prayer too?"

Carl nodded.

"Cool." She finished reading and shut the book.

After rules and roll call, new peers introduced themselves.

"Gene," said a boy on the far end of the room. "Willmar, Minnesota. Alcohol. Mushrooms. Speed. My parents said they'd kick me out of the house."

"Gary. Florida. Heroin. Speed. I was court-ordered. I don't really think I'm chemically dependent, but I don't plan to use when I get out, just in case I am. It's kind of hard to accept something that has that much power over you. Especially when you're only sixteen."

"Celeste. Houston. Crack cocaine. Alcohol. Ecstasy. I had a choice: come here or go to boarding school."

"Jenna. New York. Speed. My parents wanted me to come."

"Nate. Los Angeles. Marijuana. LSD. Alcohol. Mostly marijuana. I got picked up by the police."

Nate's mind drifted back to the day the encounter with the police was published in the newspaper. He could still feel the rush of fear along the back of his neck when he saw the headline.

A few days earlier, his parents had gone to Palm Springs for the weekend, and Nate was driving with several friends to a concert. Before they left, one of the guys had passed around some psilocybin mushrooms. The other four kids, two guys and two girls, shared six caps and gulped a bottle of Pepsi to drown the nasty taste. Nate fingered his two caps, feeling their dry, leathery texture, noticing the bluish tint and thinking they must be pretty potent. Instead of swallowing them, he put the caps back in their plastic bag, pulled his pack of Salems from his shirt pocket, and tucked the bag in the bottom of the pack.

They drove to a nearby convenience store, and the two girls ran in to cash a check so they would have cash for marijuana later in the evening. The three guys sat in the parking lot singing along with Pearl Jam on the radio. One of them, Paul, leaned down to the floor and picked up a toy gun he'd grabbed from his little brother earlier in the day. It was a small plastic gun that looked almost identical to a .45 pistol, and he pointed it at the girl sitting in the Pontiac next to them. The guys laughed at the startled look on her face. Paul dropped the gun. "Hey, guys," he said. "I think she's writing down our license plate number."

"Cool," quipped Nate. When the girls returned, they drove back to Nate's to pick up his favorite pipe, a small gold one with a shallow bowl. There was a little residue in the pipe, which he lit as he got into the car. He took a puff then laid the pipe on the dashboard. Just then, three police cars careened into the driveway. Six police officers leaped out, pointing guns. The teenagers were instructed to get out of the car and put their hands on the car roof. The police found the toy gun and lectured the boys on the seriousness of the joke. The policeman standing next to the open driver's door sniffed, then reached in and picked up the pipe. He lifted an eyebrow. "Smoking a little weed?"

"C'mon." Nate tried to bargain with him. "That's nothing, just a little paraphernalia. Look, can't we just forget this?"

The policeman lifted his hat and ran a hand over his hair. "Look, son, you're lucky it's just paraphernalia. That's just a fine. If we found a bag, I'd have to arrest you. Look for something in the mail from us," he said.

Nate's throat was dry. "Just don't call my folks, please," he begged.

"We find this again, and your folks will get a call." When they left, Nate grabbed a Pepsi from the backseat and swallowed both mushroom caps. What a close call. He could handle a fine, as long as his parents didn't find out. He would have to intercept it.

But the newspaper headlines told his parents before the letter came. When kids living in Beverly Hills got in official trouble, it could be cause for news. Nate's dad was to pick him up from school that day. All day Nate worried about the article and whether his parents had read it. His parents would be so embarrassed; they would never forgive him. Radcliffes didn't do things like this. Three generations had gone to Harvard. When his dad pulled up in front of the school, Nate was sick to his stomach. He opened the passenger door and got in, hoping his dad hadn't had time to look at the paper during the day.

"Did you have a nice day, Nate?" he asked.

"Yeah." Nate looked at him out of the corners of his eyes. Maybe he hadn't read the paper.

"Really," his dad yelled. "Is something you forgot to tell us?"

Giving Up

Nate got drunk for the first time in eighth grade. He had always been teased for being short and pudgy. It seemed to him that he was different from the other kids, that he just didn't belong, and the feeling never went away. He was sure the other kids were looking at him thinking, *He's ugly, what a jerk.* In seventh grade, he grew into his body and lost his chunkiness. But it didn't change the image he had of himself. He still felt weird and ugly.

Marijuana and alcohol helped. He felt better when he was high. In eighth grade he spent the weekend with a friend, and they found some Jamaican rum in the liquor cabinet. They drank until they were drunk, got on their bicycles, rode around the block, came home, and threw up. He tried marijuana a few weeks later, and by ninth grade he was smoking and drinking almost every weekend. He had a group to hang out with then, and all summer they spent weekend evenings at keggers. By tenth grade he was smoking every day. It didn't hurt his soccer—his team won the state tournament—or his track. It didn't even seriously hurt his academics.

His junior year was a kaleidoscope of drugs: Darvon, psilocybin, marijuana, and alcohol. A new friend, David, moved into the neighbor-hood. A year older than Nate, David wore Grateful Dead T-shirts, knew every song the Grateful Dead ever put out, and was a top soccer player. Nate wanted to be like David. They snuck out of school and smoked be-fore third-period calculus, smoked on their lunch break, and some-times didn't bother to come back to school.

In November, David brought Nate some acid. About an hour after Nate chewed the little red tab of paper, he saw the palm fronds in his yard become ghosts floating in the sky. It made him laugh. He stared at his hands and waved them gently back and forth through the air. They were forming electrical trails, leaving behind multiple images of them-selves. His body went numb, and he became a video camera, watching whatever he wanted, forming cities in the ceiling, meadows in the walls. The red in the Bob Marley poster above his dresser glowed like hot coals, and the beat of the music vibrated in his chest, moved down through his pelvis, legs, and flowed into his feet.

David had a friend who dealt grass at the end of Sunset Boulevard. It was a rush to go there, David said. Would Nate like to go along? It was a pretty rough part of the city, and Nate knew his parents would be furious if they knew. They drove down Sunset in a BMW until they began to see male prostitutes standing on corners in tank tops and tight pants. They passed female prostitutes with bright red lipstick and short skirts, smiling their cold, lonely smiles on the street corners. As they got further down Sunset Boulevard there were coffeehouses, recording studios, rock clubs, and music spilling onto the streets.

Finally, they stopped at a stucco house with a tile roof. They pulled baseball caps down over their faces, sauntered into the house, and came out with four pounds of weed. Nate made the run down to the Silver Lake District with David and his friend several times. He knew that one of David's friends had a gun held to his head in this district, but that only increased the rush. He felt as if he was putting his life on the line each time, and when he came out alive, it was like putting an-other brick in an invisible wall. If he could make it out of there, he could do anything.

He and David and a few other buddies started stealing car stereos for money, although it was David who knew how to get in and out fast. For Nate it was easier to take money off his folks' dressers. They never missed a twenty here and there, especially his dad, who carried enough cash that he didn't really keep track of it. Nate got a lot of his dope free at parties. As the winter went on, he missed more and more classes. The guys would leave school for the beach around 10:30 A.M., sometimes to trip on acid, sometimes to just lie in the sun and smoke dope. By April, they'd meet across the street from school, not even going in. The school had sent truancy notices to Nate's parents, but he had intercepted them. If his parents had come to midterm teachers' conferences, they would have discovered the absences anyway, but his dad was out of town that evening, and his mom had a meeting, so Nate was home free.

Nothing about the drug use bothered Nate until mid-April, when his girlfriend, Cindy, broke up with him. It wasn't that he was so crazy about her. But she was a symbol of everything his parents wanted him to be, everything he had wanted to be. Cindy got good grades, dressed well, was applying to prestigious colleges. She was a dancer, and she tutored younger kids at the junior high. She was mainstream. But after the night he talked her into doing acid with him, and then exploded at her for not doing it right, she split. That's when he decided to cut back on the dope. He didn't use anything for about three days, but he didn't feel normal without it. The old feelings of being different, weird, and ugly rushed back on him right away. He walked into a Friday-night party and could feel everyone turning to look at him, thinking, *What's that jerk doing here?* He couldn't think of anything to say to people. All weekend he felt nervous, off. He just didn't feel normal without the marijuana. It wasn't worth it.

In early May he came home after school and found his mother crying. He'd taken codeine that morning and was planning to meet David in about an hour to drop acid. The day was sunny and warm, and they planned to find a private spot in the hills. He was whistling as he walked into the house, his hands in his pockets where he could feel the dope under the fingers of his left hand. It was going to be a nice afternoon. His mom looked up at him when he came in and held out a piece of paper toward him. His stomach tightened. He looked down at the floor and turned quickly to go up the stairs.

"Wait a minute," she demanded.

He stood still, but didn't turn around.

"Can you explain this?"

"What? Mom, I don't know what you're talking about."

"This letter from the principal. It says you haven't been in school for a month." Her voice was strained. Nate felt caught. He turned to face her.

"Must be a mistake, Mom," he said. "That school is always screwing up."

"It's not a mistake, Nate." His mom looked pale. "I called the principal. He says your grades have dropped. You're not handing in assignments. You were getting Ds and Fs on your tests last month. But this month you haven't even been there to take a test."

"I hate the stupid school," yelled Nate. "They're a bunch of idiots. Stupid idiot teachers. I don't learn a thing there."

His mom stood with her mouth open, staring wide-eyed at him. "Nate, what's going on with you?" she yelled back at him. "When your dad gets home . . ."

Nate's head was spinning. His dad was going to be pissed. *I'll just tell her*, he thought. *Get it over with. They'll put me in drug counseling.* A couple of his friends had been through that. A few hours a week. He could handle that.

He pulled the bag of marijuana from his pocket and threw it at her. "Here. This is what's the matter," he yelled. The bag hit her right cheek and fell to the floor. She dropped her head and her shoulders sagged forward. She turned and stood hunched, silent. Nate ran up the stairs to his room.

He went to drug counseling the next week. And on Thursday, his parents left for Palm Springs for the weekend. Nate dug under a pile of clothes in his closet for his stash. There, in a small tin, were four joints. He lit one, sucked the smoke and air deep into his lungs, holding it until he felt as if he would pass out. In minutes, he felt a lightness in his head, a sense of ease washed through his body. After finishing the joint, he carefully made his way downstairs, out the front door, and into the garage. He grabbed his bicycle and began cruising around the block. The marijuana made him buoyant, and he kept getting lost in his mind. He reached the end of his block and suddenly felt as if he had just awakened. *Oh*, he thought, *here I am at the end of the block.* He turned left and started down the street, staring up at the palms against the blue sky, the color of pure lapis. As the light breeze fondled the fronds, the next two minutes seemed to take an hour. He took another left, and he started laughing. He stared down at his hands on the handlebars. They were a tawny tan, and in the sun he could see faint blue lines under the skin. Then the hunger hit him. He pressed down hard against the pedals, his mind floating backward as his body pushed forward toward home.

The next day he was arrested, and his parents read about it in the paper on Monday. Nate's dad was giving him a ride home from school, shouting. "What's it like getting picked up by the police? What do you think people are going to say at my office? How am I going to go to the club tomorrow? And your grandmother, do you know how she's going to feel?"

Once he got home, Nate contemplated suicide. He'd never go to college. He couldn't show his face to his relatives. He couldn't get high anymore. He went out to the garage and set a chair under a rafter. He stood up on it, felt the roughness of the rope he had put around his neck, and imagined it jerking tight. He looked around the garage at the shovels, the rake, his bike, and the lawnmower. He knew he didn't have the guts for it. He couldn't do anything right.

4

First Steps

NATE RADCLIFFE was just beginning to feel like his mind was coming into focus on Monday, two days after he arrived at the Hazelden Center for Youth and Families. Six young people sat around a conference table in a room with a view that overlooked a courtyard of Japanese lilacs. In May the trees were freshly green, the fragrant white blossoms waiting for warmer weather. Jim Young, a counselor, was leading the orientation group. He went over some of the rules, told them that in the next couple of days they would receive the Minnesota Multiphasic Personality Inventory and the Beck Depression Inventory to see if they needed any special counseling, and that they would also be given the Wide Range Achievement Test to check on their school skills.

The counselor seemed pretty mellow, and Nate liked him. But he wasn't sure about one of the patients, the guy who sat directly across from him. The guy had a tattoo of a snake on his forearm, and he stared down at the table, frowning.

Nate pulled his attention back to the counselor, who was still talking. "The first thing I want to do this morning is talk about alcoholism and addiction. In 1955, the American Medical Association accepted addiction as a disease. Can anybody tell me something about the disease process? What disease is addiction similar to?"

Before Nate could think of an answer, one of the other patients spoke, a guy who'd said he was from Texas.

"Cancer."

"How's that?"

"It's not your fault."

"I love it when somebody says that right away. It's a no-fault disease. I was an alcoholic waiting to happen. What else can you tell me about the disease?"

"You can't cure it," said a young woman from St. Louis.

"Exactly!" said the counselor in an enthusiastic voice.

Okay, thought Nate. *This counselor seems pretty cool, but can he be for real?*

He went on to tell them about the four ironclad rules: no chemicals, no violence, no stealing, and no sexual relations. "All the rest," he said, "are expectations because we don't want you to try to do things perfectly. Trying to be perfect is part of this disease. We all make mistakes." Then he asked, "What about narcing and ratting? Do we do that here?"

A blond-haired young man from England answered him. "One of your expectations is that we tell staff if a peer is using, right? I'd call that ratting."

The counselor shook his head. "Nope. Narcing and ratting don't take place here. That happens in penal institutions. Here we have concerns, confronting."

Yeah, right, thought Nate.

"You see somebody doing something that's hurting his recovery, you tell him about it because you care about him," the counselor was saying. "The key is you tell him directly and respectfully, out of love. A 'care-frontation.' If he's hurting his recovery, he's also creating a climate that's hurting your recovery, and you can't afford to let that happen."

As the counselor talked, Nate thought back to the "concerns" he had watched in group that morning.

Care-frontations

Earlier in the day, after having breakfast and attending a lecture, Nate had walked with his new buddy Jacob into the group room next to the girls' side of the treatment unit. Through its large window he could see still another courtyard, this one with a birdbath in the center. When they walked into the room, there were already four other young people sitting there. Only Melanie walked in after Nate. He remembered her from the Saturday-night community meeting. He had liked how she looked, the bright colors she wore, her finely sculpted features. Now she folded her long legs into her chair, and her smooth skin looked bronzed against her jade sweatshirt. Before Nate sat down, he studied the chalkboard. He saw several labeled columns and each column was filled in:

NAME	RESPONSIBLE/ IRRESPONSIBLE	FEELINGS	STEPS	DRUG
Curtis	R	tired, grateful, optimistic	1	alcohol
Peter	R	jumpy, nervous	2	cocaine, heroin
Melanie	R	proud, confident, honest, caring, worried, frustrated	1	alcohol
Dan	R	impulsive, confident, grateful	1	speed, cocaine, LSD
Tessa	R	tired, grateful, optimistic	1	pot, hash, methadone, Darvon
Mary	R	content, hopeful	3	alcohol, heroin
Jacob			3	speed, crack-cocaine

"What's that stuff on the chalkboard?" Nate asked Jacob. Jacob, a premed student who looked younger than his twenty years, had walked over to the Medical Services Unit on Sunday. He had shown Nate around the unit, introduced him to the other kids, and hung out with him.

"You gotta fill in how you're feeling this morning," Jacob explained as he walked over to the chalkboard and wrote "R" after his name, followed by "sleepy, hopeful." Nate added his own name to the board and wrote "nervous."

The last to walk in was the counselor, a slender blonde woman with a friendly, crooked grin. The group leader, Peter, stood and said, "Let's open." Everyone stood and came together in a circle, arms around each other's backs, and said the Lord's Prayer. After the meditation reading, Nate was startled by a knock on the door. A tall young man with a plaid flannel shirt and work boots came in. He pulled up an extra chair that was sitting against the wall and announced, "I have a concern for Dan. Dan, it really bugs me when you don't get out of bed when your alarm rings. You end up rushing around and barely finishing your tasks on time. You have to take more responsibility for yourself, man."

Dan pulled at his short brown hair, tapped his foot, and played with a crease in his jeans. Nate had heard that Dan was detoxifying from methamphetamines, and some guys on the unit were making his jitteriness worse by tormenting him, doing things like jumping out from behind doors, and poking him. "Thank you," said Dan. He stood, and both young men embraced before Dan's roommate left the room.

The counselor, Carol, leaned back in her chair and clasped her hands behind her head. Her brow furrowed. "Is it true, Dan? Are you really getting up late?"

Dan smiled sheepishly, said he was up only five minutes late because he was dreaming that he was on a submarine, and he had confused his alarm with a submarine warning system. Carol laughed a hearty laugh. "Oh, that's a good excuse. A submarine dream!"

Dan chuckled.

"You know what the consequences are on this unit when you get up late, right? Tomorrow you have to get up fifteen minutes earlier."

Dan's voice was resigned. "Yeah, okay."

Carol reached over and rubbed the top of his head. "Maybe we can get you out of the submarine tomorrow."

The next young man in the circle, Curtis, reported that he had also risen late, but it was not his fault. He was still sleeping on the MSU and the nurses had woken him up at 4:00 A.M. with their singing. He had a hard time getting back to sleep after this and, therefore, couldn't get up on time.

Carol moved her wiry body to the edge of her chair and raised an eyebrow. "What? This is a good one." Her voice carried amazement, not skepticism. Together they decided they would go talk to the nursing supervisor.

For the next twenty minutes there were knocks on the door, kids entering and giving "concerns" and "positives." One group member got a concern for taking a note from a girl, another for telling stories the night before that glamorized his drug use, and another for gossiping. Jacob got a positive for being especially cooperative, and Melanie got a positive for making herself available to talk to another young woman on the unit who was feeling down at breakfast. The group went on for an hour and a half, with the young people talking about their feelings, how things were going on the unit, and what they were working on in treatment.

Phat Shoes, Dude

A few days later, Nate joined several of the peers who had gone out to the courtyard. He had been on a roller coaster of feelings since he'd come. He thought about the feelings he recorded on the chalkboard during the first few days: nervous, great, hopeless, content, argumentative. But then, all the other kids had similar feelings. He was beginning to feel comfortable in the treatment center. The extreme courtesy from the peers no longer felt weird. The staff was great, and he liked being in the treatment group every morning. He liked playing hacky sack with the other kids in front of the timber retaining wall carved with the words, "Hack E. Sack." He liked the breaks, sitting in the warm sun in the courtyards rapping with the other kids. He liked the evening best of all, when they did written assignments on the Steps, and there was time for one-on-ones, when they could talk privately with other kids about their feelings or something they were struggling with. It was a time when Nate could hang out with his roommates, crack jokes, and talk. And he loved the food: tacos and submarine sandwiches and brownies and hamburgers.

By 2:00 P.M., the temperature had reached the sixties, and he felt high on the sunshine. The courtyard stilled the wind and captured the sun, and the lazy warm air was slowing Nate down. He could have sat on the wooden picnic table forever. He was looking down at his new black vinyl Nikes, the ones he bought the week before his arrest. Somehow he had imagined they would make everything in his life better.

"Phat shoes, dude," said Peter. Nate smiled. He wasn't going to let on that he didn't know what "phat" meant. *It must mean he likes them,* thought Nate.

"Yeah, they are way cool, man," chimed in Melanie.

Nate felt like he was really part of the crowd here. He chuckled inside. Maybe his shoes were making things go better. "Are you going to swim this afternoon?" he asked Peter and Melanie. Melanie said yes, but Peter was going to lift weights. They talked about high school, about the classes they'd taken, the ones they hadn't bothered to go to. Carla, a girl with long auburn hair and a star painted beside her right eye, was reading palms on the other side of the table. "You have a long lifeline," Nate heard her saying, "and you will have children." A couple of the guys were talking about their SAT scores. Nate stared at the reflection of his hair in his sunglasses lying on the picnic table as he listened to the kids chattering and joking around, and for the first time he could remember, his hair didn't look ugly to him.

After a few minutes, as the kids finished their cigarettes, mashing them out against the concrete floor and dropping the butts in the ashtray by the door, they shuffled inside to get ready for the YMCA. Nate stayed behind, putting his head back against a post that supported the shingled rain shelter over the table. He took in the sun for a last long minute. When he opened his eyes, he was startled. There, in the bushes on the other side of the birdbath, tucked in next to a variegated hosta, were three baby ducks and their mother. He felt excitement rise in his chest. "Wow," he whispered. The babies were tiny, about three inches long, and covered with brown fuzz. They walked like his little niece walked, rocking from side to side. He was glad everyone had gone inside and wouldn't scare them. He was glad, too, that he didn't feel hazy anymore; if he was messed up, he'd have thrown rocks at them or something. Those baby ducks were such a trip. Now that he was sober, he could notice the little things. *So all right*, he said to himself, *maybe it's not the shoes.*

Looking Inside

The next Monday, as ten o'clock drew near and Nate ambled toward the treatment room, he was thinking that the center felt a little like summer camp. In his feelings column, he wrote "pretty good." But when it came time to give positives and concerns, Carol got on him. "Nate, I haven't heard you give anyone a positive yet. You've given some concerns. Have any of those people changed? If they have, you have to follow up with a positive. You have to let them know that you noticed their change."

He looked down and fidgeted with his Grateful Dead shirt. Jerry Garcia stared up at him. *Okay*, he thought, *I gotta come up with something quick.* One of the guys had come to the group yesterday and given Melanie a positive for stretching herself so much, working so hard. He looked at Melanie. "I want to give you a positive for working so hard, dude," he said. "You've really been stretching yourself a lot."

Carol rolled her eyes. "That was really from the heart," she said. "You can't be a weasel here, Nate. Let's hear from somebody who really has something to say."

Nate felt the back of his ears turn red. Then Jacob was talking, giving a concern to Dan, the young man who was coming off methamphetamines, about his hopelessness. Carol asked Dan about his feelings, telling him he needed to talk to staff about them. Dan was running his fingers through his hair and looking at the floor. It was hard for Nate to watch Dan feeling so uncomfortable. Nate noticed that Jacob reached out and took Dan's hand, and he wondered how he'd feel if Jacob did that to him in group.

His stomach was tight as he watched Carol push at Dan about saying his feelings. Nate remembered Carol pushing him a couple days ago; it had seemed like she could look right inside him. Nate had been talking about his anger at Kendra, a feisty young woman who had been kicked out of treatment for drinking a beer on a trip to the YMCA. "Kendra was kind of like a role model for me. She was doing so well, and I looked up to her," Nate had told his group afterward. "I just feel betrayed by her. I'm really mad."

"Okay, Nate, but what's behind the mad?" Carol had asked.

He had looked at her quizzically.

"I think anger always has something behind it, hurt or fear or some other feeling," she had explained.

"Hurt," was Nate's reply. "I'm hurting so bad. I really looked up to Kendra. How could she do this to me?"

"Good! You say 'I'm mad' a lot," Carol had advised. "But there are a lot of other feelings you have besides that. I'm glad you could see what else there was in there. I can understand that you feel really hurt. But remember that it was Kendra's disease that talked her into taking that beer. Her disease got the better of her. You have to frame it that way, Nate."

Sometimes it was just spooky to have someone look inside you like that. He wondered what she was going to see on Wednesday when he did his First Step.

Step One

Nate did a curious thing when he wrote out his First Step: "We admitted we were powerless over alcohol—that our lives had become unmanageable." He knew his suffering was relatively light compared with a lot of the kids around him. For instance, Peter's mom had died when he was ten, and his dad had shipped him off to a boarding school. Peter felt closer to his dog than he did to his family. Melanie had been sexually abused by her uncle for years, and she was a prostitute before she came to treatment. Curtis had been drugging and following the Grateful

Dead around for three years, and he slept on the street more often than not. There was another guy who was shooting heroin, and you could almost see the bones poking through his shoulders. Despite all this suffering, the unit felt close, like a family. Nate felt accepted, close, contained. To make sure no one thought he didn't belong, he exaggerated his alcohol use.

At the same time, he didn't believe deep down that he was chemically dependent, especially the alcoholic part. Alcoholics were old men who sat around by themselves and drank Seagrams. In fact, like so many before and after him, Nate found it almost impossible to accept that he was an alcoholic. Though primary treatment was a beginning, a starting block from which he would dive into recovery, he would not fully understand his powerlessness over drugs and alcohol until months later.

He worked on his Step One all day Monday and Tuesday. By Wednesday morning he had written out fourteen pages about the topics listed on his sheet: attempts to control, preoccupation, effects on family, and other subjects.

He was tense; Carol didn't always accept people's first Steps. Yesterday she had said to Curtis, "That ain't good enough. I don't think you get that you're powerless over drugs yet. You're blowing us off. Go back and put more time and effort into it."

When all the positives and concerns were done, and they had been around the circle and everyone had checked in, Carol looked at Nate. She sat back in her chair and smiled. "You ready to do your First Step, Nate?"

He swallowed hard, then smiled back. "I guess." He started reading from his first page, the page about preoccupation. "I thought about marijuana in school, in every one of my classes all day long. I'd be worried when I walked in the door about where I'd get five bucks for a joint before class. If we were going to drop acid, I'd think about when we were going to do it and plan out how."

"Give me an example," said Carol. "What class were you sitting in?" Carol led him through an accounting of his time during and after classes. She led him through his alcohol use and his acid use. Carol pressed him for details, asking how he felt when he took drugs. He thought of how self-conscious and different he used to feel at parties, in class, even walking down the street. The drugs took that away. "I liked it," Nate said. "It was fun. I felt important, good."

Again Carol asked him for an example. The worst time flashed into Nate's mind. *Should I tell them?* he wondered. Then he plunged in. He told them how for months he had been after his girlfriend to drop acid with him. He told how surprised he was when she finally said yes, how they went to a friend's house and turned on cartoons, how he had orange sunshine and pulled off two hits for himself, a hit for Cindy, and a hit for the friend. "She dosed, held it in her mouth for about twenty minutes, and then accidentally spit it out on the carpet. I had to give her another hit, and it really made me mad."

"So what did you do then?" prompted Carol.

"Nothin' really." Nate rubbed his hands on his jeans. "I just kept watching the cartoons, and my hand started streaking. I was getting into it, and Cindy starts fussing around. Gets up and does the dishes, stuff like that. She couldn't sit still. I told her to sit down and stop it. And when she got up again, I went off on her. I yelled at her for wasting my drugs. I was thinking how well I was doing, and how much better I'd be doing if I had taken her hit too. I was yelling at her, saying I should have taken her hit since she couldn't even take acid right. Then I started yelling about everything she'd ever done that made me mad, like talking to other boys and stuff." Nate's voice had risen while he described the scene.

"And then what?"

Nate sighed, and his voice dropped. "She just sat there, bent over with her head in her hands, rocking back and forth, crying."

"So how'd you feel then?"

Words he'd heard at a lecture ran through his mind: "You won't feel the pain of your drug use until you've gone against your own values." Nate had stolen money, taken cars for joyrides, broken into houses, and stolen stereos and televisions. He had cheated in class. He had broken windows at the high school. But none of that bothered him like this did. Nate laughed a self-conscious laugh, choking back tears. "It just sucks, man. This sucks."

"So did you feel big, Nate? Did the acid make you feel wonderful? Was it fun?"

"I told myself it was fun."

"So how do you feel now?"

His voice came from so far back in his throat it was barely audible. "Like I'm dying."

Carol went on. They covered blackouts and destructive behaviors, effects on physical health, sexuality, emotional life, and finances. Then Carol asked, "How has this affected your family?" Nate had been dreading this question more than any other. He just stared at the floor. "I know this is hard, but you're doing a good job," said Carol. "It's important that you look at this stuff."

Nate pulled a foot up on his chair, wrapped his arms around his leg, and pressed his chin into his knee. "It's really hurt my parents a lot. My dad, he couldn't believe I would do this. He's a successful businessman, and me blowing off my future like this. And my mom . . . " Nate pictured his mom's face, the bag of dope hitting her. He saw her drop her head and turn to hide her tears. He wasn't thinking about how the other kids had problems worse than his. He felt his chest filling with shame, something starting at his diaphragm and heaving upward. He jumped up from his chair, walked to the corner of the room, and sobbed for a long minute. When his chest settled again, he returned to his chair. The room was silent. Everyone waited. He whispered, "My mom cried for four days when she found out."

"So your drug use has hurt others too. It's hurt the people around you pretty bad." Carol's voice was gentle. Nate sat quietly, staring at the floor.

Carol asked the group if they accepted Nate's First Step. Jacob began, saying, "Yeah, man, I know what you're going through right now. It's real hard to let emotions come out after all this time. I can relate to that. I always wanted to get messed up to hide all that. I accept your First Step."

Curtis was next. He wiped his cheek with the back of his hand. "I really felt your pain, man. I've never seen anybody open up like that before. I just felt like I was one with you. I've never felt like that with anybody before, except when I was on acid. You were really cool, man." Nate rubbed the back of his neck and looked up at the group around him. *They've heard all these awful things about me, and they still like me,* he thought.

After everyone in the group had accepted his First Step, the counselor spoke. Carol saw the defeat on his face and knew he needed to forgive himself. "You're doing a great job, Nate. You gotta look at what your drug use has done to you and to the people around you, but you also gotta remember it's the disease. The drugs and alcohol are in control of you; you've got no power over them. Nate's a super guy."

She continued, "I heard you say you had put everything behind your drugs. You say your drugs made you feel big and important. But none of the things that happened were big and fun. You know, I listen to AA tapes all the time. There's one that totally reminds me of you. It says, 'Drugs and alcohol gave me wings to fly, and then they took away my sky.'" She looked at him with a big, crooked grin. "How do you feel right now?"

"Relieved."

The Multidisciplinary Team

Carol sat rocking back and forth in the gray office chair. She and the other counselors had piles of folders spread out on the floor around their chairs. Drawings some of the young people had made during orientation group were taped to the wall: beautiful flowers slowly dying, a rainbow growing out of a black hole, a car racing into a brick wall.

Another of the counselors, Jim, went through one of his cases. He was interrupted periodically by questions from the other counselors, the unit's psychotherapist, the chaplain, the nurse, or the CD technician. The team met every morning at shift change to hear from the night techs how things had gone during the evening and the night before.

And once a week they met to go over cases in depth. Jim and Carol wrangled over one of Jim's patients. "This guy is going to make it, Carol," Jim was saying vehemently. "We've just got to give him more time."

"I think you've got your rose-colored glasses on again, my friend. This kid just doesn't care at all, and he's dragging other kids down with him."

Jim sighed. "Yeah, I know. But he's had the deck stacked against him forever. What if we send him over to extended care early?"

"I love your rose-colored glasses," Carol chuckled. "I couldn't do this work without being reminded to look for the best in the worst of them."

"Check with extended," said the supervisor. "See if they can take him now."

Carol leaned over and picked up Dan's folder from the floor. "This kid worries me," she said. "He's so vulnerable. His mom left the family when he was seven, and his dad is pretty abusive." She looked toward the psychotherapist who saw Dan twice a week in the mental health clinic. "How do you think he's doing?"

"The medication is working," she said. "He's sleeping at night now. And he's not suicidal, but he is very vulnerable. I'm seeing him this afternoon. Let's talk after that."

Next Carol retrieved Nate's folder from the floor, spreading it out over her lap. She perused the progress notes and told the team that he'd finished his First Step the day before.

"How'd it go?" asked Jim.

"I think it went well," she said. "He's such a great kid." She leaned back in her chair and frowned. "But I'm worried I'm being too easy on him."

"You?" Jim's voice sounded incredulous. "That'll be the day that I die," he grinned, singing a rough version of a sixties song.

Carol quipped back, "You're just jealous because I'm so nice."

Across the room, the unit supervisor peeled the paper wrapper off a blueberry muffin. "What are you worried about, Carol?"

"You know, it's that balance we've got to strike. By the end of his First Step, I had to scrape the kid off the floor. He was feeling so crummy about himself, and he needed some building up. But I don't think he gets the powerless piece yet, at least not about the alcohol."

The supervisor nodded.

"He wanted to do a good job on the First Step, and I'm sure he exaggerated his alcohol use. Not the marijuana or LSD. I'm sure he used every bit as much as he said he did. But not the alcohol."

The nurse spoke up. "He showed no symptoms of alcohol withdrawal when he was admitted."

"Nah, I know," said Carol. "But he doesn't really understand the cross-addiction piece yet."

"It's always a hard one for the kids," Jim answered. "They know the drugs have dragged them down, but they think they can keep alcohol in their back pocket. How many times have I said, 'You get high on alcohol, your body's gonna crave the pot, or the crack, or whatever it is you like most? Your body doesn't know the difference. It just knows it likes to get high.'"

The supervisor interrupted. "Nate can read well, can't he? Have you got that pamphlet *Cross Addiction* in Nate's treatment plan?"

"Good idea," said Carol. "He's a very motivated kid, and he's earlier in the addiction process than a lot of the kids here." She added the pamphlet to his treatment plan and shut Nate's file.

Reprogramming the Computer

Nate had been on the unit for two and a half weeks the morning he sat in the lecture hall watching the guys from the extended care treatment unit march in. They were so tight, they really seemed like a team. They sat in two rows at the back of the auditorium, and when all the primary treatment patients had finished roll call, one of the extended guys stood up at the back of the room. "Jeremy. Addict. Let's take roll," he called out in clipped tones. Then he called the room numbers, and the responses came, sharp and quick: "Number 35 . . . Terry. Addict. All here. . . . Number 37 . . . Perry. Alcoholic. All here. . . . Number 40 . . . Jonathan. Addict, Alcoholic. All here." The first guy, Jeremy, said, "Let's open."

Again, Jeremy shouted. "Big Guy in the sky, keep us from getting high."

The entire unit shouted in response, "God . . ." Then their voices dropped slightly and fell into a rhythmic, singsong pattern, almost like a chant. "Grant us the serenity . . ."

One of the counselors from extended care began the lecture. "You're ugly. You're stupid. You're too short. You're irresponsible," he started. "Most addicts have been told these kinds of things for a long time, and inside they feel like they are jerks, like they can't do anything right. They get high to escape those feelings. If you want to recover, you've got to trust somebody. You've got to let somebody love you even when you don't feel like you're lovable. Recovery is about the good part of you inside."

Nate recalled the day before in treatment group when Melanie gave him a positive for doing so well in treatment. Carol had chimed in, "I couldn't agree more. You are a real asset to this group, Nate. You're doing great!" Nate had squirmed in his chair.

"I've got a hunch it's hard for you to feel proud," Carol had said.

"Yeah," he admitted.

"Hey," Carol's voice had raised the ante. "You've got a right to feel it. Why is it it's so easy for you to feel the shitty feelings and so hard for you to feel proud? You're doing a great job. Own the good feelings too. They're part of recovery. This feeling is new, and you're just so scared you're not going to be able to hold on to it."

The lecturer was now introducing the guys from extended care, the ones who were going to do skits. He called them the Extended Care Players. A frenetic young man with a blond buzz started walking around the kids from primary care. He was shouting things at them like, "You got funny hair," "You're mean," and "All those rings in your face could set off a metal detector." A string bean of a kid with long black hair followed him, shouting, "Your hair is really pretty. I love the purple stripes," and "You are the nicest person I know." After about three minutes of this, Nate was transported home, to the craziness of criticism and mixed messages. He felt dizzy. Then the skits moved on to people pleasing, peer pressure, and perfectionism. Nate often got bored during the lectures, but this one was really fun. These guys seemed cool, as if they really got what treatment was about.

He hadn't been over to the extended care unit, wouldn't be going there, but he knew his buddy Jacob would be. Jacob really didn't want to go, but he had been through four treatments before, and his parents were both active alcoholics. Carol was telling him he'd use for sure if he went back to that environment again. Nate felt bad for him, having to stay in treatment for another three months, but as he watched these guys, he began to feel a little jealous of Jacob. After two more skits, the lecturer, a big guy with a booming voice, got behind the podium again. "Say this with me," he shouted. "Don't 'should' on me." Nate got into it, shouting along with the counselor. He shouted louder the second time. "I won't 'should' on myself."

"Finally," said the lecturer, "reprogram the computer. Get in front of the mirror every day and say, 'I love me,' until you are okay with yourself."

As they filed out of the lecture room, Nate told Jacob that extended didn't look so bad. "Easy for you to say," answered Jacob.

"I know, but c'mon, those guys were having fun."

"Do you know the guys work all Twelve Steps on extended?" Jacob asked. "They have to fill out workbooks, big as textbooks, about things like job skills. They have to write a résumé, and a lot of 'em go to school a few hours a day, get their GEDs."

"Bet you'll get more free time," said Nate. "And you'll get to go out six nights a week."

"Right. To AA meetings."

"And to the YMCA," protested Nate.

"You want to trade places with me?" asked Jacob.

"Nah, I'm going home," said Nate. It was Friday. On Sunday, two days from now, his parents would arrive for the parent program. He missed them, but he didn't relish facing them. He couldn't help thinking that in some ways Jacob might have it a little easier in extended care than he himself would at home.

Parent Program

He saw them walk into the cafeteria Sunday afternoon. His dad was standing stiffly in a gray pinstripe suit, his 6 feet, 2 inches pulled up high and his shoulders squared. The bit of gray at his temples made his southern California tan look even darker than it was. His mom, her blond hair cut short and curled around her face, was holding on to his dad's arm. She was called Gloria after her own mother's aspirations for her happiness. Gloria and Nathaniel II. While his dad looked younger than he had two and a half weeks ago, his mom looked older. Her face was drawn. When he saw her, he wished he'd changed out of his Grateful Dead T-shirt.

He took a deep breath and threaded his way through the big round tables to the far side where they were standing. He turned to his mom first for a hug and was startled, as usual, by the fact that he looked down on the top of her head now. He wasn't quite as tall as his dad, but he might still get there. Then he turned to his dad and was enveloped in a bear hug. Six other young people were also greeting their parents in the cafeteria. The parents had come from all over the country for three days of lectures and meetings; they would learn about the disease of addiction, how to help their child, and how to help themselves.

"How have you been, darling?" asked his mom in a worried tone.

"Fine, Mom, I'm just fine," Nate answered, trying to keep the irritation out of his voice. It would be so much easier for him if she'd quit worrying all the time. It wasn't that he didn't understand her worrying, but he hated it just the same.

"Nice place you got here, son," said his dad in a booming, jovial voice. "Want some lemonade?" He gestured to the cafeteria line.

Nate visited with his parents for about twenty minutes and then returned to the treatment unit, feeling both reassured and distressed. The feelings fought in him. His parents seemed honestly glad to see him. Perhaps they weren't furious with him. Perhaps they weren't going to blow up at him in the family conference tomorrow. But then again, maybe he would be the one to explode. He felt flattened by his mom's worry. It took his breath away to think he could have made her feel so awful. But still, her smell was so comforting; it made him think of his house with its vaulted ceilings and white rugs, the watercolors on the living room walls. It made him lonesome.

He had to wait and worry and wonder about the conference until late Monday, when the three of them met with a family counselor. In the office, Mr. and Mrs. Radcliffe pulled up chairs on each side of Nate, and the counselor sat straight across from him in the circle. After some introductions, the counselor announced that Nate had some things to tell his parents. He was supposed to tell them every detail of his drug use.

Nate launched into it, beginning with his first joint in seventh grade. He told them every detail he could think of and watched their faces register surprise, annoyance, and concern, but they didn't cry once. His mom reached out and touched his cheek, and he felt released of something that had shackled him since he first told them about his drug use. They were okay; they didn't hate him.

Then the counselor asked them to talk to Nate about how his drug use had affected them. His mom talked about her feelings when she'd gotten the truancy note and her constant worry about where he was in the evenings. She talked about how embarrassing his arrest was, the tones of pity in the people who greeted her in church, and how much she hated that. She said that, most of all, she felt as though he had crossed over into another world and she had lost him. That was when she began crying and saying, "I know I raised you badly. It's all my fault. I'm so sorry, Nate. I tried so hard." Though the counselor reminded her it was a no-fault disease and Nate was an addict because that's how his body reacted to the chemicals, that he really didn't have control over his drug use, she persisted in saying it was all her fault. Nate wished something would come in the room and swallow him whole, get him away so he wouldn't have to see the pain he'd caused his mom.

His dad talked about the hopes that had been dashed, how he had planned and saved for Nate to go to Harvard, and how that dream was probably gone now. He talked about Nate's soccer career, about how good he was, and about the money they'd spent for soccer equipment, team fees, and private coaching for him. He said it felt as though somebody knocked the wind out of him when he discovered Nate had endangered all that. He talked about how glad he was that Nate was doing well in treatment and said all he'd ever wanted was for his son to be happy. That's when his dad started to cry. Nate felt as if his heart was caked mud crumbling in his hand as he watched his dad cry. He'd never seen that before. He turned his body as far as he could toward the wall, trying not to look at his parents.

"Nate, it looks like it's pretty hard for you to see the effect your drug use has had on your parents."

Nate nodded.

"Are you afraid they're mad at you?"

Again he nodded.

The counselor suggested he ask his parents how they were feeling toward him now. "I'm really proud of you, Nate," said his dad.

"We just want you to get better, Nate. We love you so much," his mom added.

They parted with hugs, knowing that in a few hours Nate would have a pass and they would go out to dinner.

"Where do you want to go?" his dad asked.

"Mexican," he said. "I'm really missing the Southwest."

A Fresh Beginning

His last week in treatment, Nate did cursory Second and Third Steps. He listened to Carol lecture on how a Higher Power was the only thing that could keep him sober, and he filled out the required forms as honestly as he knew how. Carol knew this was a hard step for adolescents, who move away from established religion as a way of moving away from their parents. They needed to rely on concrete symbols, such as the ducks Nate had seen earlier in the courtyard and the relationships with staff members and peers, to communicate the reality of a power greater than themselves. During treatment Nate was getting the basic skills to use for recovery in the real world. As with his First Step, these Steps, too, would become clearer over time.

Although he wouldn't realize it on his last Sunday at Hazelden, an evening in June, Nate was about to do one of the most important things he would do in treatment. He was finishing supper in the cafeteria and was feeling a mixture of excitement and sadness. He had been in treatment for twenty-two days and was leaving in two more. He kept looking at Peter, at Melanie, thinking how he would miss them. Jacob had already gone over to extended care. Nate was amazed with how honest Jacob could be. When Jacob was leaving, he had autographed Nate's Big Book, writing, "Stay with the program, man. You're great and I know you can do it. I just worry sometimes that you don't really want to." Jacob had pinned him there. He didn't always want to do it.

Sometimes he thought about his buddies, and he just knew they were home doing something great, something he was missing out on. Sometimes he longed to get wasted with them and lay back and listen to Metallica just one more time. But how they pounded it into your head here. It's like potato chips—you can't use just once. He didn't dare chance it. Sometimes he thought he'd like to use just a little again, now that he knew how to behave, but if the staff here was right, he'd end up in the same bad place again. If he wanted to be a lawyer, he had to keep his grades up, and it was going to be the devil just to recover from the 1.4 grade point average he'd left school with.

Peter was clowning across the table, trying to balance a spoon on the end of his nose. Who was going to understand what he felt like, why he didn't want to use drugs, when these guys weren't around? It scared him. He had heard stories about people who had left treatment and relapsed. Ruined their lives. Some of them died.

Tonight a woman was coming over to pick up him and Peter for an off-site AA meeting. He knew AA could never replace his new friends. Nate walked dispiritedly back to his room for his jacket. Rain was pelting the plate glass doors that led from his room to the cedar balcony. As he changed into his black vinyl Nikes, running a towel over the toes to make them shine, he could hardly see the forest of maples and poplars that he always counted on to lift his spirits. He stared at the tiny points of hail bouncing off the balcony, imagining the meeting, a handful of old men sitting around talking about drinking whiskey. *This isn't going to work,* he thought.

At 6:30 P.M. the woman pulled up in front of the center, left the red Cutlass running, and dashed inside. She saw the two boys waiting by the front door and asked if they were Nate and Peter. Nate was surprised. The woman couldn't have been over twenty-five years old. She extended her hand and said enthusiastically, "I'm Barbara. I'm glad you can come with me tonight." They pulled their jackets over their heads and dashed for the car. They were driving to Wayzata.

The rain was sputtering out as they arrived at the church, a big modern building with a long green lawn. As they walked toward the front door, they let themselves lag behind Barbara. Peter turned to Nate and grimaced. In response, Nate hunched his shoulders and held his back. "Oh, my aching back. The old lumbago is acting up," he strained. "Got any Seagrams on you?" They laughed.

As they were about to enter the building, the sky began to lighten and they could see the sun dipping toward the horizon. "You first, my man," said Peter.

They descended the stairs to the big room in the church basement and were startled by what they saw. There must have been two hundred folding chairs set up, and the room was almost full. There were some old men, but they weren't hunched over. They wore suits or dress slacks and shirts, and stood straight and tall. There were also young men, none quite as young as Nate and Peter, but almost. The man who was wearing cutoffs and a Jim Morrison T-shirt, standing by the coffeepot to the right of the door, couldn't have been more than twenty-one. He was talking to a woman who looked about the same age. In fact, about a third of the people in the room were women. Several looked to Nate like college students.

The man in the cutoffs saw them and came over. He looked at Barbara and, like her, he spoke enthusiastically. "Hey, Barbara, who have you brought with you tonight?"

When she introduced them and explained where they were from, he said, "I'm Terry. It's great to have you here. You must be getting out of treatment soon."

"Two days," assented Nate.

Terry let out a big breath. "Whooo, what a place that is. I don't think I'd be here without them. I went through their extended care. Let me give you my number. If you ever want a ride here after you're out of treatment, give me a call." Several other people walked over to introduce themselves before the Serenity Prayer signaled the start of the meeting.

Nate continued to be startled as the night progressed. The speaker was a thirty-two-year-old crackhead who was now a public relations manager. He'd been as down and out as you get, having been beaten up while scoring his drugs. Now he had a wife and a baby. This guy was cool.

At break time Nate and Peter followed about twenty people outside to smoke. The rain had cleared entirely, though the grass was still wet. Everyone gathered on the concrete walk in front of the church. A woman and man to Nate's right were talking about a scuba diving trip they had made to the Caribbean last winter and their plans to go wreck diving in Lake Superior this summer. An older woman was telling someone that she had her first book published on her eightieth birthday, and it had been the most glorious birthday present she could imagine. The talk around Nate and Peter was excited, rapid, and punctuated by generous laughter. Nate walked on the lawn, not caring if his shoes got wet. With such a swelling of freedom, he couldn't stand still on the sidewalk. He had heard people talk about treatment highs. *This must be it,* he thought.

He felt excited about looking for a meeting when he went home to California. Attending Alcoholics Anonymous at least three times a week was part of his continuing care plan. Besides that, Carol had contacted a potential sponsor for him back home, and they had talked on the phone. After this meeting, he felt it wouldn't be so hard to follow the plan. The California meetings had to be at least as cool as the meetings in Minnesota. A man who looked to be about thirty-five walked over to Nate and welcomed him. "I'm Leonard," he said. "And you?"

"Nate."

They talked for a few minutes about the meeting, about Nate's plan to return to high school, about the color of the setting sun, about Nate's soccer games, and about his cool shoes. Then Leonard asked, "How does it feel to be here, Nate?"

"It's way cool," Nate answered. *Treatment is giving me a whole new life,* he thought to himself. *It got me sober.* He didn't know yet that AA is what would keep him sober.

5

Inside the Maze

ANDY FOLLOWED the two men along the maze of hallways that turned left and right in so many directions. He was certain that he would never find his way by himself. Fortunately, signs were posted at each turn, with one pointing to Shoemaker Hall, a men's unit where Andy would spend his first weeks in rehab.

"That's an odd name," Andy said to his counselor. Andy was uncomfortable with him carrying his suitcase. "I can carry it," he protested when the counselor first stooped to pick up his bag in the Ignatia unit. Andy wasn't used to the courtesy he received not only from the staff but from his own peer, Billy, another patient who had come along to welcome him. Billy had lifted Andy's coat out of the closet and was now carrying it over his arm to the unit.

"It was named after the Reverend Dr. Samuel Shoemaker, a close friend of Bill W.," his counselor said. "Do you know who Bill W. is?" he asked.

"Sure. He and Dr. Bob were the cofounders of Alcoholics Anonymous. I wrote a newspaper article on them once."

Andy followed as the two men turned down another corridor. A group of six women from Dia Linn, a women's unit, approached. Billy and the counselor hardly noticed as they passed. Andy smiled; one woman nodded back in response.

Once on the unit, Billy gave him a tour. In the kitchen, Billy pulled out a coffee cup with a blue and white Hazelden logo and attached a stenciled label with the name "Andy" to the cup. He hung it on a corkboard with about twenty other cups. Andy said nothing about the cup. No one but his parents called him Andy. On the street he was known as "Roey," a nickname taken from his last name—Monroe. Sal, Glamor, the guys he used with in Harlem, even his old roommates in Long Island would occasionally call him Roey. When he first introduced himself in

Ignatia, it was the counselor who suggested "Andrew" or "Andy," since Roey was associated with street life and dealing. It was strange to see the name on a coffee cup that belonged to him. He hoped it suggested a new identity.

Billy opened the refrigerator to show him the available food, and explained why he was called the "Senior Peer." He was elected by other patients on the unit to lead the meetings in the lounge, the big room just below the kitchen, where everyone met at 7:15 in the morning for meditation before breakfast. Just off the kitchen, Billy showed him the unit's computer, which would print out each patient's schedule. "Hazelden has an Internet page on the Web too," he said.

"Yeah, I know all about the Internet," Andy interrupted. "I've written essays about it for a New York magazine. I know my way around on it." Billy nodded and showed Andy how to print out a copy of his daily schedule each morning. "I used to be the editor of a technology magazine, and computers are second nature to me," Andy added.

Billy continued and pointed out the Twelve Steps of Alcoholics Anonymous on the wall. "You'll have time to read them later," Billy said.

"I'm familiar with them," Andy remarked, remembering his first treatment in New York and the AA meetings he attended later.

"Well, obviously you forgot the First Step," Billy offered, smiling. Andy looked away, and they returned to his room.

Billy told Andy he would share a room with three others: two men who had arrived several days ago and a third man who had come from Ignatia only hours earlier. This was Jay, the fifty-year-old man Andy saw in Ignatia the day before. He recalled Jay trying to smuggle Valium into Hazelden, remembered how he thought the man should be kicked out, and how Jay's yelling had disturbed him. He thought about how much older than fifty the man looked, with his potbelly, large red cheeks, fluffy mustache, and bulbous nose. Andy didn't look forward to seeing him again.

Later that afternoon, Andy met all his roommates. Besides Jay, there were Danny and Bob. Danny, who was from Laramie, Wyoming, was only twenty-five years old, and Andy felt drawn to him. Danny was a graduate theology student at Harvard who smoked pot and used Dilantin, a pharmaceutical narcotic injected intravenously. He was good-looking, thin, and agile, wore a long ponytail, and looked like someone who might enjoy shooting baskets. Bob was affectionately nicknamed by Shoemaker's patients as Dr. Bob, after the Alcoholics Anonymous cofounder, because Bob was not only a doctor but lived in Akron, where the AA cofounder was from. Bob was thirty-five years old and had a wife and two daughters. He had a small, failing medical practice in a suburb just north of Akron. Bob drank vodka day and night. He kept a bottle hidden in his office and sipped from it between patients. He drank vodka because he believed it had no odor and, therefore, could not be detected on his breath.

That first night, Andy was kept awake by Jay's snoring. When Andy finally did sleep, he was awakened after midnight by loud coughing and moaning. It woke everyone in the room. Jay, sitting up in bed now, was retching hard. Finally, he vomited on the floor in the middle of the room. Andy disliked him all the more, and would not get out of bed to help clean up. *Let him do it,* he thought to himself.

That morning, at 7:15, the four men were expected to arrive promptly for a short reading from the book *Twenty-Four Hours a Day,* a few announcements, and meditation. Fifteen minutes later, they would attend breakfast. No one was excused. There were no individual wake-up calls—no nurse, counselor, or officer knocking on their doors to wake them up. The alarm that Danny had brought with him sounded at 6:30. It was the responsibility of another peer to announce a wake-up call over the intercom. The four roommates were expected to make their beds, and Andy knew he would be the first one up and the first to have his bed made. He was determined to do things the right way, and he expected others to follow his lead.

On Monday, Andy and the others were told the housekeeping rules. They were to remove their shampoo bottles from the shower so the housekeeper could clean it. They were to pick up every towel and make round corners at the bottom of the beds. They were asked to keep their shoes and suitcases off the floor so it could be swept and mopped. The unit's housekeeper would allow two or three days before she reminded the newcomers of the regulations on keeping up their room. Most of the regulations were minor, but infractions required a fee of fifty cents, payable to the Pig, a bank shaped like a swine. Many of the men on the unit, like Andy and Jay, were not used to making their own beds. Their wives, lovers, housekeepers, parents, or children made their beds. Or they were left unmade. When Andy lived with his New York roommates, he simply kept his bedroom door shut until Tuesday, when the house-keeper came to clean. Now making his own bed had everything to do with sobriety, everything to do with rebuilding his self-respect and self-esteem, with taking responsibility. Other chores, like vacuuming the hallways and main room, dusting, washing dishes, sweeping the kitchen floor, and emptying wastebaskets, required Andy and other newcomers to work together to create a community on Shoemaker.

At the Kitchen Table

No one, Andy thought, had gained or lost as much as he had through the use of chemicals. No one's elevator had crashed from such a great height as his. He imagined himself as worse off than anyone on Shoe-maker, worse off than everyone in Hazelden, in all of Minnesota, in America, in the world. Imagining himself as such a complete failure iso-lated him from his roommates and the other men on Shoemaker. He thought of himself as a flame, doomed to spend himself, leaving only smoke and ashes.

For the entire first week, Andy tried hard to identify with the men telling their stories every morning in the lounge at eleven. The floor was vacuumed by that hour, and no one brought coffee cups into the room. On the first morning, Andy sat down in the seat nearest the stairs. Billy reminded him that the seat was reserved for Oliver, a pa-tient with multiple sclerosis who walked with canes and needed the nearest available chair. The chair at the far end of the room, nearer the sliding patio doors, was reserved for that day's storyteller. It was some-times called the "hot seat," and each day a different man would take his turn there. Once the session began, the storyteller might talk off the cuff or read from his notes for up to an hour. Some men might only take thirty minutes, while others took longer. They took as much time as they needed. The entire group, consisting of nineteen men, met there every morning after lectures. No one was excused. The storyteller's counselor would arrive as he began his story.

After the story, each group member was permitted to ask one ques-tion for clarification. The following afternoon at three o'clock, each peer evaluated the speaker's story. The peers would note the speaker's strengths and weaknesses, pointing out if he had expressed his feelings and demonstrated courage, glamorized his past drinking or using, minimized his drinking or using, or blamed others. They would also talk about whether the story showed responsibility or self-pity. After the peers spoke, the counselor spoke reflectively about what had been said by the peers.

Andy listened to Shoemaker's Dr. Bob tell his story. He talked about where he had hidden his vodka bottle from the nurse and secretary, and of his intense loneliness, which often led to extramarital affairs. Andy still felt alienated from him and the others. Andy thought his own successes made him better or more sophisticated than Danny, despite their similar drug use. And while Dr. Bob was a medical doctor whose success and wealth afforded him travel to the Caribbean every winter and a beautiful home outside Akron, his drinking couldn't match Andy's. In his opinion, men like Danny lacked success, and men like Dr. Bob lacked recklessness.

All week, Andy compared himself to others. When a businessman from San Diego who worked in the computer industry spoke, Andy could identify with his success, having been a prominent journalist in the fields of electronics and high-tech marketing. But once again, the man's history of drug use wasn't as colorful as Andy's. He identified with men who were financially successful, but none of them could really understand. Men like Jay and the heroin addict from New Jersey, who had shot up in movie theaters, had sunk to a similar degradation, he thought, but they hadn't been successful at work. In fact, they had no jobs.

Not until Andy gave his own story to the group a week and a half later did a real crack open in his shell. He walked around all day with a pencil and notepaper in his pocket, making notes for his story. He worried about telling too much, and he worried about not telling enough. He wanted to make a good impression on the guys, and if he told them everything, like about Sal prostituting moments before he arrived at her apartment, they might think he was really depraved. On the other hand, he knew they valued honesty, and it was an important rule. He wanted to be honest. He had heard men on the unit talk about the Big Book of Alcoholics Anonymous and its tenet of rigorous self-honesty; without it, a life of sobriety was out of the question. His mind circled in ever-tightening loops all day.

When Andy finally sat down in the chair and the group quieted for him to begin, his throat was dry. He usually didn't have any trouble performing before a group. His comfort with crowds was part of what had made him successful in his job. But this speech was so self-revealing; it felt like one of the hardest things he'd ever done. He took a deep breath and plunged in. "I'm afraid I haven't done as well in writing my notes as others of you have," he told the group. He apologized for sounding so disorganized as he talked, but his Harlem experiences themselves were chaotic and random. He confessed to being selfish and stupid in his behavior. He admitted to hating Glamor, the gang leader who gave orders to have him beaten, admitted to cheating Sal, his roommates, even his mother. He admitted to stealing thousands of dollars in credit card fraud from his job. He said that he lied during his Hazelden admissions about his last use of cocaine, and had been arrogant, belittling other men on Shoemaker in his mind.

"I'm sorry," he said, near tears. He said that smoking crack had irreparably damaged him, had taken his soul, and he didn't think he would ever find it again. Before he told his story, telling the truth had meant despair and hopelessness for Andy. For every breath he took in, he'd exhaled doom. But something shifted slightly during his story hour. He was remotely aware of the attention the men paid him, their nods of recognition as he talked, their occasional chuckles, and the looks of concern on their faces. And when he'd finished, they all clapped. He was surprised at how good he felt.

However, the next afternoon at his peer evaluation, Andy expected the others to criticize him for being arrogant and self-centered. And some of them did, saying they found Andy to be full of self-pity and self-aggrandizement. They found him difficult to get to know. Still, they thought he showed courage for admitting that he had isolated himself from everyone. They had noticed how Andy had separated himself by sitting alone during lectures and not talking much in the dining hall. Andy was complimented for being honest and "copping to it." His counselor, Steve Eastman, also the unit supervisor, summarized the men's thoughts and feelings when he said, "Andy, you're hurting and you have to open up your doors and let us in. We want to help, but we can't if you won't let us."

Andy wanted to open the door, let them in, or himself out, or maybe both. Maybe now the door was slightly ajar.

Later that evening, after the lecture, a group of six men sat at the round table in the lobby above the meeting room. They were all drinking coffee. Two other men stood at the counter munching on popcorn. Others pulled up chairs to be near the table, listening to Tom, an attorney from Texas, regale them with stories from his eighteen treatments at chemical dependency centers throughout the country. Andy, attempting to change, had joined the men at the table. Still, he was quiet. He felt jealous of the attention Tom was getting. Andy interrupted and said that he, too, had visited the island of Montserrat. Andy boasted about his job as a writer for the travel magazine. The men had heard about the job during his story hour. "Yeah," Andy went on, "they paid me to travel all over the Caribbean."

"Wow," Tom said to Andy, as the others in the group listened attentively. "A Caribbean writer! What a job!" Andy blushed a little and soaked in the attention. Just as Andy leaned back in his chair, Tom leaned forward across the table and added, "Too bad you screwed it up."

Everyone roared. For a moment, Andy sat still, grimacing. The other men weren't laughing at Andy; they were laughing at themselves. Each one had screwed up: jobs, families, relationships, their lives. In a way, they all had led extraordinary lives that failed. From the outside, their lives, like Andy's, might have seemed exotic, but in reality their lives were terribly marred by alcoholism and addiction. Someone standing alongside Andy slapped him on the shoulder and messed his hair. "We don't mean anything, Andy. It's all right. We're all in the same boat."

Andy looked up at the man. It was Jay—old, potbellied, and smiling. Andy still remembered the sickness that first night, but now he noticed Jay's smile, how wide and expressive it was. He smiled back and nodded. *Yes,* Andy thought to himself. *We are all in the same boat, rowing together to safety.*

For the first time since Andy arrived on Shoemaker Hall, he began to enjoy being among the men. That evening at the coffee table, many of the men recounted terribly embarrassing experiences of their using days. They laughed at each other and at themselves. Andy hadn't laughed so hard for years. His side began to ache, which only made him laugh more. Instead of seeing the differences between himself and the others, now he began to see the similarities. Both Jay and he were crack addicts and had dealt drugs. He, like Danny, was a young, athletic man ruining his body with drugs. He, like Dr. Bob, had lost his soul. Andy could identify with Dr. Bob's loneliness, even though Bob had a wife and child. And the other men on the unit—the butcher from Alabama, the chef from Florida, the corporate lawyer from Chicago, the communications director from Seattle—they would not belong together anywhere else in the world but at Hazelden. Alcoholism and drug addiction brought these men together. Andy looked at the men in the kitchen and knew he belonged with them. He was part of a fellowship.

Later that night, Andy recalled what Tom had said to him about his job. *Yes,* he said to himself, smiling, *I sure screwed it up.*

Afterward, Andy was no longer offended by the men who slept late in the mornings. His self-righteous attitude began to diminish. He no longer seemed to notice who hadn't done their chores. The less morally indignant Andy became, the more the men liked him and invited him to the patio to talk.

Choosing to Stay

The door to Steve Eastman's office was usually closed, as were the doors to most of the counselors' offices and the staff room. Andy complained to his roommates about the difficulty of getting time with his counselor. "Just knock on his door," Danny said. He was writing in his journal, but closed his notebook and talked with Andy until he finally let on why he wanted to talk to Steve. "Just knock," Danny reminded him after the conversation.

The next day he did.

"Come in," Steve called out. As the door opened and Andy came in, Steve swiveled in his chair to face him. Andy felt less intimidated seeing Steve seated in his chair. Andy often felt hesitant when Steve was standing. Because he was a tall man, large, bearded, and long-haired, he seemed imposing to Andy.

Andy noticed postcards on a bulletin board. "Nice," he said.

"Thanks. They're pictures of different paintings."

"Yeah, I recognize van Gogh's bedroom at Arles and the Renoir." Steve also had a collection of shells, arrowheads, Japanese river stones, stones from the North Shore near Duluth, miniatures of angels, Buddhas, and pictures of Gandhi and St. Patrick originally taken in Cork, Ireland, displayed on tabletops and bookcases in his office.

"I believe in bringing my spirituality to work," Steve said.

"Can I have some time to talk with you?" Andy asked.

"Sure. What's up?"

"Nothing in particular. I just haven't talked to you for four days, since my story."

"Is something the matter?"

"No, not exactly."

"Well, I don't have a lot of time to chat, but if there's something pressing that you want to talk about, I'll close the office and give you all the time you need."

"You know, if Hazelden is supposed to be one of the best treatment centers in the world," Andy started, "how come I have to wait days, almost a week, to get an appointment with you? All the doors are shut here. You guys never show up for morning meditation. If we have to, why don't you? No one is on the unit after four o'clock. What if one of us gets sick and needs to talk to a counselor? How can you expect us to take care of things? We're just a bunch of drunks and addicts. I've been in treatment before. I need more than this. I need daily counseling sessions or I'm going to relapse. This isn't enough for me. How am I going to get help? I know the Twelve Steps. There is nothing here that I haven't tried before. I need more than what you have here."

Steve listened. As someone who believes in Tao, Steve tried hard to get things done by knowing when to do nothing. Everything was in place on Shoemaker to bring the patients together, to work things out, to help each other. "Alcoholics love to wrestle with authority figures," Steve told Andy. "A person like you comes to my office and says, 'Why should I stay here?' You know what I have to ask you? Why should I have you here? Why should I keep you? Andy, there are no locks on our doors, no penalty or terrible confrontation if you choose to leave. So why do you want to be here? Ask yourself, 'What will I do if I leave?' The only thing that will help is to admit having this terrible disease that threatens to take your life. I can't do that for you, but I can step out of your way and provide you with support from peers and staff. We talked about this at your peer evaluation, after your story."

"But I need more than that. I'm hopeless. I've been through this before."

Steve looked hard at him. "Andy, you're making a convincing point.

If you are so hopeless, I can arrange for the driver to take you back to the airport. If you think you can't be helped here, I can make arrangements for you to leave." Steve looked steadily at Andy, who was breathless and afraid. He had backed himself into a corner. Steve had offered an exit. If Andy wanted to stay, he had to admit that he could be helped, that he wasn't hopeless, that it wasn't up to the counselors and peers to give him sobriety, faith, and hope. For a long time neither man spoke. Andy looked down at his feet while Steve waited for an answer. Steve could guess that something dark was nudging itself loose inside Andy, something that needed to be released. Andy was realizing that he had to bring something to his own recovery. His eyes moistened.

"I don't have anywhere else to go," Andy said, his voice catching.

"You must believe in yourself even when you can't," Steve spoke. "You have to find hope somewhere, even if you feel hopeless. Courage isn't jumping into a raging river to save a child while onlookers watch from a bridge. No, courage is jumping into your own river and saving yourself when no one is watching. You've got the guts, Andy. Look at what you've done, the fearlessness you showed in Harlem. Show some of that fearlessness here. Use that energy for yourself."

Yes, Andy had showed audacity in Harlem. His recklessness was a liability then, but now he could make it an asset. Who cared if he knelt by his bed and prayed? So what if he looked foolish to others. It would be much easier than walking around Harlem with bruised ribs.

"Yes," he said, nodding to Steve. He would give it a try. He would "act as if" life wasn't hopeless for him. He would do his own share of the work, attend group meetings without comparing himself to others, begin talking to others more, and seek out help from his peers. In the office, Steve wrote out a short treatment plan for Andy. First, because Andy was having such trouble recognizing his own powerlessness, he was to read in the AA Big Book about the limits of self-knowledge, and discuss his thoughts about it with three of his peers. He was also to complete a twelve-page Step One assessment; watch the video *Cunning, Baffling, and Powerful;* and ask others about how they pray. Andy was instructed to ask someone to watch him pray in his room. Andy wasn't to go for a walk without inviting someone else along. "From now on," Steve said, "I want you with someone else. Don't even think of walking by yourself to lecture hall or sitting alone. And I want you to ask God, a Higher Power, or the spirit of nature to come along with you." Steve wasn't trying to make him religious, but Andy did need to rely on others and a Higher Power for support and direction.

Andy felt as if he were being treated like a child; at the same time, there was relief in having such explicit instructions. He didn't feel quite so alone.

After they had shaken hands and Andy had turned to go, Steve said, "Remember: The addict is either focused on the past or on the future. Either remorseful over what he's done or fearful of what he must do, of his future. One of my goals for you, Andy, is to experience a moment of vulnerability right here and now. You can only experience a Higher Power in the present. We tell people around here, like I'm telling you, that if you project into the future, you go without God. All you bring is your own fear. And if you go into the past, you go without God. All you bring is your own self-recriminations. So stay awake to what is right here." Steve put his arm on Andy's shoulder as they walked to the door. "Okay?"

The next day in his room, Andy explained to Danny and Jay how his counselor wanted someone to watch him pray. But praying made him feel like a fake. He wasn't opposed to his roommates or anyone else praying. He was glad it worked for them. In his own heart, however, he believed prayers were useless. After some resistance, Andy got down on his knees, humbling himself in front of the two men, and found himself praying silently and earnestly. Danny and Jay watched him kneeling at the side of his bed like a child. No one spoke. Except for Andy in the privacy of his soul.

After a minute or two, Andy started to feel self-conscious and silly. He stood up. "I feel like I'm cheapening your own prayers by doing this. Prayers work for you, but not for me. I'm acting like a hypocrite. I don't believe in it, but I'm trying to 'act as if,' like Steve told me to."

"What did you pray for?" Danny asked.

"I prayed for some other answer to this, because what I'm doing on my knees feels so phony."

"Why don't you pray for the ability to pray?" Danny said.

Jay agreed. "That's it. Pray to pray."

That seemed feasible to Andy. It became an intellectual gateway to spirituality for him, a kind of logic that allowed him to pray, to act, as Steve had encouraged him to do, as if there were hope.

A Way through the Maze

It was the beginning of Andy's third week on Shoemaker when an unexpected event suddenly caused him to end one aspect of his treatment plan. All four men were still sharing the same room. When other rooms, smaller ones that offered more privacy, became available, neither Danny nor Dr. Bob, who had seniority, requested to move. The four men had come to depend on each other. In the middle of one night, long after everyone had gone to sleep, Andy was awakened by strange animal-like sounds. He heard gasping and grunting from across the room and saw Bob thrashing in bed. Danny and Jay woke in turn. "What is it?" Andy shouted. Danny turned on the lamp. "Jesus!" Andy cried out. "He's having a seizure."

Bob, though a doctor, had long minimized the significance of his own diabetes. At home, he had continued to drink excessively despite his high blood-sugar levels. He had kept his diabetes a secret from everyone, including his roommates. Now, Bob had gone into insulin shock.

"Stay with him," Andy shouted to Danny and Jay as he ran for help. Andy had never mastered the hallways and depended on the signs and other patients to find his way to lecture hall, Cork athletic center, and even the dining hall. That night, however, Andy found his way through the maze of corridors without stopping to read the signs. Something inside him knew when to turn right and when to turn left. Afraid for his roommate's life, Andy ran down one dark corridor after another. He turned right, straight toward the library, past the dining hall to Ignatia. It seemed as if he had learned his way without trying. His fear and worry for Bob—his emotions—set him on the right track. He knew the way to Ignatia without knowing. He had trusted himself. It was the first time sober that Andy felt anything so intensely. Never before had he been afraid for anyone other than himself. He flung open the Ignatia door and raced to the desk. It was his first time at Ignatia since he was admitted. "Hurry," he yelled to the nurse. "Bob is having convulsions." She dropped her pen, picked up a blood pressure cuff and other supplies, and with Andy, raced back to Shoemaker.

Bob was still thrashing in bed. His tongue was bleeding, and Danny and Jay were standing beside his bed, trying to calm him, when Andy and the nurse arrived.

Andy stood next to Danny while the nurse worked. It was the first time Andy prayed without anyone watching him. He didn't pray to pray; he prayed for Bob's life. Andy felt so small, so powerless to effect any change in Bob's health. He prayed because he didn't want Bob to die. Andy needed him. Everyone on the unit needed him. Danny cried. And Andy cried for the first time since he was a child. After that night, no one needed to watch him pray anymore. In fact, it was deleted from his treatment plan. Andy no longer struggled to pray. It was clear to him how much he needed others. And just as important, he could see how others needed him. On the night his roommate almost died, Andy discovered that spirituality wasn't reached through prayer and meditation alone. Sometimes it could be found by running like hell to save another man's life.

Andy no longer considered himself unique. His fall from grace into alcoholism was not the longest and worst fall. No. He began to be more humble. Humility felt like clothes that fit. He described himself to Danny as a circle: they were all circles, and yet each man's life overlapped with others, forming concentric centers, common bonds, and wasn't that, he told Danny, the definition of humanity?

Still, his hopelessness waited deep inside of him, like a shadow. It would resurface whenever Andy felt lonely, confused, or vulnerable. Andy knew he needed continued support and feared he wouldn't get the extra help. He believed he needed Jellinek, a long-term unit at Hazelden. A part of him wanted the longest possible confinement. He had no home to go back to in New York: his roommates had locked him out, his mother couldn't afford to help him, he had lost his job, and his prostitute girlfriend had kicked him out of her Harlem apartment. Even the drug dealers didn't want him back. Where could he go?

6

The Good Patient

JOANNA never entirely gave herself over to the business of treatment in the winter of 1994, and so she never felt quite at home on the Lilly unit.

On Wednesday afternoon, she met with her counselor, Marilyn Jasperson, who was also the director of the Lilly unit, to look over her treatment plan. The first item read, "Understand powerlessness over alcohol and other drugs: Do Chemical Dependency Assessment Worksheet." The second item stated, "Shame and spirituality: Let go of shame." Marilyn talked to her about the difficulty alcoholics and addicts have believing that they cannot control their drinking. She also talked about how addicts are ashamed of the things they have done while in the grip of their disease. For women, this often took the form of letting their children down or failing to protect them. Many addicted women often feel like failures as mothers. Marilyn talked to her about how deep-seated the shame is and how it sabotages healing. If Joanna could accept that her negative behavior was influenced by her disease, it would help her to get sober.

Marilyn was pretty and seemed kind, but she was about twenty years older than Joanna. How could Marilyn know anything about her life? How could Marilyn know what Joanna had done to let her daughter down, or if she'd done anything at all? It made very little sense to her, but she knew Jeff wouldn't let her come home until the counselors said she was ready. She nodded her head to Marilyn that she understood and would work on it.

Marilyn told her it was also important to talk with the other women on the unit. "They have had similar experiences, and they will know what you feel. Sharing secrets is the first step to getting over the shame. Don't isolate yourself. When you are tempted to stay alone in your room, make yourself join the other women."

Joanna's bedroom on the unit was referred to as "the bunker." A shared room, it was lower than the other rooms and at the end of a tunnel-like hallway that connected the Lilly unit to the rest of the Hazelden complex. Her bed stood next to sliding glass doors that were adjacent to the patio, which flooded her personal area with light. Her desk was bare except for a notebook, her treatment plan, and the Big Book. Her shampoo, hair curlers, and makeup were piled neatly on a shelf next to a photo of her, Jeff, and Molly. In the glorious half hour of free time she had each day, that's where she wanted to be, quietly alone in her circle of sunshine.

Though she had roommates, she paid little attention to them. If she didn't talk to them much, and stayed by her bed in the far corner of the room, it was almost like being alone. Her bedroom and her wish to be alone pulled at her all day long, but she resisted. During her first treatment in Chicago, she was accused of isolating herself. Here, she would try to please Marilyn. Joanna made herself stay out in the lounge, the central gathering place, during her little free time. She disliked being kept so busy. First, there was morning meditation together, breakfast at 7:30, a lecture at nine, and group afterward. And that was only the morning regimen. After the long afternoon of lecture, story time, counseling sessions, group rec time, and after they marched as a group to the evening lecture where they sat together, Joanna wanted nothing more in the world than to sneak off to the bunker, crawl into her bed, and curl into a ball under her blue coverlet.

However, when Wednesday evening came, she went back to her room, changed into a sweat suit and slippers, put on fresh lipstick, dropped off her notebook, and forced herself to walk back up to Lilly's kitchen. Several women sat at the three round tables, the morning newspaper scattered over them. Joanna tried to glance surreptitiously at the names emblazoned on the women's coffee cups. Even though she had been on the unit for three days, she was so foggy from the Librium, and now the phenobarbital, that it was hard to remember names.

The mugs told her that Polly sat at the table to her right, and Susan sat next to her. Carter's was the only mug she could see on the table to the left. *I wonder if they'll notice me,* she thought. *If I'm going to sit with them, I'd better get some coffee.* Self-consciously, she walked over to the wall where the cups hung from a corkboard, grabbed the mug labeled

"Joanna," lifted the nozzle to the coffeepot, and let the dark brown, bitter liquid fill her own mug.

She saw Susan lean toward Polly. "You keep your paws off my yogurt, honey. And don't you tell a soul it's there. I don't want to get in trouble with the kitchen." Susan was single and from San Francisco. She sizzled with energy, and her words seemed to trip over each other in their rush to get out. She had carefully combed brown hair that hung past her shoulders. She was maybe twenty-eight or twenty-nine years old.

"Well, pardon me," said Polly, a housewife from Tennessee, with exaggerated dismay. Polly's face was round and dimpled. Joanna guessed she was in her mid-forties.

Carter, the woman sitting next to Polly, looked up from the article she was reading. She had an aristocratic air and spoke with a slight accent. "All right, ladies, back where I come from in Montreal, we share and share alike." She winked at Susan. "You go ahead, take my blueberry yogurt."

Joanna was drawn to their banter. They looked as if they were actually having fun. It had been like that in the morning, too, after breakfast. They gathered, she discovered, in the lounge every morning for meditation. The leader that morning was Carter, and she read the December 28 entry from *One Day at a Time*. Everyone was quiet. Another woman read a paragraph from the Big Book, and another quoted a poem by Galway Kinnell. Then Susan, the bubbly one from San Francisco, quoted Peter Pan. "'I don't want to grow up,' by Peter Pan." Joanna couldn't tell whether she was serious. After a few minutes of quietness, all the women stood, closed the circle until they were shoulder to shoulder, and held each other's hands. Joanna was between Carter and Polly. They said the Serenity Prayer together, ending with "So be it." When Carter squeezed her hand, Joanna felt a longing to be part of this sorority of women, and yet another part of her resisted identifying with them.

Today, in the kitchen, the women were talking about Abby's story. She had told her story after dinner, sitting in the lounge, everyone in the unit gathered around her. Abby had said the words matter-of-factly.

"I'd buckle the boys in their car seats—they were two and four then—and drive for an hour to San Antonio to get my heroin. It was a crummy neighborhood, gunshots, the whole bit, and I'd leave the boys in the car when I went inside to shoot up. Near the end it got really bad. Jimmy and Sam would be in the car for three hours, while I sat in the bathroom, my arms all bloody, trying to find a vein. But I didn't dare stop. I would be sick if I didn't get it in me. After that the boys' dad took them, I lost my apartment, and I had run out of unemployment. I started walking the streets.

"You gotta understand. I shot heroin in the morning so I could cope with walking into a bank and writing a check. I shot heroin in the morning so I could cope with making my bed. I wasn't getting high, I was just trying to stay normal. I woke up sick in the morning, and if there was no heroin, I thought I was gonna die. I'd drag myself out of bed, turn a trick, and I'd have enough money to score. As soon as I got the heroin, I'd feel better. And then I'd go earn enough money to stay high for the rest of the day."

"I don't know what I'll do when I tell my story," Joanna said to the women in the kitchen. "It'll sound so boring compared to Abby's." What she didn't say was how relieved she was. She wasn't so bad after all. She never left Molly in the car, not for more than ten minutes anyway. And that was in a good neighborhood. And she never drove around high on heroin with Molly in the car. She might have been a little fuzzy from alcohol, but never heroin. At least she hadn't lost her child. At least she wasn't a hooker.

"Every story's important," Carter answered, her voice shifting to high-octane intensity. "And underneath, every story is the same. We're more alike than we are different."

Joanna smiled. "I'm sure you're right," she said.

Making Connections

Joanna went through the next four days in a phenobarbital haze, remembering snippets of conversations, bumping into furniture, and plotting her escape, the day they would let her out. She talked to Jeff at least three times a day, telling him how much better she was, how he should bring her home before Molly's birthday. Sometimes her speech was slurred from the tranquilizer.

Jeff would say, "Joanna, you are so out of it." Joanna struggled to speak clearly when she talked with him. If she was going to convince him, she had to sound together. She also had to convince her counselor.

She wrote out her Step One worksheets. The forms asked her to write out how much alcohol she drank, when and what she drank, how much it cost, and what happened in her life as a result of drinking. It was shocking to see the amount and the progression. She questioned her memory, thinking, *I couldn't possibly have drunk a fifth and a half of vodka a day.* She finally began to see the problems her drinking had caused. She wasn't away from Molly for Christmas because she was a poor housekeeper, cook, or wife. She was beginning to see that she had missed Christmas with her daughter for one reason only: she got drunk.

On January 4 there was a storm, almost a blizzard. She woke to the howling of the wind. It seemed to beat like a fist against her windows. Outside, the bare branches were bending, the snow obscuring the stone wall that ran along the outdoor walkway. The tranquilizer was starting to clear from her system, and it was not quite so hard to get out of bed. The first thing she saw as she stood up was the photo of her, Jeff, and Molly. That morning, Joanna dressed in black leggings and an over-sized purple sweater. She listened to her roommates talking as she put on her makeup, pale green eye shadow, mascara, and light red lipstick. Put together, she was ready to go out to the lounge.

Everyone wore heavy sweaters as they milled around the coffeepot in the kitchen before breakfast, picking up their schedules for the day. The women from the South, especially Abby and Claudia, were complaining about the cold. But the building was warm despite the wind, giving a feeling of coziness that Joanna loved, a feeling difficult to duplicate any other time of the year. The network of hallways that connected the complex meant they never had to brave the cold unless they wanted to. If she chose, Joanna could go anywhere in her slippers—to the cafeteria, the counseling center, the bookstore, the lecture hall, even to the gym and swimming pool.

In the evening, Joanna was still wrapped in her oversized sweater. She had grudgingly come to look forward to this time of day, the time when all the structured activities were over, a time when they did their worksheets, read the books they'd been assigned, or sat in the lounge joking, teasing, dropping in and out of intense conversation. Abby, the woman whose story had shocked her a few days ago, was completing an assignment for which she had to collect fifteen positive attributes about herself from different peers. It was often one of the hardest assignments the women did. They found it very difficult to think of things they liked about themselves, and they were embarrassed to ask others to say good things about them.

"Oh, shit," said Abby. "I've collected seven. So, who's gonna give me another one?"

"Honesty," observed Claudia.

Abby laughed. "Isn't that amazing? Me? The prime scuz ball of the world. A dirty heroin addict who'd lie, cheat, and steal to get high. 'Honesty,' says the lady."

Joanna sat quietly, watching.

"C'mon," said Carter, "you know that was your disease. You're not getting high now, and you are one of the most honest people I know. Remember in split group? How you told us about the sexual abuse? That took guts." Twice a week, so they could talk more easily, the Lilly unit was divided in half for smaller group sessions.

Joanna sat up. "What was that?"

"I'm sorry, Abby," said Carter. "Maybe I shouldn't have said anything."

"Nah, it's okay," Abby answered. "It's good for me to tell it. It helps me understand why I feel so crummy about myself." She diverted her piercing green eyes to the floor. Her long blond hair overflowed the clip that held it loosely at the back of her head. Freckles dotted the bridge of her nose. She told Joanna the story of her brother, ten years older than she, coming home to visit when Abby was fifteen, coming into her bedroom at two in the morning, getting under the covers, covering her mouth, warning her not to tell their mother or father because they'd never let him come home again. She talked about his hands pulling down her pajama bottoms, the horror and pain when he pushed inside her.

Joanna could feel herself trembling inside. She looked at her hand resting on the tabletop. It was shaking ever so slightly. She felt light-headed. "I think I know how you feel," she said. "Something sort of like that happened to me in college."

Carter, who sat next to her at the table, slipped an arm around Joanna's shoulders. "Oh, honey," was all she said. Joanna had kept it hidden for so long. She couldn't imagine what had made her tell these women now. When she finished recounting what had happened that night after she left the bar, she felt strangely relieved.

Abby sat up and leaned toward her. "Hey, it sure as hell wasn't your fault, Joanna. Have you told the counselors?" Abby reached out and put her hand on Joanna's leg. "You've got to tell Marilyn. This is the place to deal with that stuff, Joanna."

Joanna sighed. "I don't know." She got up, excused herself, and walked down the stairs to her room.

About 10:30 P.M., while Joanna was brushing her teeth and getting ready for bed, Abby came down to the bunker. "I've got something to show you, Joanna." She handed Joanna her Significant Event Sheet, a yellow sheet of paper on which the women wrote their feelings, thoughts, and observations, a kind of diary that they gave to their counselor each morning. It was a way to help the counselors track a patient's progress, and a way for the patients to communicate with the counselors. On Abby's SES, she read, "Marilyn—Joanna told us something tonight. She was raped in college, and she's having trouble talking about it."

Joanna's hand trembled again as she handed the paper back to Abby. If Abby turned in that SES, Joanna would have to talk about the rape, get it out in the open, and deal with it. She wouldn't have a choice anymore. She would have to decide now. "Okay," Joanna said. She turned away and walked back to her bed. She felt frightened and relieved.

Post-Traumatic Stress Disorder

The next morning the storm had stopped and was replaced by the same blinding sunshine as on the day Joanna had arrived. She had nightmares during the night and dreaded her meeting with Marilyn. But Marilyn did not scold her about keeping secrets, did not lecture her about responsibility and how rape wasn't an excuse to drink. "Joanna, I think you might find it helpful to talk with Donna O'Brian. She's the therapist you saw who interpreted your MMPI and the Beck Depression Inventory, you know, that psychological test that showed you were depressed. Is it all right with you if I set up an appointment?"

Later that afternoon, Joanna walked toward Cork, where the Center for Ongoing Recovery was located. The maze of hallways seemed to go on forever, and the carpet muffled her every step. As she came out into the vaulted atrium of Cork, she could look out on the frozen lake, all white and indistinguishable from the lawn.

The steps to the second floor, where Donna's office was located, went on and on. For Joanna, climbing the stairs felt like slogging through mud. When she pushed open the door to the receptionist's area, the butterflies in her stomach took flight and made her voice quiver. "I have an appointment with Donna O'Brian," she said.

The receptionist smiled. "Have a seat. I'll tell her you're here." *What am I doing here?* wondered Joanna. Her shoulders were tight, her breathing shallow. In a few minutes, Joanna was following Donna toward the back of the building and into her office, noticing the sign on her door, which read "Wild Women Don't Get the Blues." Joanna smiled in spite of her nervousness. The therapist's hair curled around her face, and her dark eyes crinkled when she smiled. She had an almost elfin, mischievous look. Donna sat down in one of the upholstered chairs and invited Joanna to sit in the other. Her voice was soft and welcoming. "What can I help you with, Joanna?"

Joanna stared out at the white lake while recounting bits and pieces of her story.

"After an experience like that, people often develop something we call post-traumatic stress disorder, or PTSD," explained Donna. "They may become afraid of the dark, afraid to stay alone, especially at night. They often have nightmares and flashbacks in which they relive the experience in a terrifyingly real way."

Joanna closed her eyes and bent her head slightly forward. She realized that her cheeks were wet, and she reached up to pat them dry. The therapist handed her a tissue, looked at her attentively, but remained quiet. Joanna was remembering.

She remembered waking to the sound of her own cry, to Jeff's hand shaking her, his voice urgent. She would lay perfectly still, frozen, trying to pierce the dark, to discover where she was and whose hand was on her shoulder.

Two months ago, the gray of the November sky felt as though it was erasing her very existence. The sun didn't rise until 7:30, and even then it was clouded over. Jeff would call in the mornings when he got to work, when the curtains of the bedroom were still drawn to hide the darkness. Joanna couldn't leave the room until daylight. She waited there for his phone call, for when the phone would ring in the early morning darkness, and she would feel the jangle race down the length of her spine and radiate into her legs and arms. Even before she could connect the ringing of the phone to the threatening calls she had received after the rape, she would hear in her mind the breathy voice: "I'm watching you" and "You keep your mouth shut, or I'll shut it for you."

When Jeff traveled to San Francisco or Miami on business, or when he was in Phoenix on a golfing trip, she would go to the post office for the mail. The memory of finding a letter in the mailbox at home, seeing her name spelled out in sloppy crayon, pricked across her skin. But the ringing of the phone was worse. On that November day, she couldn't do it anymore. She turned off the ringer and called Jeff at his office, told him about the rape, and her terror. He accused her of lying, of making an excuse for her drinking. The gray sky sealed the morning. On the outside, Joanna looked as if she still existed, but on the inside, she had been entirely erased.

Now, hearing the therapist tell her that these feelings were normal, they began to pour back in.

"Can you put some words to it, Joanna?" asked Donna.

"I shouldn't . . ."

Donna waited through the silence again, then asked, "Shouldn't what, Joanna?"

"I shouldn't be bothered by it anymore."

"Of course you are bothered by it. It was a terrifying experience, and you've lived alone all this time with that terror. That's devastating."

Joanna could no longer hold back her tears.

During the rest of the session and a second one the following week, Joanna began to connect the terror and the drinking. She realized her binges got much worse in the fall, the same time of year when she was raped. She realized she had begun to drink heavily and constantly in the dark of the evenings when Jeff was at the graduate school library until after midnight. His packing a suitcase, preparing to leave town on business, often precipitated a drinking binge for her.

"If people do not deal with sexual abuse or other traumas, it is very difficult for them to maintain sobriety. People who are chemically dependent simply can't afford to use alcohol to numb their pain. When they don't deal with past traumas, the painful feelings about the abuse can become what we call 'a relapse trigger,'" the therapist told Joanna.

"I think it would be a good idea for you to attend our Survivor's Group, which meets twice a week. There you can hear from other women who have been through similar experiences."

Joanna would face other dreaded feelings over the next months, more than she could fully explore in this phase of primary treatment. She did talk about putting Molly in her crib, leaving the rail down, passing out, and then, when she came to, finding Molly crawling on the floor. "Once," she told Marilyn, "I'd passed out on the floor by the bed, and when I woke up, Molly was crawling around at the top of the steps. It's a long staircase that leads to a hardwood landing."

She still hadn't admitted to driving drunk to the liquor store with Molly in the car. She believed that if she admitted to everything, all her secrets, she would have to stay in treatment longer. And, if she talked about all the secrets, how could the other women know she was different from Abby, who had lost her children to their father?

Face Down

On the evening of January 11, Joanna called home. Every day she used her fifteen minutes at the pay phone to call Jeff, and he called her at least twice a day. But this evening was different. She was dreading this call; it meant she had not made it home for Molly's birthday.

"Can I talk to Molly?" she asked.

"Oh, Jo-Jo, she may be asleep by now. But she had a wonderful birthday."

Joanna worked hard at keeping her voice up. "I'm so glad, Jeff. Tell me about it."

"Your parents came over and had dinner with us. I made spaghetti, and bought an ice-cream cake at Baskin Robbins. It was in the shape of a doll, and you should have seen Molly's eyes light up! She couldn't be happier."

When she finished talking, Joanna hung up the phone, ran to her room, grabbed her jacket, boots, and hat, and raced toward a door that faced the lake. As she stepped into the darkness, she felt a high keening begin in her chest.

She walked a narrow, trampled path of snow. It was very cold, and the stars hung in the distance like tiny sparks of flint. There was just enough light to see the path in front of her and the darkening that was the stand of wood in the distance. The snow crunched beneath her boots, but she didn't notice the sound. Instead, she saw Molly with strawberry ice cream smeared on her face, waving her Peter Rabbit spoon in the air. When she had walked all the way to the edge of the trees, her wailing began to subside, and she turned back.

Joanna was entirely spent and chilled when she opened the door again. She walked quickly, head down, past the library and the lecture hall, through the glass doors that separated Lilly from the rest of the complex. She walked past the women gathered on the couch and chairs in the lounge. She walked down the steps to her room and saw the photo of her family. They were sitting together in front of the fireplace, all of them smiling. Molly was about ten months old in the picture, and her hair had grown long enough to curl at the nape of her neck. Joanna turned the photo face down, and fell into bed.

Fear of Anger

One and a half weeks before she was due to finish primary treatment, Joanna was told by Marilyn that the staff was recommending she go to a halfway house. "You will benefit by practicing your sobriety," said Marilyn. "Do you know how powerful the craving can be?"

Joanna thought to herself, *But I'm not a heroin addict! I'm not a cocaine addict! I don't even drink daily! I can go for weeks without craving a drink. And now that I understand how drinking a bottle at a time could have hurt Molly, well, I just won't do that anymore. Now that I understand, I'll just drink a glass or two to take the edge off, or when Jeff wants company.* But to Marilyn she said, "Believe me, I know how powerful the craving can be. I'll never take another drink. You don't have to worry about me."

"I've talked to Jeff. He understands the need for it."

Does he, wondered Joanna, *or is it something else?* On the phone the night before, he had been his usual concerned self, and then he had slipped one in like a knife. "Molly and me, we're doing just fine. In fact, Jo-Jo, the longer you're gone, the more I realize how well I can get along without you." She had felt stricken when he said it, but not entirely surprised.

As long as she'd known him, he'd come out with little zingers like that from time to time. Like last year when he told her that she didn't deserve a Valentine's Day present because she'd gotten so fat, and he took back the necklace he'd bought her. But it was out of character for him; most of the time he was so nice it was hard to believe he'd really said those things. Still, "I can get along without you" kept playing through her mind. And now Marilyn was telling her she should stay away longer.

"You what?" Joanna said. Her own volume surprised her. She gripped the arms of her chair, clenched her jaw.

"We think you need to spend some time in a halfway house before you go home."

Joanna stood up and put her hands on her waist. "You what?" she said again. Her voice became even louder, and she chopped the air with her arms. "You told Jeff before you talked to me?" She stomped to the other side of the office. "What were you thinking of, going to him first? I can't believe you did that." She was yelling now.

Marilyn sat down in her chair and watched. *Ahhh, there is the anger,* she thought to herself. *Thank God.*

"I'm sorry, Joanna. You're right, I should have talked to you first."

"Yeah, well a lot of good that does. Now Jeff's gonna say I can't come home. Anyway, what do you know about how much it hurts to miss your child?"

Marilyn's voice was very quiet and measured. "You're right, Joanna, I should have talked to you first," she repeated, "but I do know about missing one's children. Alcoholism took me away from my sons."

For a moment, Joanna remembered this woman was her friend. But her thoughts quickly returned to Jeff and her fury rose. "You think he's the one in charge? Is he my dad or something? Why am I always the little one, the kid, whenever Jeff's around?" She stomped out of Marilyn's office and slammed the door. She was about to go to her room, but noticed Abby and Carter sitting in the lounge. She marched through the kitchen area and down the four steps to the lounge. With force, she lowered her feet on the coffee table in front of the women.

"Hey, girlfriend. What got into you?" asked Abby.

"I can't believe her," Joanna yelled. She told them about the halfway house and Marilyn's call to Jeff.

"All right," said Abby. "Maybe she shouldn't have called Jeff first, but Jo, you have got to take what they say seriously. You know what the Third Step says. You have to be ready to turn your life and will over to the guidance of a Higher Power. For now, you've got to surrender. These folks have been in the business for a long time. They know what you need. Do it."

Images, thoughts about the Twelve Steps, and memories rushed at Joanna.

"Powerless." How she hated that word. It signaled weakness, her body a doormat for Jeff, her dad, her mom, for anyone to trample. She was sick of being the weak one, the child, and she wasn't going to be powerless over this stupid idea of a halfway house.

"Insanity." Another stupid word in the Big Book. An old book written by old men many years ago. She wasn't going to let anyone call her insane.

"Higher Power." She didn't want anything to do with some authoritarian God acting like her dad or her husband, telling her what to do and how to do it, telling her she wasn't good enough.

·She wanted to yell. She wanted to be like that younger woman, Maria, who showed up on the unit three days ago, snarling at everyone, telling everyone to go to hell. But that wasn't Joanna. Instead, she sighed a heavy sigh, got up from the couch, and walked away. She did not feel the same as these women, even if she did admire them. That night she wrote in her journal, "I'm so pissed I feel like I could kill somebody. I'm so scared of my anger."

The Medallion Ceremony

Feeling uncomfortable over the anger she had expressed, and the anger she had hidden, Joanna kept some distance from the other women on the unit the next day. After dinner they were having a medallion ceremony for Abby. Each woman received a medallion upon successfully completing primary treatment, and the ceremony was charged with significance. The quietness during these ceremonies had a sacred quality to it.

By the time the women gathered, sitting in the couches and chairs that formed a large circle in the lounge, they were in high spirits. Polly moved the rich, red amaryllis, its double-headed blossom standing a foot high, so she could put her feet up on the coffee table. Susan, wearing jeans that hung low on her hips, was sporting a bright yellow Walkman, gyrating to a secret sound. "I found some good weed," she sang, slightly off tune. Then she looked up, smiled, and shook her finger.

"That's a trigger," she said. She plopped into a chair next to Maria, who was new and still angry, sitting with her shoulders hunched and her face down. Joanna hid her own face behind the newspaper.

Abby pulled a gold coin from her pocket, took the chair next to Susan, and handed the medallion to her. Susan turned it over in the palm of her hand, studying it. Then she placed it between her fingers, held it up so the side with the missing piece—a clipped corner caused an imperfect circle—was visible. The roomful of women hushed, filling the lounge with an air of expectancy. All eyes looked to Susan. "This is the part of the medallion you leave here at Hazelden," she said. Then she moved it around between her fingers until the unflawed portion was visible. "And this is the side you take with you when you leave."

She turned the medallion over. "And on the back is the Serenity Prayer, and each time you read it, think of us and remember all of us, and know we are with you." Susan leaned over and hugged Abby tightly. Her long brown hair fell over both of their faces. "Always remember, we are looking at the same moon." Susan wiped her cheek and handed the medallion to the woman sitting next to her.

Each woman in turn took the medallion, wished Abby well, kissed the coin, and passed it on to the next woman. Their urgent wishes were fueled by fears of their own potential relapse. Polly spoke, and her voice had a begging quality, "You go to your meetings just as often as you need to, you work your program, you be strong and stick with it." Tears ran down many faces. Finally, Abby received her medallion and spoke of how much the women meant to her. She paused, looked silently around the room at the circle of faces, and whispered, "I love you guys." The group stood, slipped their arms around each other's waists, and chanted the Serenity Prayer together. Even Maria moved reluctantly into the circle for the closing. Magic was released into the air. There were hugs and sloppy cheek kisses, and the women, heady with the first warm day in a long time, dispersed toward Bigelow Auditorium for the lecture, sweeping Joanna along.

The women of the Lilly unit entered the auditorium noisily, taking seats where they always did. Joanna sat in the twelfth row back, behind all the other women, and waited quietly for the lecture to begin. The man at the podium paced back and forth, his hands deep in his pockets, looking nervous. There wasn't any particular gesture that told Joanna he was nervous, but there was no mistaking it.

The speaker talked of watching a twenty-two-year-old friend die of alcoholism, of holding his girlfriend as her heart stopped from an overdose, of burying a friend in the dead cold of winter. And still he had been unable to stop using cocaine. It was a story filled with pain, and the pain filled the auditorium. He talked at length of the incredible gifts he'd been given during his six years of sobriety—the view of a clear moon, the wonderful woman he had met and married, and the most incredible gift of all, witnessing the birth of his son, and just seven weeks ago, watching the birth of his daughter.

"And despite these wonderful gifts, sometimes I still want to get high. Sometimes I still have to sit on my hands," he said. And Joanna didn't doubt it for a moment; his pain was palpable, as if it were touching her shoulder. She looked around the lecture hall. It was perfectly quiet. She watched the women of the Lilly unit, her comrades. Carter was looking at Abby, squeezing her hand. Abby, in turn, reached over and patted Claudia's thigh. Polly laid her head on Susan's shoulder. Even Maria let one of the women put her arm around the back of her chair.

The speaker ended his lecture by saying, "I love this place, and don't you doubt it for a moment. Peace."

Another Perspective

"Joanna is absolutely refusing a halfway house," Marilyn told the treatment team during a case review meeting the next day. "She is so anxious to get home."

"Does she have kids?" asked another counselor.

"A girl, just had her first birthday."

"What do you think? Can she handle it?"

"She's a bit naive still about how powerless she is over alcohol," replied Marilyn.

"Does she think she can handle controlled drinking?" asked the other counselor.

Marilyn frowned. "Well, she says not, but I think she may be covering. She seems driven to get back with Jeff as soon as possible."

"What about Jeff? Does he understand that she'll lose control if she drinks again?"

"He didn't attend the family program," said Marilyn. "I don't have a good grasp of where Jeff is."

"What's her aftercare plan?" asked another counselor.

"She'll go to AA meetings in Chicago, of course," reported Marilyn. She paged through Joanna's file. "She plans to get a sponsor immediately. Donna reports that the depression seems to be lessening, but Joanna needs additional treatment. She has agreed to see a therapist when she gets home."

Marilyn took a piece of candy from a bowl on her desk and passed it to the counselor sitting beside her. "I was encouraged by the anger she showed the other day. And Donna says she is speaking in the survivor's group, seems open to working on the residue of the rape."

"Sounds to me like, on balance, you think she'll be okay."

"I think if she follows her aftercare plan, she'll be okay," answered Marilyn.

A week later Jeff drove to Center City to pick up Joanna. She had watched two new women arrive on the unit, frightened and angry. One of them had even threatened to hurt herself if they didn't get her some heroin immediately. Joanna had noticed Maria's body and spirit beginning the transformative journey of healing. Her shoulders relaxed and her face lifted toward the room. Her voice gained confidence as she began to talk with other women. Joanna watched Maria begin to feel like part of the group.

Joanna had gone through her own medallion ceremony, regretting only that she hadn't been as honest as Abby or some of the other women. She was pleased, however, that she had convinced the staff to approve her departure. And their approval would please Jeff. There would be no halfway house for her. Her arms were aching for Molly. She would go home and be a good mother. And she would go home and cook and clean and look pretty and make passionate love and prove to Jeff that he needed her.

7

Who Is My Higher Power?

THOUGH IT WAS mid-February, the group of eight women sat outside on the patio talking. They had just finished lunch, and the sun was shining, bringing the temperature into the low seventies. A cloud of cigarette smoke drifted from the patio into the courtyard. Many of the women in their twenties and thirties smoked, and Liz had to move away from them, since the smoke made her cough and breathe heavily. She stood up and moved her chair next to Vera, who had just arrived at Hanley-Hazelden a couple days before. At seventy-one, Vera was just a year older than Liz. The two older women were quiet as the young women talked.

"This was the kind of weather I liked back in Columbus, Ohio," Ann was saying. "But it didn't get this warm until May." Ann was in her twenties and was the most outspoken woman in the group. She had been in treatment before.

"I remember sitting on the patio of a bar, picking up this guy who was as drunk as I was," Ann continued. "I had just broken up with my boyfriend weeks earlier, and maybe that was my way of getting even with him."

"Is that when you got pregnant?" another young woman at the same table asked.

"No, that was another guy, a couple of months later. This guy offered me twenty-five dollars. Can you believe that?" Ann asked. "I was going to slap him, but instead I said, 'Make it fifty.' He offered forty."

Sitting across from Ann, a young woman with a tattoo of a rose on her upper arm, said, "Well, did you take it?"

"Yeah I took it. I was drunk. I had never done that before. *Why not?* I thought. I didn't have enough money with me to buy another drink." She shook her head. "Still, I can't believe I did that."

Liz winced. The story disturbed her. She looked away from Ann and stood up from her chair. "Vera, do you want to take a walk?"

"Where can we walk? We can't go off the grounds," Vera replied.

"Hey, Liz, am I bothering you with this story?" Ann asked. "I'm sorry for talking about it if it troubles you."

"No," Liz lied. She didn't want to bother the group with her concerns.

"It's okay. I think it's just the smoke. I'm going inside to sit in the lounge."

Vera got up, too, and together they walked inside. The two sat in the lounge and looked out the patio door. The sunlight was intense. "Sometimes I don't know if I belong here with these young women," Liz said to Vera.

"It's not Ann, it's the disease in Ann," Vera answered. Liz had heard the counselors say things like that, and she knew Vera was quoting them, trying to explain Ann's behavior both to herself and to Liz.

Liz sighed. "I suppose it's a generational difference. Girls these days do things like that. And they do have such difficult things to face."

"It's still jolting, though," Vera admitted as she shook her head. "Sometimes I feel like I don't have much in common with them, still trying to raise families, start careers."

"Yes. I just keep reminding myself of what my counselor said. 'Focus on what you have to do, not what they are doing,'" said Liz.

"Anyway, I'm really glad you're here, Liz. And Sophie too." Vera looked around. "Where is Sophie?" she asked.

"Taking a nap," Liz answered. Sophie was another older woman on the unit who had arrived in early February, just a few days after Liz. The older women were strongly encouraged to go back to their rooms to nap or read. They weren't required to attend all the functions and activities the younger women attended. "Sophie won't even sit outside on the patio if anyone is smoking," Liz told Vera. "She has some kind of chronic bronchitis and stays far away from any smoke that might be shifted by a breeze and blown toward her."

Liz walked over to the coffee machine and poured herself a cup. "Would you like some?" she asked Vera.

"No, caffeine upsets my stomach."

"Where are you from, Vera?"

"I lived most of my life in Billings, Montana, and came here to

Florida to retire with my husband about seven years ago. He died last year. I live in a town called Melbourne, north of here."

Liz put her cup on the coffee table and sat back down on the couch.

"I'm sorry to hear about your husband. Mine is in Iowa right now, but he'll be back when I finish inpatient treatment. We're both going to stay at a local hotel while I finish two more weeks of outpatient treatment."

"You mean you're leaving soon?" Vera sounded surprised and disappointed.

"Oh no, not really. I just won't be sleeping here, but I'll be here from breakfast till bedtime. You can count on that," Liz said. "My insurance will only pay for two weeks of inpatient treatment and an additional two weeks of outpatient. It's almost the same.

"Oh." Vera seemed relieved.

The two sat quietly for a short time, then returned to their earlier conversation. "You know, some of the girls here call me 'Mom,'" Liz said. "I actually think they would prefer to call me 'Granny,' but don't out of courtesy."

"I think that would be nice," answered Vera. "How do you like having such a young woman for a roommate?"

"I like it. You know the girl sitting next to Ann? Well, she's my roommate, Sharon. I feel like a mother to her sometimes. I never had a daughter of my own. She asks me all kinds of things at night before we go to bed. She has talked about cocaine and sex, and it's hard for me to listen to it all sometimes, but I'm trying not to be judgmental. There isn't a drug she hasn't tried. Her parents lived that way and she was just doing more of the same. I feel sorry for her, because she hasn't been taught anything different. She seems so lost."

"I'll bet she's happy to have you," Vera said.

"Well, I think I've been helpful to her. I reminded her that we can turn to one another, and she has started to come out of her shell and interact with others. I think the girls are going to like you a lot, Vera," Liz said. "You've only been here a few days, but you watch, the girls will start calling you 'Mom' pretty soon."

"I like being around younger people, but they are so busy raising children, getting jobs and careers, dating and getting married," Vera said. "I've done all that. My husband has died, my health isn't so great, and my own parents and one brother died long ago. Many of these girls have never been ill and they've never had someone in their family die. How can they understand where we are?"

Liz tilted her head and smiled. "I know what you mean," she said. "But there are plenty of people in the senior groups who can help us with our drinking problems."

Vera's eyes opened wide. This was the first time her drinking had been mentioned by any of the patients. She had almost pushed it out of her mind. But now that Liz had mentioned it, she couldn't avoid talking about it.

"Do you really think you have a drinking problem, Liz?" Vera asked. "You know, I'm not sure. I never drank that much, only six or seven ounces a day."

"Well, at our age, it doesn't take that much to get drunk."

"It sure isn't much compared to the quarts these girls can drink. And all the drugs they use. We didn't have that when I was young."

"We have to focus on our drinking, not theirs," Liz said. "Otherwise we won't get well."

"Do you think you're sick? I don't. I mean, I never drove when I was drinking. I wouldn't do anything that might harm someone else."

"What about your grandchildren?" Liz asked. "Did you feel bad about that?"

"What do you mean?"

"You know." Liz nodded her head. "Your children wouldn't let you babysit your grandchildren because you were drinking, right?"

"Oh, you heard me mention that at the senior grief group. It's nothing, really," Vera said.

Our Daily Bread

The Sober Seniors' meeting met Wednesday at noon. Everyone rose and stood in a circle as the leader of the group began the closing prayer. "Our Father, who art in heaven . . ." he began, and others in the group joined in.

Liz felt connected to everyone there, and liked how the people held hands and formed a circle at the closing, but she didn't care to say the prayer. Saying the prayer seemed like a challenge to her agnosticism, even though she didn't mind everyone else saying it.

Liz had talked to her counselor about feeling uncomfortable with the invocation at the end of meetings. Her counselor assigned her a chapter in the Big Book titled "We Agnostics." It stressed the need for the individual to find his or her own conception of God, not a borrowed one from the clergy or a religion. The chapter also stressed the importance for alcoholics of finding some kind of Higher Power, but Liz felt suspicious of the words "Higher Power." They seemed like code words for God.

Halfway through the prayer, Liz looked up and saw Vera with her eyes closed, solemnly praying out loud with the group. Liz knew from talking with Vera how much her religion and church attendance meant to her. Liz felt envious of Vera's beliefs. Liz wanted to believe, and feared that if she didn't believe in a Christian God, she wouldn't do as well in recovery. She had no Higher Power, and it worried her.

Standing next to Vera was Sophie. Sixty-eight years old, she had come to the unit a few days before Vera. While the group prayed, Sophie furrowed her brow and squinted. She wasn't saying the prayer at all, but looked straight at Liz, who then looked away.

After the meeting, Sophie and Liz took the elevator downstairs and passed the outdoor pool on the way back to their unit. "I saw that you didn't say the Our Father," Liz said to Sophie. "Are you agnostic?"

Sophie smiled. "No. I'm Jewish."

"Oh," Liz nodded. "So that's why you didn't say the prayer."

"Right. It's not my prayer. It's not a one-size-fits-all prayer."

"I know what you mean," Liz said. "I'm agnostic, and I feel the same way about the prayer."

"I believe in God, but not Christianity. I find this pretty difficult," Sophie said.

"I hear there are Jewish AA groups not far from here," Liz answered. "You might try one of those after treatment."

"The chaplain mentioned that to me. I'm sure I'll do that."

"I wish there were groups for agnostics," Liz said. "I don't believe or disbelieve. No one can know for sure. I definitely don't believe in a God who sits in heaven listening to our prayers and needs, as if he could wave a wand and grant our wishes."

As they walked across the campus back to the women's unit, Liz continued, "I don't know about this Higher Power stuff. It still seems like you have to believe in God. My counselor told me I didn't. She said I could believe that the AA group is a Higher Power, as long as I was willing to step out of myself and seek help from something bigger than me. I just don't know what to think of that."

The following day in the cafeteria, after they had finished eating, Sophie, Vera, and Liz walked out of the building and paused near the women's unit. "Let's go over to the pool before the AA meeting starts," Liz said to the other two women. "It's such a beautiful evening."

Like Vera, Sophie also lived in Florida and was surprised that Liz found the evening so beautiful. The temperature was falling below seventy, and Sophie was wearing a sweater.

"It's probably below freezing in Iowa. And I bet it's snowing, or maybe it's thawing and slush covers the streets and sidewalks. I just want to take advantage of this sunlight," Liz said.

"Sure, let's," Vera said.

"I've been thinking about what you said on the patio before," Sophie said as they sat down on lounge chairs. At first, Liz didn't remember what she was talking about. "You know, about the Our Father and being agnostic."

"I didn't know that," Vera said, surprised. "You're agnostic, Liz?"

"Yes. I've always been agnostic, for as long as I can remember," Liz answered.

"You mean you don't believe in God?" Vera exclaimed.

"No, it's not that simple. I just don't think anyone can know for sure."

But Vera and Sophie knew for sure. Both women approached the idea of God quite differently, but they had strong beliefs.

"I talked with the chaplain here," Liz added. "I guess I complained to him about the Our Father prayer." Liz lifted her glass of mineral water and sipped.

"Sometimes I get scared that I won't recover unless I believe like everyone else does and say the prayer. My counselor reassures me that everyone can recover in this program. I don't have to be a Christian."

"What's wrong with being a Christian?" Vera asked.

"Oh, Vera, I don't mean to insult your beliefs. In fact, I wish I could believe like you do, and say the right prayers at the right time, and draw some kind of sustenance from religion. I envy you, Vera. But not everyone believes like you do. Did you know that Sophie is Jewish?"

"No," Vera said. Vera looked at Sophie, sitting in a chair across from them both. Sophie smiled and nodded her head.

"I feel stuck," Liz continued. "If I don't pray, I may not stay sober. And how can I pray if I don't believe in a Higher Power that is God?"

"Hi!" hollered one of the younger women from the unit who had come to swim. "Do you want to join us?"

"No, thank you," Liz hollered back as Sophie waved.

The younger woman turned back and stepped into the pool. The sun would set in another hour, but the water in the pool was still quite warm.

"Maybe it will just take some time for me," Liz said.

"My counselor said, 'You have to go beyond seeing Alcoholics Anonymous as a Christian religious program, and see it as a spiritual one instead. Then, these problems will resolve themselves.' Do you think that's true?" Liz asked, glancing at Sophie and Vera.

"I hope so," Sophie said.

"Maybe you'll come to believe in God," Vera ventured.

"And maybe not," snapped Liz.

"I'm sorry." Vera averted her eyes. "I don't mean to be telling you how to live your life."

"I know," answered Liz. "It's okay. I just have a different way of looking at things."

Over the next few weeks, Liz stood silently as others in the meeting said the Our Father prayer. In time, Liz would ask her AA group at home in Iowa to say the Serenity Prayer to close the meeting. Her group would happily accommodate her after she explained her difficulty with the prayer.

A Difference

The chaplain drew a triangle with a red marker on the easel. All the women were gathered in the large open room where community meetings were held. Vera sat next to Sophie on the couch, while Liz sat across from them in one of the chairs. The unit housed twenty women, and all of them were present in the room. The chaplain would meet with the older women, Liz, Vera, and Sophie, in the Life Transition group, which also included older men from the male unit, but this meeting was a general discussion about spirituality. Liz was glad it was happening now.

"How many of you have ever been in an emotional triangle?" asked the chaplain. Some of the women laughed. Nearly half of them raised their hands. Liz was surprised to see Vera lift her hand.

"Well, I'm going to show you a different emotional triangle, a spiritual one." He held up a small gold coin in front of the group.

"This," he said, as he showed the coin around the room, "is an AA medallion. On the back of it is a triangle. Its three sides represent unity, service, and recovery."

"This triangle," he said, pointing to the one on the easel, "represents a different kind of relationship than the one that made you laugh."

The chaplain identified the sides of the triangle with a word at each point: Self, Others, Higher Power.

"This," he said, "represents spirituality. Spirituality is based on the relationship that you have with yourself, others, and your Higher Power or God, if that is what you call your Higher Power."

Liz put up her hand. "May we ask questions?" she asked.

"Of course. Feel free to interrupt any time you want. I'm here not to lecture you, but to start a discussion," Jerry said.

"Well, I'm an agnostic, and my idea of God is quite different from yours, all of you. Even the words 'Higher Power' make me feel uncomfortable. What do I do about that?"

"People have many ideas about what a Higher Power is," the chaplain said. He felt relieved. He had hoped someone in the group would bring up this point. "Does anyone else share Liz's feelings about God?"

Other women spoke up. In no time, it was clear that everyone in the group had very distinct and intense feelings and ideas about God. They ranged from a religious devotion that included attending church every Sunday, as expressed by Vera, to a denial of the existence of God, as expressed by a younger woman who identified herself as an atheist.

Liz remarked, "But a recovering person seems to need religion. Some of these Steps even use the word 'God' in them. It seems if you don't practice some religion, you'll never understand the concept of God or a Higher Power. If our conceptions of God don't matter, then why do they always say the Our Father after meetings? It is, after all, a very Christian prayer which espouses a belief in God, who is the Father.

My friends Sophie and Vera have very different ideas of God, but at least they have religions. I don't. So what do I do?"

"Liz, Alcoholics Anonymous is a spiritual program, not a religious one. It is important to note the difference. Let's try this," Jerry said. He wrote two words on the top of his easel and drew a line down the middle. One column was titled "Religion" and the other "Spirituality." "Let's go around the room and say words that we associate with religion and with spirituality." The women called out their answers, and he recorded a long list for each of the words:

RELIGION	SPIRITUALITY
God	God, Higher Power
Church	Centered
Sacraments	Serenity
Confession	New Age
Organization	Peace
Guilt and shame	Connected
Black and white	Inner strength
Punishing	Trust
Penance	Lack of stress
Showy, rituals	The stars and the universe
Priests, ministers, men	Earth
Laws and commandments	Rivers, streams, lakes
Fundamentals	Acceptance
Patriarchy	Blue water, rain

"Notice the difference between these two lists," the chaplain said to the women. Liz was amazed at how distinct the meanings were for all of them.

"Religion is more structured and external. Spirituality is freer, more personal, broader. Ideally," Jerry added, "religion helps you achieve spirituality, but if it doesn't, then set it aside for a while.

"Liz," he said, "you asked about differences in our conceptions of God and religion. Do you see how this might help? You don't have to accept anyone's notion of God or religion here. I am only asking you to find a spirituality that will enable you to change and stay sober and straight."

Liz nodded. She was thinking about spirituality. She did believe that the universe itself, the earth and the cosmos, formed a kind of unity that would outlast all humanity. It existed before man and would exist after him. *So why can't the universe itself be my Higher Power?* she wondered to herself.

Next, Jerry took a medallion from his pocket and showed it to the group. "This is my medallion," he said. "It has the Roman numeral six on it and symbolizes the number of years I've been sober. On the back is a triangle that reads: 'To Thine Own Self Be True.' It appears in *Hamlet.* In your relationship to your inner self, this dictum is critically important. Be honest with yourself, with others, and with your Higher Power."

"Can I see it?" Ann asked. Jerry passed it to her.

"What do the letters H-O-W stand for?"

"HOW the program of Alcoholics Anonymous works: Honesty, openness, and willingness," Jerry replied.

"Cool," Ann said.

"Yes, it is cool," Liz added.

Ann smiled.

Days later, the women would find a second triangle drawn on the easel, only this one would mean something entirely different. They were in the same room, listening to Jack Pearson, a specialist in the area of relapse.

His triangle represented an iceberg. He drew a horizontal line indicating the water level, with only the tip of the iceberg showing above it.

"Alcoholics love the idea of controlled drinking," Jack said. "They want so desperately to be able to drink that the very notion of controlled drinking, which some treatment programs believe possible, seems like a miracle. But the Big Book says on page 30, 'The idea that somehow, someday he will control and enjoy his drinking is the great obsession of every abnormal drinker.'"

"If you think you can drink just one and control yourself, you are mistaken."

Vera listened closely. Relapse was her problem. Liz touched her hand because she saw Vera get teary-eyed and sensed that she was remembering past experiences.

"The top of the iceberg," Jack said, "was the behavior, the trouble we got into as a result of drinking. You can see that part, the lost jobs, the anger, the poverty and desperation, the wasted hours spent sipping whiskey, drinking beer, doing drugs. After you sober up in treatment, the top of the iceberg looks relatively harmless. You might think, 'Well, I've got it all under control now.'"

Some of the women nodded their heads.

"But underneath the iceberg, when you try to drink just one, a molecular response occurs, and you don't see it because it's invisible, below eye level like the iceberg. By taking that one drink, you trigger the craving, which is the disease. You've activated your illness. Maybe you won't immediately feel a compulsion to take another. And maybe next week, when you return to the bar and have another drink or two, you still won't feel the compulsion. But before you know it, the desire for drink or drug will bear down on you."

"I know what you mean," one of the women said. "I've experienced that strange need to drink. I could be enjoying myself, listening to music, when I say to myself, almost out loud, *I need a drink. It would make everything perfect.*"

"That's right," Jack added. "Then, in a very short time, the top of the iceberg, your behavior, changes and you become visibly troubled. All the crappy behavior returns in no time, but it was already unfolding with your first drink."

Liz put her arm around Vera, who was crying now. "I did that over and over," she whispered.

On the Rocks

It was Liz's turn to tell her story. Everyone, especially Vera and Sophie, was eager to hear it. Even the younger women, new to the unit, had wanted to hear how or if an older woman's story of alcoholism was different from theirs.

"For sure," Ann said to the woman sitting next to her. "I can't imagine Liz doing the stuff we've done on crack. She's too sweet, too much of a grandmother."

Liz had started her story with an apology. "I'm afraid some of you might find my story kind of boring. My life isn't nearly as interesting as yours." Liz was to tell her story as simply as possible, saying what had happened and what it was like.

"I was born in 1921," she began. "In a little town in Iowa. Well, it isn't that little. Ames, Iowa. My father was Danish and came to the United States when he was a young man. In 1929, when the Depression hit the country, we were quite poor, but my mother made sure we were educated. I went on to graduate from school and become a lawyer; then after the Second World War started, I left Iowa to work in New York City."

The other women were stunned. Some of them had never met anyone like Liz before. She was not only an older woman who was a drunk, but a lawyer as well, and at a time when few women worked outside their homes.

"Imagine," one of the women whispered to Ann. "A woman going to school in the forties and becoming a lawyer."

"I returned to Iowa from New York after the war," Liz continued. "I was quite depressed. Both my parents had returned to Ames, Iowa, too. They had been living in Detroit, where my father was working for the war effort as an architect. In a short period of time, both my father and mother died, my father from a heart attack and my mother from cancer. I started seeing a psychiatrist for depression, and I began drinking in the house where I had grown up, but now owned. I wasn't much older than some of you," she said, lifting her hand and gesturing to the group.

"I went through different phases. There was my sherry phase. It was more acceptable to drink that. Then I started drinking rye, gin and tonic, and when vodka became more available in the mid-fifties, I began drinking vodka martinis, highballs, and manhattans, straight bourbon and vermouth. People always said that vodka couldn't be smelled on your breath, so I drank it, hoping no one would detect it. Sometimes I had my drinks on the rocks, but I didn't realize that I was the one on the rocks. My doctor once asked me if I had ever gone a whole day without drinking. I tried it, and it was easy. So I resumed drinking the next day."

The women in the group laughed, and Liz smiled. She hadn't realized how illogical that sounded. "Yes," she said, "I could be abstinent one day, but that was all. I don't think I ever missed a day of drinking after that." Again, the women laughed. Except for Vera.

"I didn't get married until I was forty-six years old, in 1967. I still feel embarrassed about that. I think I should have married when I was younger, that maybe I didn't get married until then because I was unattractive." Many women could identify with Liz. They nodded.

"I worked as general counsel for a university. And when I drove home from work at five, I often stopped at the corner liquor store. Eventually I'd get home and get supper ready. When dinner and the dishes were set out, I was ready to start drinking my bourbon and water or bourbon and soda. Highballs were my favorite. I always asked my husband if he wanted a drink. 'Jonathan,' I'd say, 'how about having a drink with me?' He'd always agree, though he'd nurse one drink for the whole evening. I thought that as long as I didn't drink alone, I wasn't an alcoholic. I'd probably have three or four before supper, and another after supper while Jonathan did the dishes and cleaned the kitchen.

"In the evening, we might sit together and watch the news. Or I would press clothes for work the next day. Sometimes I would do the wash, which I didn't mind because I would take my drink downstairs and sip from it. Every night at about eleven o'clock, I would read. I'd keep a tall glass of bourbon and soda on the nightstand. I loved the taste of bourbon. I think I used to pass out while drinking, and when the booze wore off, I would wake up at three or four in the morning, feeling anxious. I was worried about being laid off from my job before retirement. I began to see myself aging, not fitting in with the younger people at work. I couldn't go back to sleep; I worried I'd be too tired to work, which made me more anxious. Mostly I was afraid of people breaking into my house. Someone did once when I was alone, but I don't want to talk about that.

"Some mornings I would lie in bed until my husband got up and made coffee. I never drank in the mornings," Liz said. "Except under one condition."

The women laughed again. They knew as well as Liz that alcoholics will make rules to control their drinking, then find an exception for every one of them. "If my car didn't start because of the cold," Liz said, "I would come inside and drink. That was a rule. It was the only time I allowed myself to drink in the morning. Living in Iowa, which gets mighty cold in the winter, gave me many chances to drink. My battery never seemed to work."

"I bet you intentionally left your headlights on," a woman in the group said. Liz smiled.

"Things went on like that day after day, year after year. Come home from work, prepare supper, drink a highball or martini, eat, drink until I passed out, and wake up in the middle of the night afraid. That was my life. I never did anything terrible. I mean, I didn't hurt people. I never drove drunk, and hardly ever missed a day of work.

"I guess I did get angry when I was drinking. If my husband went somewhere with his brother without telling me, I would worry about him, and then become angry. I might throw things, like plates and glasses. Sometimes I felt so out of control, I'd say, 'Help me, help me.' I couldn't stand having knives out on the kitchen counter. I didn't know if I felt like cutting myself or someone else. My bizarre behavior vanished when I stopped drinking. One evening in a bar, I felt sure that Jonathan was going to tell me something terrible. I thought he was going to say he didn't love me anymore.

"'What is it, Jonathan?' I asked him.

"He said, 'Liz, you know you don't have to finish your drink in order to leave.' I was relieved that that was all he had to say, but what he didn't know was that I had to finish my drink. I needed it. I wasn't his first alcoholic wife. He had had another, his first wife, whom he divorced. She was beaten to death in a bar in 1972, only forty-two years old. Her son, my stepson, is also a practicing alcoholic."

It was nearly two o'clock in the afternoon and Liz had finished telling her story and sharing her life with these women. When they stood and looped their arms over each other's shoulders, she felt closer to them. They closed the meeting with the Serenity Prayer, a prayer that Liz was now saying out loud with the group.

The following Thursday, having already begun her outpatient treatment, Liz left her husband Jonathan at the hotel restaurant, where he was eating breakfast. Liz had joined him, but only for coffee, since she would eat breakfast with her friends in treatment. Though she was thrilled to have evenings with Jonathan, who had arrived a week after she had begun outpatient treatment, Liz was still excited every morning to drive back to Hanley-Hazelden.

That morning, after socializing with the women on the unit, Liz was glad to attend the aftercare group. Many alumni from the senior program at Hanley-Hazelden came for the meeting, but it was mandatory for all the older adults, men and women, currently at Hanley. It was one of her favorite groups, next to the senior AA meeting on Wednesday.

In the aftercare group, she sat between Sophie and Vera. One of the counselors who worked only with seniors opened the meeting. Then came the introductions. When it was Liz's turn, she introduced herself.

"I'm Liz. I'm an alcoholic."

"Hi, Liz," the group answered. Sometimes Liz disliked the predictability, but not this morning. She was grateful to hear from the seniors who had a couple years of sobriety, who had been through what she was experiencing now. With them, here, she could talk about the losses, not only of people like her parents, but of dreams. And the loss of health. Here, everyone understood when people talked about arthritis, sore hips, fallen arches, and more serious diseases.

Vera was one of the first to talk. "I think I'm an alcoholic, but I'm not sure. I want to be honest with all of you, because you all have been so honest with me. I'm not entirely sure, but I've talked a lot with Liz and Sophie here, and I'm beginning to understand a little about this drinking."

The counselor encouraged Vera to talk more about her First Step, how her life had become unmanageable from drinking too much. "I don't want to bore people," Vera said.

"Oh, Vera," Liz interrupted. "You can put aside that worry and just tell everybody about yourself. Tell them what you've told me."

Vera began telling her story, or a piece of it, that late morning. She would glance at Liz as if she needed her encouragement. In less than a week, Liz finished her two weeks of outpatient treatment and was discharged from Hanley-Hazelden. She would attend the aftercare meeting a few times before she and Jonathan returned to Iowa. At home, Liz could count on Vera and Sophie to send cards and call occasionally, as Liz would too. But that morning they didn't know they would remain lifelong friends. And Liz didn't know that she was forming her own conception of a Higher Power.

8

A Life-or-Death Matter

"I ARRANGED an appointment for you at Jellinek at three this afternoon," said Steve, Andy's counselor.

Andy sat back in his chair, relieved. He had been careful not to insist on going to Jellinek for extended care. He had learned from listening to other men on Shoemaker that if he insisted on designing his own after-care, telling the counselors where and when he should go, it wasn't likely to happen. He had watched his peers try to manage their own treatment and had seen their plans backfire. So when Andy had completed three weeks of primary rehab, and it was time to discuss his aftercare, he tried not to sound too enthusiastic about the extended care program.

Jellinek seemed a good place to hang his hat for a while longer, since he had nowhere else to go. Unlike the other men, who wanted to return to their homes and jobs, Andy had no wish to go back to Queens, to Sal, or to work. Besides, no one wanted him back. At Hazelden, he was treated well, respectfully. He exercised regularly at Cork, the center that housed the gym, pool, basketball and handball courts, and a weight room. He was eating nutritious meals and running each afternoon on the trail that wound through the Hazelden grounds, through tall pines and poplars. In Andy's mind, Jellinek offered a reprieve. It was too early to leave. He was just beginning to understand that though his addiction would never be cured, his hopelessness might be.

Now that Steve had got an appointment for him at Jellinek, he felt encouraged. "It might happen," Andy told his roommates.

His appointment that afternoon was with Thomas Novak, the supervisor of Jellinek. Weeks earlier, Andy had heard him speak at Bigelow, where they went for lectures three times a day during primary care. Andy had taken prodigious notes and perused them before leaving for his interview.

The Interview

Andy walked along the corridors until he had crossed through Tiebout Hall, another primary treatment unit for men named after a friend of Alcoholics Anonymous, Dr. Harry M. Tiebout. From there it was a very short walk outside to Jellinek. It was late August, a hot and muggy afternoon, and lawn chairs sat outside the door and on the grass. A receptacle for cigarette butts stood next to a chair. Jellinek was a unit for both men and women, a much different situation from other units where men and women were housed separately and discouraged from even talking to each other in the hallways or dining room. It was strange for Andy to see one of the Jellinek patients, a man, talking to another patient, a woman, near the phone. He nodded hello, and they both greeted him heartily.

Though Andy thought the rule against socializing between the sexes was more for adolescents living in dormitory-like situations than for grown men and women, he wouldn't have even considered breaking the rule.

For Andy, rules were important now. He wanted to do things right at Hazelden, and the rules told him what those things were. He didn't know any other way to act in recovery. Following the rules was always a solution. It relieved Andy of having to consider feelings.

By focusing on the exterior rules, Andy was able to ignore the inner rules, his own beliefs, conscience, and values. It was easier for him to obey a rule imposed upon him than to consider what rules he needed to impose upon himself. In treatment, he followed the rules, not because he valued harmony and peace, but because he was afraid of being engulfed by his own disorder and chaos. Rules made the path seem straight and simple; whereas inside him, the path was crooked, obstructed with secrets, resentments, and fears. For Andy, it was better to pay blind allegiance to rules and regulations than to ferret out for himself what was right, what was wrong, and what was both.

"There is a difference between compliance and surrender, between 'should' and 'want,'" Steve had said at a group discussion about behavior. "'If I follow the rules and be good, can I get to do the things I want? Can I be in control now?' Ultimately," Steve continued, "that is what lurks behind compliance. Surrender is about acknowledging that we don't get to control our life. That our old life is dead and we live at the will of a Higher Power. That our life belongs to that power or God. And that means growing up. That means not hanging on to this relationship, or that job. Not hanging on to the status quo. Not hanging on to the pieces of your life that you think keep you safe. Bill W. said that once a person surrenders, they walk through the dark one step at a time."

For Andy's treatment plan, Steve had told him to read the pamphlet *Surrender vs. Compliance,* as well as "Doctor's Opinion" from the Big Book. He was to discuss the readings with his peers.

Andy could recall the lecture as if it were happening at that very moment. As inspiring as Steve's words were to him, Andy still preferred to know exactly what was expected of him, what he could do to demonstrate his willingness to change. Not knowing worried him, and because his interview with Thomas was uncertain, he worried more.

As a newspaper reporter and editor, he had done countless interviews with presidents and vice presidents of major corporations, prime ministers of the Bahama Islands and Montserrat, and celebrities, but the interview with Thomas Novak provoked more fear in him than any of these. If he didn't pass the interview, he would have to leave Hazelden. Where would he go? When Andy knocked on the office door, Thomas called out for him to enter. Wearing blue jeans, loafers, and a white shirt, Thomas stood up from behind his desk and walked toward him.

As the interview progressed, Andy felt more and more relieved; he was answering the questions correctly. Thomas asked what he thought about the Twelve Steps of Alcoholics Anonymous. "I see them as a set of directions," Andy said, remembering that Thomas himself had said the very same thing in his lecture. Andy was quoting Thomas to Thomas. It was exactly how he had described the Twelve Steps. It did not go unnoticed.

Thomas smiled, then asked Andy if he would be able to handle being on a unit with women. Would he be able to stay out of romantic relationships with them?

Andy had the right answers on matters like the Twelve Steps, on powerlessness and unmanageableness, but he hadn't considered what Thomas was now asking. He didn't know how he might act around women. He stuttered, started his sentences over. "Well, I think I could . . . I think I could . . . manage." Thomas studied him carefully from the other side of the desk. Andy crossed and uncrossed his legs, rubbed his chin. Thomas had read in Andy's chart about his destructive relationships with Sal and with Kathy, a woman he had dated for over eight years.

Andy sensed Thomas's doubt, and it worried him that he might not be allowed on Jellinek. Without prepared answers for these unexpected questions, he resorted to telling the truth. "Honestly, I haven't thought about it," he blurted out. "I know I am a very needy person, and I have used women in the past, but the Hazelden program has taught me that I need to stick with the guys for now. I'm so scared of leaving or getting kicked out of Hazelden, I think my fear alone will keep me from getting into bad relationships, any romantic relationships now."

Andy was capable of being honest, Thomas observed, and accepted him at Jellinek.

On Time

Andy never missed an activity and always arrived on time for group functions. On the fourth morning of his stay at Jellinek, he was the first to present one of his sections, a "Kind, Amount, and Frequency" (KAF), an inventory of his drug and alcohol use. Andy had worked on his KAF until two in the morning, typing over six pages that listed his use of chemicals dating back to 1976. He read the entire six pages to the group. His history was broken down not only into years, but into months, even days.

As Andy read what he had used, when, how much, and how often, it began to sound like a chant. "June 4 to 6, 1990. Crack. 30 grams, one time. June 7 to August 3. 2 grams, one time. January 1 to 5, 1991. 50 grams, one time total. Heroin. 1.4 grams, one time. January 28 to February 13. 140 grams, one time total. Heroin. 2.1 grams, one time." He tallied having spent over $142,250 on drugs, alcohol, and related costs in the last eight years.

For his feedback, which peers gave at the end of the section work, patients called his KAF "thorough, painstaking, detailed." He wanted them to like what he did, to find him exceptionally honest and forthcoming. He wanted everyone to like him. Only a month ago, when Andy was in the detox unit, he had scrawled in a diary, "I resent people because I have to go so far to get them to like me." He felt good about being congratulated on his KAF section work. Andy considered that if he kept writing extensive section work, twice a month for four months, fifteen pages each time, he might have over 120 pages, half a book, perhaps a novel, about recovery.

From then on, he typed his sections more purposefully. He'd begin at night, after his roommate had gone to sleep. He took his portable electric typewriter to the art room downstairs and set it on the long wooden table in the center of the room. He opened a bottle of mineral water, sat down on a stool, and began typing. He wrote until three, sometimes four in the morning. He tried hard to write exceptional metaphors, similes, dialogue, vivid imagery, and precise detail to describe his powerlessness and unmanageability. He became like a character in a novel, wearing blue shorts and a sleeveless shirt, sniffing cocaine with a friend outside the locker room before a soccer game. He described the field, the crowds, the coach.

His sections and writing met all the requirements. Peers had noted his honesty. "It felt so real," they'd say. He had included many of the terrible consequences his crack use had on his relationships, jobs, and school. Andy was struggling hard to be honest, but he took an intense pride in what he wrote. He wouldn't have called it arrogance, but he did believe that he wrote the best section work. He was a writer, after all. Why shouldn't he? And he was the only person in the room who had played intercollegiate soccer, the only one who had performed in front of a stadium of people, the only one who had met with Caribbean prime ministers and traveled free of charge to exotic countries. A part of him saw his story as a made-for-television movie.

Moderation: A New Word to Learn

Six weeks into his stay at Jellinek, Andy was called to his counselor's office. When he entered, he saw not only Rick Gilinski, his counselor, but also Ruth Singer, one of the supervisors and personal trainers at the Cork recreational center.

"No," they said, when Andy asked if he had broken some rule at Cork. "Of course not," they reassured him. He had obeyed the letter of the law, but it was the spirit of the law that concerned Rick and Ruth. Everyone was allowed fifty-five minutes a day to exercise, and they were glad that Andy took advantage of the time to run, swim, play basketball, and lift weights. But something seemed wrong. He was waiting at the door when the gym opened for Jellinek patients, and he was the last to leave when it closed. There was something obsessive about his routines. His situps were too strenuous; no one at Hazelden had ever done them using weights. When he used the free weights, lifting them up from his sides, his face turned red from the tension, and he groaned loudly. His workout clothes were soaked with perspiration. "You must realize," Rick said, "you are recovering in a rehab center, not training for the Olympics." Ruth, too, said, "When other patients lift weights, the repetitions are fewer, to give muscle tone. But you seem to be doing bodybuilding. Then afterward, you go outside and run." It was true. Andy had built up his running to eight miles a day. "Alcoholics and drug addicts," Rick warned, "don't know what moderation means."

Andy took offense. "Doctors say that exercise can keep us healthy, and isn't that what Hazelden is all about? Staying healthy?"

Rick anticipated Andy's argument, and that was why Rick had invited the physical fitness trainer to sit in on their meeting. Rick wouldn't argue with Andy. Rick and the trainer presented an exercise option for him, and if he didn't accept, they would pull his green fitness card, leaving him with no pass to Cork Center.

Ruth proposed that she would coach Andy and help him improve his exercising techniques. She would give him one-on-one training and show him the proper way of strengthening his abdominal muscles. Eventually, he would spend less time working out, but would get in better shape. In exchange, Andy would run once every three days, not daily. On the days off, he would not exercise. He could, however, walk the trail, but not alone. From now on, he had to invite someone to join him, whether he was shooting baskets, swimming, lifting weights, running, or just taking a walk. He had to learn that he wasn't in treatment to become a professional athlete and that he could no longer isolate himself when exercising.

Andy agreed to the plan. He soon noticed the new exercises seemed to work better. Though his old regimen was more strenuous, he felt the new plan was equally beneficial. He welcomed the requirement to invite someone to work out with him. He had wanted someone to join him on his walks, but couldn't bring himself to ask. Now, he had an excuse. It was part of this treatment plan. *Thank God*, he thought. He began to understand what Rick had told him about moderation. But Andy had one more hard lesson to learn before he would realize that physical fitness wasn't the answer to his spiritual unrest.

Andy, like many of the patients at Jellinek, felt such intense camaraderie among his peers that it was easy to imagine himself as part of an especially unique group of people, unlike any group that had been there before. They thought their stories created a composite picture or fingerprint that had never been seen before at Hazelden. And in a way it was true. No other room so well accommodated people from all walks of life, education, class, race, or belief. Crisis united plumbers, school teachers, clergy, doctors, athletes, the unemployed, the old, and the young together in ways they wouldn't have imagined. The long days living closely together had created a fellowship and support system that seemed even deeper than the closeness they had experienced in primary treatment. The group rallied for each other. Late one afternoon, however, Andy would undermine that fellowship.

No competitive sports or pickup basketball games were allowed at Cork Center or on the court outside of Jellinek, but some patients did play competitively after the counselors had left the unit. Though Andy wasn't one to break rules, his desire to look good and athletic among his peers made the risk worthwhile. Besides, since the counselors had all gone home, the risk was minimal.

After supper, six men broke into two groups of three for a basketball game. Andy always played against Billy, a young man from Long Island, a crack addict, whose story seemed too grandiose to Andy, though it contained the same gunfire, credit cards, gangs, prostitutes, and rolls of money found in Andy's story. Andy thought he was a bad apple. While Andy tried to be honest, Billy seemed to exaggerate his life as a "roadie," someone who loads and unloads sound equipment, for the Rolling Stones. For every story Andy told about using crack, Billy told one that seemed wilder and more dangerous.

Billy was taller and younger, and he seemed quicker than Andy. When the games started, Andy never played on the same team with Billy. The six men started games right after supper. Andy was the only one quick enough to cover Billy. For Andy, it was win or be beaten, shame or be shamed, humiliate with feints and layups or be humiliated. The men played hard, sweating and panting in the late-afternoon heat. They seemed to like the attention from their peers, who watched from the picnic tables. Everyone knew competitive playing was against the rules, but no one intervened. Andy's team was down six points when Billy pressed hard and dribbled straight toward the basket. As he leaped in the air for a layup, Andy, too, leaped, ramming himself into Billy, intentionally fouling him. Billy fell. As he got up from the concrete, he stared steadily at Andy. Andy rested his hands on his hips, defiantly standing his ground. The basketball had rolled away. Usually, someone ran after it before it rolled into the lake. But not this time.

Billy dashed toward Andy, and the two stood face to face, inches apart. "Lost your cool, man," Andy taunted him. Andy wouldn't swing; he felt in control of himself, but he knew Billy wasn't. If Billy took a swing, he would be kicked out of Hazelden. Andy wanted him to swing, and the other men knew it. Andy put his hands behind his back, his body language saying, "Go on, hit me. I dare you." Finally, one of the other men stepped between them, and Billy walked away.

Billy wouldn't walk away from another fight, and within two weeks of Andy's departure from Jellinek, Billy would be kicked out of Hazelden for fraternizing with a female patient. However, the other men no longer trusted Andy. He had become a dangerous person, someone you couldn't trust. No one would play basketball with him again. In fact, the court and net would be dismantled months later and moved. But that late afternoon, no one came up to Andy and put their arms around him, saying, "Hey, relax. We're all in this together." Instead, one man said, "You can behave better than that, Andy. You're missing the point. You were provoking him. You wanted him to swing. There's something about you, a look in your eye, and it isn't fun to be around you when you get like that. You just have to win."

"I'm supposed to play in a game and want to lose?" Andy retorted. "Are you saying it would have been my fault if he had hit me? Come on, man."

No one bothered to reply. They left the court and went back inside the building.

Andy stood alone under the basket. He knew he was right, but he did not know why he felt so bad.

When Looking Good Is Looking Bad

Not long after the incident on the basketball court, a full group was announced. Everyone discussed it for days. These large group meetings from which no one was excused, not even the counselors, weren't held often. Nevertheless, they could shake the earth underneath a patient who had grown too complacent. The full group meeting went from early morning to late afternoon, from eight to four. All twenty-nine patients and unit counselors attended. After the session began, the door was closed and no one entered or left, unless to use the rest room.

The group members took turns talking about how they were doing on the unit, what their treatment plans and goals were, and what issues they were working on with their counselors. When one person was done, he or she would say who in the group, in his or her opinion, needed extra group attention. They had to explain why they thought so. And finally, the counselors would select two patients from the group, and the rest of the session would be focused on those people, on their behavior, their issues, and their recovery.

Many of the Jellinek patients suspected Billy was sneaking out at night and seeing a woman in primary, at Lilly. In Andy's mind, everyone there, besides a few close friends in the group, was a candidate for group attention. There were five particular patients who were mentioned most frequently as needing extra time. No one had mentioned Andy. *Why should they?* he thought to himself. He was never too intimate with women on the unit, had written the best sections, typed out his notes, worked hard on reviewing other patients' sections, vacuumed the halls, made his bed in the morning, always attended meditation, and cooperated with Ruth on his new recreational workouts. He was one of the few people who wanted to be there. He was, in fact, a model patient. Mr. Recovery. He had broken the rule against competitive basketball, but since there were five other men involved, no one was likely to mention it.

The first patient selected for extra time was a woman named Jill, who fed the ducks in the lake despite repeated requests not to from the counselors and landscaping crews. She broke many other rules as well, but not to be defiant or belligerent. Jill was a quiet, self-effacing patient. When she fed the ducks or slept in, it wasn't to rebel; she simply wanted to satisfy her desires. She meant no harm to the ducks, whose food-gathering instincts could be impacted, preventing them from flying south during cold Minnesota winters. Wherever she went, Jill appeared sad and lonely. No one seemed especially bothered that Jill broke rules. They felt sorry for her. But that morning, the group challenged Jill to begin doing those things that might brighten her life and push away the self-pity and sadness. Many peers identified with Jill, including Andy, who also felt isolated and alone.

After lunch, when the group reconvened, Thomas started the meeting with asking, "Andy, how are you doing?"

"Good," Andy said, mentioning all the hard work he was doing. Andy startled and sat up in his chair when Thomas announced that he wanted him to have extra time from the group for the rest of the afternoon. "Why?" he asked. "I don't need time," he said, futilely protesting the decision.

People spoke at random about Andy, about their impressions of him. Most thought he worked hard at his recovery, was active, friendly, and supportive of others on the unit. But his peers also would use words like "intimidating" and "tough" to describe him. Another man said, "You always need to be right." One of the six men who played basketball that day said, "I think you have an attitude about exercise." One of the women remarked, "You criticize everyone about smoking, but you'll chew tobacco. It makes you sound arrogant, as if you think you are better than everyone."

Andy sat still, stared at the floor, and fidgeted with his watchband. After the comment about him criticizing others, Andy sat straight up, ran both his hands through his hair, then said to Thomas, "Do you mind if I talk now? I have something to say." Thomas nodded.

Andy stood up and walked over to the man who called him intimidating, then turned toward the others who talked about him in group. "I am troubled by the fact that all of you need the safety of this forum to make observations about me," Andy said. "If this is how you see me, I'm wondering about your collective lack of intestinal fortitude. Nobody has the nerve to talk to me directly. It seems cowardly of you all for not speaking up to me before this." Andy's face reddened. He had a way with words and the other patients were no match for him in this situation. "Is there anybody in this room," he added, "who could tell what the hell their problem is with me? Have I done something wrong?

Is there some rule I've broken? Do I sleep in and miss breakfast like Billy and Jill did this morning? Well, tell me. What have I done?"

No one in the group had criticized Andy for failing in his duties or responsibilities. On the contrary, he was praised for being reliable, for attending all the activities and being on time, for writing lengthy sections and detailed work. "Well?" Andy added.

The group kept silent. No one spoke for the longest time, it seemed. "So?" Andy said.

"Andy, the fact that nobody wants to talk to you directly may not be your fault, but I've got news for you," Thomas replied, "it's your problem. People here may want to talk with you, but no one can."

Andy stopped roaming inside the circle of patients and sat back down in his chair. In his heart, he knew Thomas was right. It was his problem, not anyone else's, but he couldn't admit it.

"You may not know what you do to put people off, to put them on the defensive, but it's clear now, Andy, that unless you find a way to be with others, you will continue feeling alone and isolated. The payoff is," Thomas added, "you get to use drugs, because that's what will happen if you continue isolating yourself. Your peers need the safety of the group in order to feel comfortable talking to you. Whatever stands in the way of your relationships with these people stands in the way of your recovery. You keep people at a distance with your rugged individualism. And the danger to your sobriety lies in wanting to be liked for what you do, not who you are."

Andy had invested so much time and energy in doing the right thing on the unit. Shocked that others did not see him as the good guy, Mr. Right, the patient working the hardest in his recovery, Andy felt despair tighten around his throat. Yes, he was doing things right, but for all the wrong reasons. "Sometimes," Thomas added, "when you're looking good, you're looking bad. When you have to be right, you're probably wrong."

His peers waited for him to respond. He sat dumbly, looking dejected. His eyes grew moist. "No matter what I do, no matter how good I try to be," Andy said in a voice that quivered, "I can't satisfy anyone around here. I've tried to be less self-centered, more caring and concerned about you guys, to make friends and build relationships. I screwed up once on the basketball court, and I'm sorry about that.

I have tried so hard to hold up my end of things. I'm on time. I follow directions, 'act as if' there were hope when I feel there is none, and I pray to learn to pray as I was told in primary. Jesus, I do the right thing, but none of you like me."

Again, the group kept silent, feeling the pain that Andy was in. It was Reggie, an overweight twenty-three-year-old bass player and crack addict, the one Andy had criticized for eating too much red meat and dessert, who spoke. "You can make us angry with you, Andy, make us frustrated with you, make us dislike you, but you can't ever make us stop loving you. We will always love you, Andy. You are one of us."

It hit Andy hard. He had a visceral reaction, as if something inside had risen up from his abdomen to his chest and into his throat. When it reached his face, he began sobbing hard. Reggie got up and put his arm around Andy's shoulders.

One Step Back

Over the next three days, Andy took a step back in his recovery. He retreated to his room. He stopped attending his meetings, arrived late, and sometimes not at all, for group sessions. He received notice for not making it to breakfast.

Andy could defend himself against his enemies, like the gang members, but he had no defense against a group that loved him in spite of his own arrogance and shortcomings. He couldn't face them. At mealtime, he often sat by himself, or if he sat with others, he kept silent. He stopped eating salads and ate, instead, the red meat he had criticized Reggie for. In the afternoon, instead of exercising, Andy went to his room to page through a magazine and be alone.

Rick, his counselor, confronted him. "This is enough, Andy. You're worrying us. There are plenty of good things about you that we all like. You can change and connect better with people. These last three days you have stepped back instead of forward. It's time to stop wallowing and start changing."

The two men spent the next hour listing things Andy could do to change his behavior. From that day forward, he would redefine his struggle. Recovery no longer meant being more honest than others, doing the right thing, attending every meeting, and jotting lengthy notes on each lecture. He might continue doing these things, but they were no longer the focus. Recovery now offered Andy another direction, other possibilities, more hope. Before, having others feel bad made him feel good. Now, he wanted to help bring out the best in the people he knew. He wanted them to feel good and happy in his presence, to have fun with him, to enjoy and trust him. Now, it wasn't only his small clique of people that he sought out, but everyone on the unit. Everyone seemed to have something to teach him about how to be a friend.

When Andy wrote his sections on relationships, how his drinking affected them, he no longer sat up past midnight typing lengthy notes for inclusion in his great American novel. Andy had learned some hard lessons, on the basketball court, at full group, in his counselors' rooms, and while taking walks with his peers. From now on, what he wrote came from the heart. He didn't dress up what he had to say with poetic images designed not to communicate his feelings, but to conceal them. He might write only two or three pages. He might throw them away after reading them to another peer. It didn't matter as long as he felt— felt something.

He began writing about his grief over his father's death and over losing Kathy, the only person who connected him to a sober world. He began to see how important relationships were. Andy wrote his sections on relationships in his room. He didn't use his typewriter. Slowly and carefully, line after line in longhand, he exposed himself as an emotional fraud, someone who desperately wanted connection and love with others but who couldn't develop and maintain relationships. It was his disease, his addiction, that isolated him from others. Once again, he felt in touch with his loneliness and despair, and he cried.

Yes, he had taken a step back into despair, but by the next morning at breakfast, Andy was ready to talk about his loneliness with his peers. There were still things he was holding back from the group, but he would share them during his Fifth Step while at Fellowship, a halfway house in St. Paul. In the meantime, he was resuming his journey forward. He had patience and would give himself the time he needed to heal. He didn't expect himself to instantly vanquish all his shortcomings and his deep isolation. Being right was no longer a priority. In fact, if being right would make him wrong, he wanted no part of it. It would take time—and love from others—but he would change. And the change he wanted to make in his life would require others; it wasn't on his shoulders alone, and he felt delightfully relieved of a burden. Needing others wasn't a shortcoming. It was a blessing.

Saying Good-bye

Most closing ceremonies at Jellinek included a few gifts, which were paid for with a collection taken up by the patients. It was customary to give each graduate an inscribed medallion and a copy of the book *Hazelden: A Spiritual Odyssey*. Because Andy had read parts of it and could purchase a copy for himself, he had asked for a T-shirt from Serenity Corner, the Hazelden bookstore. The shirt depicted a coyote and a wolf howling against a southwestern sky. The words "You Are Not Alone" were printed below the animals. Andy asked everyone in the group to sign it with a permanent marker. A man named David, a heroin addict from Detroit, drew an obscene cartoon of a woman on the shirt. When Andy saw it, he became mad. He wouldn't be able to wear the shirt in public now. It was ruined and David was to blame. Months later, upon hearing that David had relapsed and died of a cocaine overdose, Andy found himself praying for him. Andy also prayed for himself to become more tolerant of others.

Five other patients from Andy's days at Jellinek would die. Larry died from AIDS. Jerry, an overweight veterinarian, died from a heart attack at the age of fifty-two while on leave from Jellinek; he had consumed nearly a full bottle of vodka. Randy, a cocaine addict and weight lifter with two kids, hung himself in jail after a drunken head-on collision with an elderly couple. Sally, a fifty-one-year-old alcoholic, was shot at a bar two months after leaving Jellinek. And Karen, who had called Andy at Fellowship, died after she stumbled down a flight of stone stairs near her home in Kansas.

No one heard from Billy after he was kicked out of Hazelden. But Andy loved Billy, for Billy had inadvertently showed him the importance of connecting with others, and that recovery really was a matter of life and death.

9

Waiting for the Lightning Bolt

WHEN JOANNA THOMSEN arrived at Jellinek, she was in a very different place than when she left primary treatment a year and a half earlier. At that time, she thought her biggest problem was being an imperfect wife. Her primary goal had been to get home as quickly as possible. Now her only goal was to survive.

After leaving the Lilly unit, she went to a few AA meetings, enough to satisfy Jeff, but she soon stopped going. She made a gourmet meal one February evening, and Jeff suggested they have some wine, one glass, with the meal. She was afraid to say no, and perhaps, at some level, glad to say yes. She knew he craved normalcy for them. He opened a 1985 Bordeaux, and when they toasted their happiness, clinking the crystal goblets they had received nine years earlier as a wedding present, he said, "I'm so glad you can drink a glass of wine now and then. I really enjoy this." Joanna, too, was glad she could drink a glass of wine now and then. Perhaps she wasn't powerless after all, she thought.

She became pregnant with Stacey nine months after leaving treatment and, as with Molly, was able to remain sober throughout her pregnancy. However, unlike her pregnancy with Molly, she was severely nauseated and threw up frequently. She was also severely depressed; it seemed as though she cried all the time. Jeff was overwhelmed and afraid to call her from work anymore. Joanna tried not to cry in the evenings when Jeff was home, but as soon as he went to bed, she'd sit down with a magazine or in front of the television and start crying again. More and more frequently, she found her mind wandering to vodka and lemonades. Two weeks before Stacey was born, alcohol had become an obsession again. Joanna fought it, but six weeks after the birth, she gave in to the desperate desire.

After her binge, she went back to Hazelden's Lilly unit for ten days, and there they tried to convince her to enter Jellinek. Marilyn, her counselor, said to her: "Joanna, this is a disease. A chronic illness. You cannot recover from this disease by yourself. You have said to us that you know you are powerless over alcohol, but I don't believe you have accepted that yet. There is a difference between acknowledgment and acceptance." Joanna cried and said she accepted it, but she had to go back to her babies. She'd be more careful this time.

Marilyn's voice was gentle, and Joanna felt loved, even through the difficult words. "You can't take care of your babies while this disease is active. Primary treatment is like a jump start, Joanna. It's a quick education by immersion. Extended care is like a long, slow bath. There is time for the lessons to be integrated, for insight to deepen, for understanding and acceptance to soak in all the way to your bones. Then you can take care of your babies the way they need to be taken care of. But first you must take care of yourself."

Joanna was afraid not to enter Jellinek, but she was more afraid that three or four months of extended care would endanger her marriage. And the idea of being gone from Stacey, still so tiny that Jeff could hold her in the length of his forearm, was unthinkable. In the evenings, when she sat in the lounge with the Lilly women, her mind would wander to Stacey. She would think of changing Stacey into pajamas, kissing the top of her head with its wisps of cornsilk hair, and nursing her to sleep.

And there was Molly, already so upset about having a new baby in the house. To leave Molly right now would create severe feelings of abandonment. Joanna called Jeff every night from the unit's pay phone, saying she couldn't go to Jellinek, she needed to come home, she needed him, and the children needed her. She said she'd learned her lesson this time. Finally, he relented. "But Jo, you can't do this again," he said, his voice grave. She could imagine him sitting, holding his forehead in his hand.

Exactly five weeks after she got home, Joanna took another drink. A friend from her first stay at Lilly, almost two years ago now, phoned her, asking if she could stop by for a visit the next day. Joanna told her she'd have to take a rain check; an old high school friend was coming to stay for a couple days. At two o'clock in the morning, the phone rang again. It was Polly, saying she was on her way. Joanna hung up and awakened Jeff. "She's drunk, Jeff. I could hear it in her voice."

"Well, call her back. She can't come." Jeff's voice was urgent.

Joanna shut her eyes. "I can't stop her. I already told her she can't come. She's on her way."

For the next four hours Joanna tossed in bed, waiting for Polly to ring the doorbell. Finally, she got up, showered, ate breakfast, and made Jeff a sandwich to bring with him to the golf course. At 7:30 A.M., Polly rang the bell. As she walked into the house, Joanna could smell whiskey on her breath. She made breakfast for Polly and showed her where the shower was. When Polly came out of the shower, she went out to her car for a sweatshirt. Joanna made coffee for Polly, listened to her cry, and begged her to go back to AA. As the morning wore on, Polly made repeated excuses to visit her car, her words becoming more and more slurred, her feet more stumbling.

As Joanna watched Polly and smelled the alcohol on her breath, she began to feel restless. A pressure built slowly, beginning in her abdomen, moving up through her chest, traveling out through her limbs. She started tapping her fingers on the table as she listened to Polly, and soon she began to pace the floor. She thought a long, exhausting walk might get rid of the pressure, but she didn't dare leave the children with Polly.

After lunch, Polly lurched into the bedroom and fell asleep. *I've got to find the bottle and pour it out,* Joanna told herself. She went to Polly's jacket, got her keys, and walked out to the car. She found an overnight case with a half-empty bottle of whiskey. She pulled the bottle out, walked back to the house and straight into the kitchen. Cradled in her right hand, the bottle fit in an alarmingly familiar way. She reached the sink, unscrewed the top, and brought the bottle to her nose. The smell seared her throat. Instead of pouring it down the sink, she screwed the cap back on and hid the bottle behind a box of cereal. *This stuff costs a fortune,* she told herself. *It's like pouring out gold. I'll just put it away where Polly can't find it.*

As she cleaned up the kitchen, she kept feeling the shape of the bottle in her hand. The pressure continued to build, and all she could think about was the whiskey, placed so carefully behind the cereal box. She fed Stacey, played paper dolls with Molly, vacuumed the living room, and all the time, the whiskey bottle kept appearing before her eyes. She began to fix lasagna for dinner, and when she walked into the pantry for noodles, she stopped in front of the cereal and pulled out the bottle. Her hand shook as she filled a tumbler. The whiskey slid down her throat and defused the pressure immediately.

She awakened the next morning and thought of nothing but vodka. After she'd set a bowl of cereal in front of Molly, and before the baby woke up, she phoned a taxi driver she knew. "Carl, I want you to do an errand for me," she said. "I want you to stop by the Depot and pick up a gallon of vodka for me." As she stood by the front window in her pajamas watching for the taxi, her mother pulled up in front of the house. As her mom walked into the kitchen to see Molly, the taxi arrived. Joanna charged down the driveway, paid the taxi driver, stashed the vodka under the bushes by the drive, and ran back into the house. Her mom came into the living room just as Joanna was walking in the door.

"What was a taxi doing here?" she asked.

"Oh, that," said Joanna. "I took a cab home from a meeting last night, and I didn't have any cash. I didn't want to wake Jeff, so I told the driver to come by this morning for the fare."

Joanna ran her fingers through her tangled hair.

Her mother frowned. "Are you all right?"

"Yeah, I'm okay, Mom. What do you think? I'm just tired. It's exhausting being up all night nursing a baby."

"But you seem almost . . ."

"Good grief, Mother. Get off my back."

When her mother left, Joanna ran out to the bushes, got the bag, and hid it in the front closet behind the vacuum cleaner. Not five minutes later, her mother pulled up again. Joanna went to the door, and her mother asked, "Are you sure you're all right?"

"I'm all right. I'm all right. Okay?"

The next thing Joanna remembered was calling a woman she had met in AA. It was mid-afternoon. The woman knew she was home alone with two children and that she was in trouble, but Joanna had no memory of their conversation. Jeff later told Joanna that the police broke down the door, that they found her passed out on the couch, and that Molly was frantically crying. The police took Stacey and Molly to a neighbor's and put Joanna in an ambulance. The neighbor called child protection, and before they would let Jeff pick up the children, he had to assure them that Joanna was not in the home.

Saturday's Entertainment

The leaves on the poplars were brittle and yellow when Joanna arrived at Hazelden for the third time. Kate, a peer who was assigned to be her buddy, came up to the Lilly unit, where Joanna had spent ten days going through a case evaluation and waiting for a bed to open up on the extended care unit. They walked together through the long maze of hallways to the northern edge of the complex, and then outside for the short walk to Jellinek. It was the place Joanna had dreaded most, the place where the really bad people go. She carried a suitcase and walked next to Kate, who was carrying her other suitcase. Kate talked about their schedule, and about how glad she was that Joanna had made the decision to come, but Joanna kept her head down, and silently stared at the path in front of them.

She had a private room on the north side of the building on the second floor, the women's floor. Joanna wept as she hung up her blouses and dresses; she wept as she put away her shampoo and stationery; she wept as she taped photos to her desk; and she wept as she sat down on her bed and stared out the window.

About seven in the evening, a tall man with a noticeable Adam's apple stopped in front of her open door. He knocked on her doorsill. "You mind?" was all he said.

She looked up at him, not bothering to hide her tears. She didn't say anything.

"Hard day, hmm?"

Joanna sniffled and gave a half-smile.

"I'm Sam," said the tall man. "Hey, it's Saturday night. How about a little entertainment? There's a state-of-the-art art room downstairs. I'll show you."

The tears started down her face again, and she shook her head no.

"Aww, c'mon," said Sam, jerking his head in the direction of the hall. "I'm cool. I don't care if you cry while you color."

Joanna got up off her bed and followed him passively down the length of the hall, turned left, walked down two flights of stairs, took a right again, and there, at the beginning of the basement floor, was a room walled in shelves. The shelves were cluttered with paint and paper, plaster molds, baskets of red maple leaves and yellow birch leaves, and squares of brown leather. Sam pulled a box of forty-eight crayons off the shelf and flipped up the top to reveal ascending rows of colors. "This is for you, my lady," he said. He also pulled out a box of Cray-pas, thick, oil-based pastels, which sat in a long row like candy sticks, and set them on the table next to the crayons. Then he opened a cabinet door and knelt to get a stack of placemat papers. "Hey, what's your name, by the way?"

"Joanna." She chuckled in spite of herself.

"Well, Joanna, I'm here for alcohol. And you?"

"Alcohol."

"Fish," he directed, and he sat down on the stool across the table from her. He pursed his lips as he studied the box of crayons, pulled out a forest green one, and sketched a fish the shape of a large bubble. Then he chose turquoise and carefully drew in scales. Joanna took a gray Cray-pas and drew a long, skinny fish with sharp gray teeth.

"Ouch. That one looks like it could hurt you," Sam observed.

"Damn right," said Joanna, smiling as she added sharp fins, but the tears started again. She reached for a blue Cray-pas. She cried through the blue and through the taupe. She cried through the pink and the purple. Sam reached across the table. "How about we let this fish see what it's doing." He colored in a large brown eye. His fingers were long and his nails well-groomed, the cuff around his wrist slightly frayed. "This is your first day here, right?"

Joanna began to cry. "My daughter, Stacey, is only six weeks old. What's she gonna do without me?" asked Joanna. "And Molly, my other daughter. Do you know how mad she's going to be at me? Four months. I'm supposed to spend four months in here." She picked up a new piece of paper and shifted to crayons. "Molly was hanging on my leg when I left. She was saying, 'I want to come with you, Mommy.' I had to tell her no. I told her, 'Mommy has an illness and has to go away to a hospital for a while to get better.' But she doesn't get it, you know?"

Sam listened quietly. "I know," he said.

She drew a tropical fish with yellow and black stripes, although she had never seen one.

"Molly loves yellow," sniffled Joanna. She pulled a tissue from her pocket and blew her nose. "Stacey might not even know who I am when I leave this place."

"That must feel awful," Sam responded.

Joanna drew in seaweed and conch shells. Sam added a stick-man scuba diver. They drew frogs on lily pads and swamp grass. Joanna cried and Sam listened. Joanna drew a whale and Sam drew a shark. They both drew dolphins leaping over waves. "What's that?" laughed Sam. "It looks like an uncooked omelette."

Joanna began to laugh too. "Yeah, well, yours looks like a wet noodle." She reached over and shaded it in with a magenta crayon.

"Can you believe this?" asked Sam, rolling his deep brown eyes toward the ceiling. "Two perfectly sane grown-ups spending Saturday evening together coloring fish?"

"The Big Book says we're insane," retorted Joanna. She looked at the stacks of paper covered with fish of every variety and scattered across the table. Then she laughed again, a nervous tension-releasing laugh. "And I believe it now."

Drink It Down

Joanna's recovery began with a new kind of honesty, an honesty she had never experienced before. She met her new chemical dependency counselor, Vivian Hogan, on Monday, two days after she arrived. She walked into the office and was struck by a huge hand-drawn poster on the wall. In the center of it was a heart that must have been four or five feet long, and inside was a splash of brilliant yellow.

"I'm very glad to meet you," Vivian said, "and I'm glad you're here. Tell me something about yourself."

"I don't think you want to know about me," said Joanna. She had reached the place of exile, the place she had always tried to avoid, and she had nothing left to fear. This was the beginning of surrender. Over the next few days, she saw Vivian several times, and each time she revealed more of herself. She even told Vivian about conning the counselors when she was on the Lilly unit, about how she didn't like AA, didn't bother to go, never intended to go.

She talked to Vivian about a feeling of hollow darkness, a feeling of emptiness beyond pain. Her limbs were heavy in the morning, and her back bent under the weight of something invisible and unknown. She dreaded opening her eyes, knowing that daylight would only bring another shade of darkness and a heavy stone in her stomach. Together they charted her mood against her menstrual cycle to see if she was suffering from premenstrual syndrome. But the darkness was omnipresent; there was no season of relief. After five weeks, Vivian suggested she consult the unit psychologist, who in turn suggested she see a staff psychiatrist for medication. When Joanna protested, saying she didn't want to be on drugs anymore, the psychologist explained that antidepressant medication is not addictive.

The psychologist told her that depression is a complicated illness with many possible causes. Sometimes it's caused by brain chemistry, and medication is an invaluable tool in healing. Sometimes it's influenced by the way a person grows up, the way she is treated in her family, and the things she sees her parents do and hears her parents say. Even the most loving parents make mistakes, and even the happiest children can be very sensitive to hurts. Depression can also be triggered by losing people who are important to you or having important dreams thwarted. Some people describe depression as anger that is turned inward against yourself. And, since alcohol is a depressant, drinking can also contribute to depression.

As when Donna O'Brian, the psychologist she had seen when she was in primary treatment the first time, had recognized her post-traumatic stress disorder and given it a name, Joanna now felt the enormous relief of not being alone. The next week, Joanna saw a staff psychiatrist and started taking Zoloft, an antidepressant known as a serotonin re-uptake inhibitor, and soon felt the heaviness begin to lift.

During their early sessions, Vivian and Joanna reviewed the various assessments Joanna had filled out: the spiritual, psychological, social, frequency and quantity of use, and recreational assessments. Vivian showed her the treatment plan, which had been developed based on the assessments. Joanna read the goal: "To personalize the disease that keeps bringing me back to treatment." She nodded her head. She was to read chapters 1 and 3 in the Big Book again, and write the Step One sections. Joanna detailed her attempts to control her drinking, wrote down the kinds of substances she had used, the amounts, the frequency, and really understood for the first time that her willpower was useless against alcohol.

Vivian had written another goal for Joanna: "To do with my Jellinek family what I could not do with my family of origin." Again, she was to write, this time about her childhood home and growing up. It was during this time that she learned how her father's drinking, and her mother's fight against it, had affected her. She learned how her relationship with Jeff paralleled relationships in her childhood, and how she continued to live by patterns established long ago.

"I want you to learn here how to do what you could not do at home as a child—to develop trust, to take risks, and to share yourself openly," Vivian told her.

Joanna began by making notes to herself. She sat at her desk after breakfast. Because her window faced north, the light was soft and diffused, made even more so by the fresh snow on the trees. It was the same stand of woods she had walked to late in the night when she was staying on the Lilly unit. It seemed like such a long time ago. She was beginning to feel the lessons she had learned back then taking form and shape in her life now.

How was drinking done in her family? "My dad gulped a glass of brandy as soon as he came in the door," she wrote. "He walked straight to the kitchen sink, took out the brandy, and poured a shot. He gulped it, poured another shot, and gulped that one too. Then he would start to slow down. He'd pour a third drink, but he carried that one around with him and sipped it." Memory pushed her hand across the paper.

How did her family's drinking affect her? The work sent her traveling backwards. She put her chin in her left hand, her elbow on the desk, and stared. On her wall, she had taped a picture of a living room from *Home Beautiful*. The windows were tall, almost floor to ceiling, and slatted white shutters let in an autumn sun. The walls had a subtle red glow to them, the sun shining on them through a brilliant red maple outside the window. A rose-colored Persian rug sat under a glass coffee table next to an ivory couch. Joanna stared at the couch, overstuffed and inviting. She could picture herself as a child sitting on the couch with her dad, his brandy glass in his left hand, his right arm slung over the back of the couch. Her legs, which didn't reach the floor yet, were folded under her. She loved this time of day, when her dad was so relaxed. During commercial breaks, he would ask about her day. She would tell him about the school's hamsters, about playing dodgeball.

It was so much better than the mornings, when she would wake to the agitated sound of clanging pots and pans as her dad would empty the dishwasher and make coffee. Many mornings she would stay in bed as long as she could, hoping he would leave for work before she had to go downstairs and eat breakfast. When she couldn't wait anymore, she would walk down quietly, hoping her dad wouldn't pay attention to her. If she spilled her cereal or her milk, he would glower at her. "Jo, get the sponge and wipe that up."

"Okay, Dad." If she turned to put the cereal box away first, he would bark, "You gonna get the sponge or not? You're so irresponsible. Why can't you kids learn to clean up after yourselves?"

In the evening when he came home again, Joanna would wait for the sound of bottles clinking against each other, the sound of the ice cubes cracking as he poured brandy over them. They were good sounds, the sounds of a father who would be calm and nice.

Joanna returned from her reverie to look at the half-empty paper on the desk in front of her. Where would she find the words to write this down? She extended her legs in front of the chair, leaned back, and closed her eyes. "Jo-Jo," her dad would say with a big smile, "give your old dad a hug," and she would gratefully throw her arms around his neck. She would settle in again and watch his television program with him. Soon he'd be nodding off, and her mom would be angry, complaining to Joanna about her irresponsible father. Though Joanna felt guilty for not defending her dad, she'd listen to her mom and nod her head. She didn't want her mom to be upset.

Joanna opened her eyes, sat up at the desk, and wrote, "Dad's drinking made me feel confused, scared, and sad." Then she put down the pen, overwhelmed by the way she had just betrayed her parents, and walked down the hall to the kitchen. She made herself a cup of hot chocolate.

Over the next week and a half, she talked about the section in her sessions with Vivian, about the guilt she felt at saying and thinking these things about her parents. One Thursday afternoon, she was sitting in her customary chair under the big heart in Vivian's office, saying, "I felt like I always had to fix everything. I was always sitting on that couch trying to fix my family."

"Such a big job," responded Vivian. "Do you still try to do that?"

When Vivian asked the question, Joanna felt her ears get hot. She was caught in her seat, afraid of what she would discover if she answered the question. Her mind went blank, and she felt like she had a vise fastened to the top of her head.

"I can't remember what I was going to say."

"No rush, Jo."

Joanna sat quietly, and the thoughts came back to her. When she married Jeff, she believed that she was leaving the tension of her family's living room; instead, the tension existed in a new setting. She could hear Jeff say she was gaining too much weight, and frantically she began to diet. She thought of the evenings that she cooked elaborate dinners—beef Wellington, ratatouille, Caesar salad, French silk pie—to fix the drinking she had done earlier in the day, the drinking he wasn't even aware of.

"I might," Joanna whispered. "I think I try to make everything okay with Jeff the same way I tried to make it okay with my mom and dad."

When Joanna left Vivian's office, she could not go back to her own room. She was too charged to be alone. She walked to Jellinek's lounge, the big room on the west end of the unit that looked out over the lake. She could generally count on finding a few people gathered there, and today both Sam and Kate were sitting among a group of people talking about sections they had worked on that morning. Sam looked up at her.

"Lady, you look like something the cat dragged in. Do you want a hug?"

Joanna smiled at him, and took a chair in the group. She sighed. "What a session I just had," she said. She didn't want to ask the questions, but something inside was driving her. She had to know what her friends thought. "Do you think I try to make everything okay for Jeff? Do you think I behave with him like I behaved with my mom?"

Kate, her original buddy and a woman Joanna was becoming very close to, crossed her legs and said wryly. "Yeah, Jo, I'd say that's probably true."

"This is no joke, Kate," said Joanna. "Do you really think I've been living my life with Jeff like I lived my life at home, afraid to say what I think, afraid to stand up for myself, wanting to keep the peace?"

"You've said it yourself, Jo. When Jeff does something you don't like, you shut up and drink it down."

The words hit home like a dart hitting a target. *Drink it down,* she thought. *That's it.* She remembered the last time Jeff announced he was going on a golfing trip. Two little babies to take care of and he was going to leave her. She bit her tongue; she didn't want him to be mad at her, nor did she want to be mad at him. Then Polly showed up drunk at her door, and the rest was history.

"I've spent a lifetime saying what I think other people want to hear, doing what I think they expect me to do." Joanna's voice was heavy with grief.

Rebecca, a younger woman from Miami, who had been on the unit for a month now, reassured her. "You're not so different, Jo. It's a problem we tend to have. Taking care of everyone else. Being what everyone else wants us to be."

Joanna's voice remained heavy. "I don't think I know who I am."

Stacey and Molly

Joanna fussed in her room, making sure the photos were set neatly on her desk, the bedspread pulled tightly across the bed. She brought up crayons and paper from the art room and laid them out on her desk. She tried to read while she waited, but found herself pacing instead, then standing by the window and staring out.

This would be the first time the children had seen her in the place she had called a hospital. On the phone yesterday, Molly had demanded, "I want to talk to the doctor, Mommy. I want to tell him to make you better faster so you can come home." Joanna was glad for the moment that Molly couldn't see the water welling in her eyes. Molly had wanted to know, "What is the color of the carpet? What is the color of your walls?" It was as if she were trying to make Joanna real to her.

Joanna couldn't sit still. She was so eager to see her babies. Would Stacey know her? She knew that the baby, though only six weeks old, had learned to recognize her before she left, because she quieted in response to Joanna's voice when nobody else could calm her. But it had been a whole month now, and Joanna had no milk to give her, no milk with which to comfort either the baby or herself.

It seemed like hours before Jeff was standing at her door with the girls. His face was rosy from the November chill, and his dark hair in disarray from the wind. In his right arm he held Stacey, completely hidden by a bulky blanket. Holding tightly to his left hand was Molly, her hair matted against her cheeks, curls sticking out from under her hood. In mint green snow pants, her short legs looked stocky, and the tip of her nose was pink. Her blue eyes were as bright as the winter snow. Wide-eyed, she looked at Joanna, smiled so the dimple in her chin appeared, and pushed her face against Jeff's leg. Joanna rushed over and knelt on the floor in front of her. She reached her hand out to touch Molly's head. Molly turned toward her, threw her body against Joanna's chest, and wrapped her small arms around Joanna. Joanna swooped Molly off the floor, burying her face in Molly's warm neck.

"Where are the babies with the pink and blue hats?" Molly demanded.

"Oh, honey, this isn't that kind of hospital," Joanna said. "Would you like to see our kitchen and our lounge?"

After a tour, and after Molly was settled at the desk coloring, Joanna laid Stacey on the bed to look at her. Her wispy brown hair had thickened a bit, and her arms and legs had filled out. Jeff leaned over to babble at her, and Stacey's legs started to cycle. As she waved her arms, Joanna noticed that her hands had gotten pudgy too. "My turn, Jeff," she said, and reached over to pick up the baby. She cupped her hands on each side of Stacey's chest, wrapping her fingers under the baby's arms and around her back. "Oh, my sweetheart, I have missed you so much," she said, picking her up. But Stacey's cycling arms and legs went stiff, and she started to whimper. "Baby, it's your mama. It's okay, Stacey," Joanna cooed. "Give me her rattle," she said sharply to Jeff. She shook the pink rattle gently in front of Stacey's eyes. She blew softly on her forehead, kissed her nose, walked with her, whispered in her ear, and swayed back and forth with her. Stacey could not be comforted.

Though the room was flooded with bright sun, Joanna felt a gray mist envelop everything. She handed Stacey to Jeff and went to sit beside Molly. For every minute of the next hour she could not make herself forget, not even for a second, that Molly and the baby were leaving again. As dusk approached, Jeff took the diaper bag and a bag of snacks out to the car. He came back, tucked Stacey into her snowsuit, and turned to Molly, who looked up from her spot next to Joanna on the bed. "Bye, Daddy," she said.

"Pumpkin, you're coming with me," Jeff told her softly.

Molly threw her arms around Joanna's neck. "Honey," Joanna said, willing her voice to be calm. "You can't stay here with Mommy. It's not a place for children. I'll come home to you soon." Jeff pried Molly's hands off Joanna, wrapped her in her coat, and carried her to the car. Joanna followed with Stacey. As Jeff pulled away, she watched, her feet rooted to the floor. Molly's face was pressed against the glass.

Judgment Calls

Joanna participated in the family program six weeks after she arrived on Jellinek. She went to the program feeling angry; it was a new posture for her. Anger was something she had rarely let herself feel, let alone display, but she was being encouraged to know this part of herself. "Your anger can be a source of strength and knowledge," said Vivian. Joanna allowed herself to explore this, and she discovered a well of anger in her belly, much of it directed against her family. After the first treatment, they had quietly excluded her from family vacations. She felt like an embarrassment to them. None of them had called since her arrival at Jellinek, and they hadn't returned her calls. It seemed fine for her dad to be an alcoholic, as long as he didn't admit it, but if she talked about alcoholism, she was an outcast. The more she thought about it, the angrier she got.

She arrived at the expansive lounge in time for morning roll call. The room was three times the size of the lounges on the individual units. She would spend the next five days there, on the opposite end of campus from Jellinek, beginning right after breakfast. It was curious to see the expanse of couches and chairs filled by such a variety of people, most of them looking nervous. She counted four couples, three older women, five women who looked to be in their thirties, men in their forties, and a couple with a son who was perhaps seventeen. They looked drawn, tired, many of them holding the traditional Hazelden mug. She noticed a couple of her peers: Rebecca, the woman from Miami; and Carl, a pilot from Seattle, whose wife was leaving him if he didn't go to treatment. There were a few others she had seen in the dining room from time to time; most likely, they were from primary.

A staff person welcomed them and called off their names. He explained to the newcomers that the program would help them to learn about the disease of addiction and how it impacted the families of an addict, and to discover ways they could help themselves. "It is critical that families stop focusing on the chemically dependent person and tend to themselves," he said.

Yeah. You tell 'em! thought Joanna.

The family program would also give them a chance to hear from some people who shared the disease that plagued their loved ones, he continued. After breakfast, they would come back here for a lecture, followed by small-group discussions, during which they would talk about the worksheets they had filled out. Despite the beautiful oak furniture, the jade plants and palms, despite the polite smiles around her, Joanna felt antsy and a little lonely. She felt like an outsider and wished she could go back to Jellinek. She was grateful, however, that patients attended the family program at a different time than their own family members. It would be easier, she thought, to talk to other patients' families than to her own.

The lecturer talked about the disease of alcoholism and addiction. She spelled out very clearly that alcoholism is a disease, that the addict is truly powerless over alcohol and drugs, and that no amount of good intentions could enable them to control their use. As she listened, Joanna was glad that Jeff would be attending the family program the next week. The lecturer explained that the disease affects families profoundly. "The disease creates an atmosphere of unpredictability that raises anxiety in family members. You're always wondering what's coming next, trying to compensate for their behavior when they're drinking or drugging. And your reaction to their behavior gets you emotionally drunk." Joanna thought of Jeff. When he was trying to keep her from drinking, he seemed as crazy as she did.

The lecturer stressed that family members are not responsible for the addict's behavior. She drew three large Cs on the board and said, "If you bring anything home with you from this week, I hope it is this: You didn't cause it. You can't control it. And you can't cure it." Finally, she talked about trust. "A common effect of the disease is a profound disturbance in our trust. It takes time in recovery before that trust can be reestablished."

Joanna met with a group of six people for the morning discussion after the lecture: Ken, who was in primary treatment at Shoemaker; a gray-haired woman named Irene, whose son was at Shoemaker; a young woman named Angela, whose mother was at Dia Linn, the other primary treatment unit for women; Tom, a dark-haired banker from Michigan, whose wife was in Lilly; Judith and Marion, both homemakers with young children, whose husbands were at Shoemaker. Each person had filled out a worksheet called "What's My Part?" The first question read: "Is there a family situation (or relationship or work problem) that I wish would change?"

Judith, one of the homemakers, began the discussion by saying,

"I just keep thinking about what the lecturer said. You know, about every chemically dependent person needing someone to blame, and it's usually the people closest to them. That's one of the things I'd change. My husband keeps telling me it's my fault that he's drunk."

"Yeah," agreed Marion, the other woman with young children. "It makes you crazy. Here he is blaming me, when he's the one who's spending so much of our money that we have trouble making the mortgage. He's the one who doesn't bother coming home until all hours of the morning."

Judith's voice was gaining intensity. "It does make you crazy. Last time he didn't come home, I was hoping he was dead. I was planning his funeral. I thought, *People will know he died of an overdose, and they won't feel bad. And they shouldn't. He deserved to die.* That's the insanity."

"I'm just shattered and so afraid. I can't go back to living like that," said Marion.

The gray-haired woman, Irene, looked at the floor. "I actually wished my son was dead, because it would be easier that way." Her voice was very quiet.

The family counselor spoke up. "It's normal to feel angry at the addict who has made your life so miserable. They may have a disease, but their behavior has still affected you."

"Does it help with the anger to know it is a disease?" asked Joanna.

"Yes, it does," answered Marion. "It helps with the anger. And it helps with the shame."

That evening, sitting in the lounge on Jellinek, Joanna's anger was palpable. "They talk about the alcoholic or the addict blaming loved ones. Good grief, I felt like I was the one being blamed," she exclaimed to Kate and Sam.

Sam's voice was very gentle. "Don't you think you're being a little judgmental, Jo?" he asked. "You know, when you pass judgment on these people, you're missing an opportunity to hear some important things."

"I remember when I attended family," said Kate. "It was so hard to hear the pain I had caused my family."

Joanna crossed her hands behind her head, leaned back, and closed her eyes. She didn't want to hear this. But she knew they were right; the people in the family program weren't blaming her. She was hiding from the pain that she had caused.

For the next several days, she listened to lectures, participated in small-group discussions, ate lunch, and even hung out in the evenings with the families attending the program. At the end of the fourth day, late in the evening, she came back to Jellinek utterly drained. "I'm confused," she told Sam after dinner. "I've been so mad at my family. I mean, look at my dad, at what he's drinking. Look at the way he's acted. How dare he turn his back on me. I'm only doing what he did, what he taught me how to do. At least I'm trying to get better; he's not. And yet, my whole family is acting like I've got some horrible, contagious disease."

"Uh-huh," nodded Sam.

"But I sit and listen to the families talk about sisters, husbands, wives, and parents. This one woman said she began to avoid her son. She said it was easier to say nothing than to say the wrong thing. Maybe my family just needs more time."

"Family's a real eye-opener, isn't it?"

"Listening to them has turned out to be a blessing. They've told me things my family, and Jeff, for that matter, couldn't tell me."

"And you've probably told them things that you couldn't tell Jeff or your parents. Do you think?"

Joanna stopped to think of something from the discussion group earlier that morning. It followed a lecture about detachment with love. Ironically, the husband of a woman who was in primary treatment on Lilly asked her, "What does this detachment-with-love thing mean to you? I've told my wife if she starts using again, I'll leave her, and I feel terrible, like I'm being horribly unsupportive."

Joanna's stomach tightened. Jeff had yet to say he would leave her, but he had probably thought it a million times. Before Joanna had time to answer, one of the patients from primary said, "If I were your wife, I'd want to know that I have to pay the consequences. You can't make your wife stop drinking, but there's more of a chance that you'll help her by setting limits than by hanging in there and tolerating it. I'm an emergency physician and I do things that hurt people—chest tubes and things like that. We do things we have to do at the moment, even if it causes pain."

The family counselor added, "Detachment with love can feel very confusing. But the point is, you have no power over the alcohol. You cannot control your wife's drinking. She is responsible for her own recovery. She's the only one who can make the choice to follow her program, and you can only take responsibility for yourself. You are a bigger help to her as a calm, healthy adult. That's not abandonment."

"If I stumble, my wife will cut me loose," volunteered Carl, the man from Shoemaker.

"I think it's one of the scariest things you can hear, but it helps me to face reality," Joanna said, her heart in her mouth.

A Long Journey of Small Steps

Joanna sat in Bigelow Auditorium, listening to Marilyn Peterson talk about a spiritual awakening. "On page 569 of the Big Book, it says that a spiritual awakening is a personality change sufficient to bring about recovery. For a lot of you, this is the first time you're experiencing being honest with yourself. That's a change. You're beginning your spiritual awakening. That doesn't have to mean flashing lights. It begins the moment you begin to change. It's a springboard. It's going to take time to grow, but it'll be stronger for taking the time to grow. Get your passion and joy from being who you are. You are intelligent, beautiful people."

After the lecture, as Joanna pulled her coat tightly around herself and ran across the short, open walk back to Jellinek, she noticed flashes of light in the gray sky. They were incongruous with the snowy landscape. The thunder rolling in a few seconds later declared the rare but possible thunderstorm during a Minnesota winter.

Something about the storm made her remember Abby and the days back on the Lilly unit. Abby had experienced a sudden spiritual awakening. Joanna remembered Abby's description of it when they were sitting together in Lilly's lounge late one evening. It had been mid-December then, too, but the cold had come late that year. The lake was covered in ice, but it wasn't yet thick enough to walk on. Usually, by that time of year, you could see pickups driving on the lake and icehouses sitting on the far side. But that year the lake was still empty. Abby had told Joanna, "I didn't care anymore. I just walked outside. It was already dark, and I stood there looking out at the lake. You couldn't tell where the ground ended and the lake began. It looked like an endless white lawn. I stood there thinking, *I can just walk out right now to the middle of that lake.* There were warnings to stay off the ice in the papers and on the radio. I knew if I kept going, I would fall through. I'm a good swimmer, but with that cold water, I knew I wouldn't get myself out. But something turned me around and started me back toward the building. I walked back inside, and for the first time, I actually heard the lecture I was listening to. Afterward, I came back to Lilly and a peer sat down next to me. I looked at her and said, 'I wanted to kill myself tonight.' She said, 'I know. I have wanted to kill myself sometimes.' That was the night I surrendered. That was when I knew I couldn't do it alone, and I didn't have to. There was something out there that cared if I lived or died."

Now, as Joanna shut the door against the wind and sleet that was pelting the ground, she thought of Marilyn's words. For a long time Joanna had thought that she wasn't the kind of person who could be spiritual. She had tried so hard to experience that transformative moment, to have Abby's lightning bolt, but she just didn't get it. But as she lived these long, intense days of tending to herself on Jellinek, she could feel a slow shifting inside, a definite sense that she wasn't alone. Marilyn's words made sense to her. Change after slow change. A long journey of small steps. The slow dawning of what had been inside her all along.

The next morning she woke up to Kate's voice at her door. "Sleepyhead, you gonna get out of bed and come to breakfast with the rest of us?" It was only a week before Christmas, her second Christmas at Hazelden. A light snow was falling outside her window. She heard the other women milling around in the hall, cozy voices calling each other's names. She heard Sam's voice booming out from the kitchen. "Deck the halls with boughs of holly," he sang in a deep bass.

Rebecca chided, "Sing me a Hanukkah song."

Sam responded, in a strange chant, "Hanukkah, Hanukkah, Hanukkah's coming."

"Knock it off, Sam. If you don't know about Hanukkah, just admit it. We're a minority here like everywhere else."

Joanna could hear the exaggerated sound of Sam blowing a kiss through the air. "I love you and you love me, whether it's Hanukkah or Christmas."

Joanna stretched and threw off her down comforter. She looked forward to joining this batch of friends for breakfast. They knew her like no one else in the world knew her. She didn't bother to put on makeup. She pulled on a pair of sweats and an old T-shirt, misshapen from many washings. As she ran a brush through her hair, she thought about Stacey and Molly. She missed them terribly, but, curiously, today she didn't want to be anywhere else.

Joanna would be spending Christmas Day with Molly and Stacey, and she was excited about that. Using catalogs, she had ordered presents for them: clothes, a doll for each girl, a stuffed whale for Stacey, and a stuffed frog for Molly. She sometimes had to put their pictures away because it was too painful to look at them. She knew, nevertheless, that she was just where she needed to be. She was perfectly content. She couldn't remember having felt quite this way before. She felt a kind of fullness, as if she were an hourglass, and each day another grain of sand filled her with a new thought, a new feeling, a new friend, a new kind of loving. *I guess it was happening while I was waiting for the lightning bolt,* she thought.

10

One Foot in the Real World

JOANNA WAS SCHEDULED to leave Jellinek on Valentine's Day and had told Molly she would be coming home when big red hearts started to appear everywhere. That was before her counselor told her they were suggesting she go to a halfway house after Jellinek. It was early January, and Vivian's recommendation wasn't entirely unexpected. Many who went through extended care were recommended to a halfway house. What did take her by surprise was the suggestion she go to Fellowship Club in West Palm Beach.

"What?" Her voice had registered shock when Vivian told her.

"We feel very strongly that you need to go to a halfway house, Joanna, and you know you can't go where Sam is," explained Vivian. Over time, Joanna and Sam, the patient who first made her feel at home in Jellinek, had grown much closer and had developed a mutual attraction. When staff members and other patients observed how emotionally intimate they were becoming, Joanna and Sam had been asked to take a step back. They were not allowed to be alone. Joanna understood the reasons. Often people in treatment are raw and vulnerable and can form romantic relationships out of weakness rather than strength. But just as important, she had begun to notice that focusing on Sam kept her from focusing on her own personal recovery. When Sam had moved on to St. Paul's Fellowship Club, Joanna was relieved.

"Besides," Vivian was saying, "Hanley-Hazelden's Fellowship is much smaller than St. Paul's, about half the size. It's quieter, and we think you will find it a better fit."

Joanna trusted the staff completely and was prepared to follow their advice. But Florida? Joanna shook her head. "I don't think so, Vivian. That's three months without seeing my children."

Vivian knit her brows. "I know, Jo. We thought long and hard about this recommendation. All of the staff members were reluctant to suggest you separate for such a long time, but we don't really see an alternative."

"You know how much I trust you guys, but this is out of the question. I can't go to Florida."

She struggled with Vivian, and she struggled internally with the recommendation. A few months earlier, before returning to Lilly after a rough relapse, she had resolutely refused a halfway house. Of course, it was easier now to see what a mistake that had been. She was still powerless over the alcohol, and she hadn't had enough time to practice turning over her obsession to a Higher Power. It wasn't second nature yet.

About three weeks before her expected discharge, Jeff called. Joanna had been arguing with a peer in the lounge. In group session, he had observed that she behaved in manipulative ways, similar to those she disliked in her mother. It had been a very difficult week; she continued to confront realizations about herself discovered during family weekend. Her mother's undermining gossip was the last behavior in the world she wanted to imitate. Her peer had pointed out something that had produced the same effect as her mother's gossip. His comment stunned her, left her feeling raw and scathed by her own actions. When she was called to the phone, she grabbed some tissue, sniffled, and tried to pull herself together. Jeff's voice sounded its baritone bell into the line, and Joanna felt her mask fall into place.

"How're you doing, Jo-Jo?" he asked cheerfully.

She answered with an equal measure of good cheer. "I'm doing great, Jeff."

"Terrific. You're sounding better all the time."

"Oh, I am. Every day I feel better." Her voice chimed back, a bright soprano. It was entirely automatic; Joanna became what she thought Jeff wanted her to be.

Three months of learning how to be who she really was came to her rescue now. She recognized the distance between her voice and her interior reality, and the mask cracked. She thought, *I'm not strong enough to go home and do what I need to do, to be myself regardless of how it affects Jeff. I still want to control the outcome, to behave as he likes so that he'll want to be with me, and that gets me crazy inside.*

She thought back to the week before Christmas, to an earlier, more honest conversation with Jeff. He had called as she and her Jellinek friends were transforming the "Twelve Days of Christmas" into the "Twelve Steps of Christmas." She had gone to the phone determined to be honest with him. She told him she had started smoking cigarettes. He became silent, and she felt terrified by his withdrawal. They argued. She was becoming a different person, he said, and he didn't know if he could live with this new woman. Finally, he'd said, "If you don't quit smoking, don't bother coming home." She was frightened by the conflict her honesty had stirred up, but she felt more solidly aligned within herself. The honesty had diminished the frightening feeling of craziness inside. She brought the memory of that earlier phone conversation to the current one. *If I slip into the old doing-everything-perfect mode, what is real and chaotic will build inside me like a volcano, until I try to put out the fire with alcohol,* she thought. When she hung up the phone, she walked down the hall to Vivian's office and knocked on the door. "You're right. I'll go to Fellowship," she announced.

A week before she was to leave for Florida, she decided she would tell Molly on the phone instead of going home. She feared she wouldn't have the resolve to leave again if she went home. Joanna dreaded the conversation. How could she make this young child understand how much she loved her and that she wouldn't stay away from her if it wasn't a matter of life and death? How was she going to bear Molly's disappointment and tears? Could she keep her resolve on the telephone? Finally, as Valentine's Day approached, and the red paper hearts went up on the front door of Jellinek, she called.

"Honey, I'm still sick and I have to go to a different hospital in Florida," she explained to her daughter. *It's true,* she thought fiercely, fighting her guilt. *If this were thirty years ago and I had tuberculosis, no one would question that I needed to be away from my children in a sanatorium. Well, alcoholism kills too.* "I can't come home when the hearts go up. But I'll be there when it starts to get warm. When all the snow is gone, and the flowers are starting to bloom, that's when Mommy will come home."

"Will the doctor go with you, Mommy?" Molly asked.

"No, honey. I'll have a new doctor."

"Okay, Mommy," was all that Molly said.

Joanna was startled. She didn't know which was worse—to have Molly cry and argue, or to have this easy acceptance.

When Jeff picked her up at Hazelden this time, Joanna felt very different from the way she had felt two years earlier when she left primary. She left determined to show the real her, even to Jeff. They had a surprisingly wonderful drive to Florida. For four days they visited and laughed, sang with the radio, stopped for ice cream, and watched the snow disappear as they headed south. Jeff drove, and she read to him the sections she had written in Jellinek. He was frequently surprised. "I didn't know you felt that way," he'd say.

On the Wednesday night before they arrived in West Palm Beach, they stopped at a roadside motel in Georgia. They ate at a little café with Formica tables. It was not how they were used to living, and in this uncharted territory, Joanna wondered if they might find a new meeting ground. They returned to the motel and slipped under the covers of the double bed. Jeff rolled onto his side and put his hand against Joanna's hip. In turn, she rolled toward him and felt the full length of him—her toes touching the tops of his feet, her mouth touching his, and her body yearned for this man who was the father of her children, for this man with whom she still fervently hoped she could build a life. She didn't know it was the last time they would be together in this way.

The Isolation of Masks

At first Fellowship Club was a disappointment after Jellinek. It wasn't that the staff wasn't caring. In fact, Joanna found she could talk to her counselor, Fred Gordon, about anything, and she had enormous confidence in his wisdom. It wasn't that the other patients weren't good people. In fact, she found Phoebe there, a roommate who would become one of the best friends she had ever had, a friend who would see her through the challenges that awaited her as a recovering alcoholic. But Fellowship did not have the cozy, contained feeling of Jellinek. It was structured to launch her into the world.

She was greeted at her room in the women's wing by her new roommate, Phoebe, who was about the same height as Joanna, and wore her dark brown hair loose to her shoulders. Phoebe sat on her bed and kept Joanna company as she unpacked. Phoebe had been divorced a couple years ago, and, like Joanna, had two girls two years apart. "You miss them?" Joanna asked.

"Every day, every minute," Phoebe answered.

"You think it's worth it?"

"You think we have a choice?" Phoebe answered.

Phoebe showed Joanna around Fellowship, walking her through the U-shaped men's and women's wings, the central kitchen and lounge, both brightly whitewashed, and the pleasant grounds with tree-lined sidewalks, tropical flowers, and a swimming pool. They discovered during their walk that they had more in common than anyone could have anticipated. Not only were their families similar, but their fathers both went to the University of Chicago, and Phoebe's maiden name was the same as Joanna's grandmother's maiden name. Their way of looking at the world seemed similar too. *I'm going to like this woman,* Joanna thought. "Do you think it was a mistake, not stopping at home to see the children?" she asked Phoebe.

Phoebe pinched the bridge of her nose. "Oh, Joanna, who knows?" she sighed. "I don't know if there's any good way to do this."

"What I'm most afraid of is that Stacey will forget who I am. She's hardly seen me in her entire life."

"Joanna, you have to turn this one over to a Higher Power," Phoebe advised. "This is one of those things you can't control, and it'll drive you crazy if you try." She paused, and then added in a quieter voice, "Perhaps Stacey needs to forget you for a little while. She's being well cared for. That's the important thing. You can't tell your Higher Power how to run your life. All you can do is have faith."

Back in their room, the two women sat up until four in the morning talking of what they had learned in their respective treatments, what they hoped for now, and how hard it was to keep going. *What a lucky fit,* thought Joanna, as she drifted off to sleep a few minutes before sunrise.

Over the next three weeks, Joanna and Phoebe became closer and closer to each other. Sometimes other patients, too, would join them in their room late in the evenings, and it would feel like a pajama party to Joanna. Talk between them was easy, whether serious or silly. The laughter rose spontaneously and often. They talked about getting older and whether to dye the gray streaks some of them were getting. They talked about children, jobs, books, husbands, boyfriends, and sex. Joanna had never before experienced such freedom of feeling or such intimacy with women.

Part of Joanna's treatment plan required her to find employment. Full-time employment was hard to find in the area and public transportation was limited, so many patients at Hanley-Hazelden Fellowship Club worked part-time. Joanna got a part-time job at the telemarketing company where Phoebe worked. Jeff had flown home, leaving Joanna the car. She drove to work each day at 8:30 A.M., and at noon, when both she and Phoebe were done working, drove to the beach for the afternoon.

Joanna would hoist a beach bag over her shoulder and walk from the parking lot to the edge of a beach called Singer Island. Eager for the warm sand, she'd slip out of her sandals and search for a good spot to sit. The touch of the warm grainy texture on her toes, on the soles of her feet, even against her ankles when she sank deep enough, traveled upward through her body. She and Phoebe would lay their towels at the edge of the hard-packed sand. They would slather sunblock over themselves, and Joanna would read a book titled *The Cinderella Complex*, the only assignment her counselor had given her. Many patients were given writing assignments, but Joanna had completed almost every feasible such assignment when she was in primary and extended care treatment.

She found the book uncanny in its ability to articulate her feelings and experiences, her wish to be saved by a white knight, her belief that she would always be part of someone else, and her feeling that she was responsible for other people's happiness rather than her own. She and Phoebe, and sometimes others from Fellowship who had come to the beach with them, would get into long discussions about the book. This, too, was part of Joanna's treatment plan: interacting with others, becoming more skilled at developing and maintaining relationships. In these long afternoons of spirited discussions, many of the women appreciated the book's description of becoming the person that others wanted them to be.

At five, they would pick up their beach bags, shake the sand out of their towels, and trudge back to the parking lot. Dinner was at six, and everyone was expected to be there. They attended groups each evening after dinner: grief group, spirituality group, Big Book group, or, Joanna's favorite, the women's group, where they talked about any issue that concerned them. From there it was to an AA meeting, three each week outside the compound, and they had to return by eleven o'clock. After she'd been at Fellowship a while, this curfew was extended to midnight.

After a month, Joanna was anxious to leave but she still needed time to practice what she had learned in treatment. Her first big challenge came when Phoebe got romantically involved with a new patient. Trevor was classically good-looking, and he was also very charming. Joanna instinctively mistrusted him. Trevor began writing beautiful, poetic letters to Phoebe, saying she was the angel he'd always wished for and that he wanted to spend the rest of his life with her.

"I'm worried about this," she told Phoebe. "He hardly knows you. How can he say he wants to spend the rest of his life with you?"

"I don't care," Phoebe answered. "I'm just glad he wants to." She closed her eyes and smiled. "He is so sexy, Joanna."

"That's the other thing, Phoebe. What you're doing is against the rules. You could get kicked out."

Joanna's first thought was to protect Phoebe and to protect her own relationship with Phoebe, who was her closest friend. Joanna could hardly imagine Fellowship without her. But as time wore on, she became increasingly uncomfortable. Every day she agonized over what to do. If she reported Phoebe to her counselor, Phoebe would be gone. Would that hurt Phoebe more than the illicit relationship was hurting her? If she reported Phoebe, she'd lose her roommate for sure, and probably her best friend. Phoebe would be furious. If she didn't report Phoebe, Joanna could get herself in trouble. And what if Trevor turned out to be as untrustworthy as Joanna suspected? Then she'd feel really lousy. She began being more and more preoccupied with this dilemma.

One night as Phoebe was setting her alarm for 3:00 A.M., to get up and sneak into Trevor's room, Joanna told her, "I can't do this anymore. If you're going to continue this relationship, don't tell me about it."

Phoebe seemed shocked. "You just don't like Trevor," she retorted.

"I've told you that," said Joanna. "I don't think he's good for you. I don't trust him."

"Well, I think he's great for me, and it's my call."

"True. But it's not fair to ask me to lie for you." As Joanna spoke, she began to realize how exasperated she felt. "Honesty is one of the foundations of this program. It's how we stay sober, and you're asking me to lie. It's a way of betraying myself." She dropped the pitch of her voice and said with evident sadness, "If you talk to me about this again, I will go to staff."

Dazzled by Trevor's eloquence, Phoebe was reading his cards to Joanna within two days. The next day Joanna talked to her own counselor, Fred. Both Phoebe and Trevor were asked to leave. As she packed, Phoebe would hardly talk to Joanna. She shook her head. "Some friend you turned out to be," she said.

Joanna, questioning her own loyalty, wondered if she was a bad friend. Fear and love pulled at her. "I didn't do it to hurt you," she told Phoebe. "I did it because I'm worried about you."

The next morning at breakfast, several men and women were talk-ing about the scandal.

"Can you believe someone would tattle like that?" asked a woman who had recently arrived from New York.

"With friends like that, who needs enemies," commented the man sitting next to her.

Joanna listened to the conversation for a couple more minutes, thinking, *Okay, now I have another choice. Do I stay quiet and let them think it was somebody else? If I pretend I don't know who did it, I'm wearing the same damn mask I've worn all my life. If I tell them, they're going to be angry with me.* Joanna looked up from her granola and cleared her throat. "It was me," she said softly.

The whole table fell quiet and all heads turned to her.

She felt compelled to justify herself. "I had to. I was living a lie, and that's not good for any of us." She told them of the long days of inter-nal struggle about reporting Phoebe, how worried she was about the ef-fect of the relationship on her friend, and, finally, how it was disrupting her own personal work. By the end of breakfast, it seemed that the oth-ers were beginning to understand; nevertheless, guilt haunted her.

She sought out Fred after breakfast, and received reassurance. "The bottom line is that you have to do what you need to do for yourself and not worry about the outcome," he said. "This has been a big issue for you." He walked over to his file cabinet and pulled out her file. He opened it on his desk, leafed through it, and pulled out a copy of her treatment plan. "It's right here in your treatment plan," he said, point-ing at the top line. 'Develop relationships: Ask others for help. Be hon-est in expressing your needs to other people.' Remember, if you're not honest, people can't know the real you, and then your relationships aren't real. Masks keep you isolated. And when you're isolated, it's harder for you to resist when that good old friend, alcohol, comes knocking at your door."

Joanna thought way back to the chaplain on the Lilly unit. Some-times it took so long for the words to really make sense. The chaplain had spoken of the Higher Power as three points on a triangle: your rela-tionship with yourself, your relationship with others, and your rela-tionship with a Higher Power. Here, her task would be to work on the integrity of each point on the triangle, beginning with honesty.

The God Box

The following Tuesday, Joanna woke with a start from a rare afternoon nap. She had been dreaming about her house in Chicago, with its wide, open spaces and huge windows. In her dream, she was in the kitchen looking out at the golf course, and Jeff was about to open the top drawer of her desk. She wanted to rush to her desk and slam the drawer shut, but it was too late. The dream had been so real she thought for a moment she would find Jeff standing beside her. She lay still on her bed in Fellowship, looking at the ceiling. She slowly remembered why the drawer was so unsettling.

In December, while she was still in Jellinek, Jeff had discovered a list in her desk. She had kept track of all the time he spent golfing and she would total it each week. He was upset when he phoned, reminding her that she never complained to him about the golfing. In fact, she went out of her way to be nice about it, baking muffins for him and his friends and bringing them to the deck as his party approached the tenth fairway, where their house stood.

"My friends were envious of me," he told her. "They always wished their wives were as nice about the golfing as you were. And now I find out it wasn't real?" He yelled at her then and said he wasn't going to give up the golfing. He worked fifty and sixty hours a week and needed golfing to relieve stress.

Joanna stretched and sat up in bed. One of the other patients knocked on her door; she had a phone call. She walked to the tiny phone room located next to her own room.

"Hi, honey," said Jeff.

"Jeff! I was just dreaming about you."

They chatted casually for a few minutes. Then Jeff told her he'd been thinking about their marriage. Joanna felt her stomach tighten. "Do you ever think about separating?" he asked her.

"I don't know, Jeff," she answered. "I can't really think about that now. It's too much." *I must be honest,* she reminded herself. She continued, "When I think about our marriage, I don't know what will happen. I know things have changed a lot, and it will have an impact on us. We're going to have to take it one day at a time when I get home. We'll have to work together."

"I know, Jo. I'll try. But honestly, I'm scared. You know, when I attended Hazelden's family program, it helped me understand that your alcoholism is a disease, and it helped me feel less resentful of your binges. I mean, I used to think it was a weakness, but after the week I spent in the program, I got that you couldn't stop yourself. But still, it does something to a person's trust."

"Of course you're scared. Of course it's hard to trust me," she answered, gripping the phone receiver tightly. "I know I have to earn your trust again. But I can't do that unless you give me a chance."

"We've always been pretty different, Jo. I think you take life a lot more seriously than I do."

This time Joanna didn't answer, but waited silently.

"I've got some pretty big news. There's a large environmental services company in Minnesota that's offered to buy out my company and give me a position with them—vice president of development. It's tempting, Jo. It's a good offer, and St. Paul is a good place to raise kids."

Joanna was stunned. A move to Minnesota could be wonderful for her. It would be easier to stay in touch with the friends she had made at Hazelden. They discussed the pros and cons, and Jeff told her he had flown to the Twin Cities and looked at property on a golf course near Stillwater, a small town about thirty minutes east of St. Paul.

Joanna's reaction was instant. "I don't want to live on a golf course again, Jeff," she said. "And if we're going to move to Minnesota, I think I would like to live closer to St. Paul "

"I thought you loved our house on the golf course," he protested.

"I do love our house," answered Joanna, "but I don't love the golf course."

Over the next few weeks, each time they talked on the phone, Joanna felt more confidence in herself, more able to be real with Jeff.

Joanna had been at Fellowship for six weeks when she received the shattering phone call from Jeff. "Jo-Jo," he began. "I've been thinking long and hard about this, and I've made a decision."

Joanna felt a chill. As soon as she heard the words, she knew what he was going to say.

"We're too different. This isn't going to work anymore. Really, I'm not sure it ever did work. I've always been frustrated by the way you try to be what you think I want you to be. I don't have the energy for this anymore. I'm sorry, but I can't keep on."

Joanna swallowed. "Are you sure?" she asked quietly. She had been counseled many times at Hazelden not to make any big decisions about her life while she was in treatment. Patients are too vulnerable, too unsettled, to make major decisions, staff members said. "But Jeff, we had such a nice time on the ride down here. I thought we were really doing better."

"Jo-Jo, I just can't do this anymore."

"Jeff, can't this wait? Can't we talk about it when I get home?"

"Why?" he asked with a heavy voice. "I'm not going to change my mind. I've felt for a long time like we've been growing apart, but you've been unwilling to discuss it. I didn't want to push it; you seemed too fragile. But when we were driving to Florida, I don't know, you just seemed stronger. Like you can stand on your own two feet now." Then his voice took on a more determined tone. "Joanna, you've been gone for months. I'm making a new life for myself. It's too late."

Deep inside of herself, despite her terror, Joanna thought it might be true. Maybe it was too late. Stunned, she hung up the phone, walked directly to Fred's office, and knocked on his door.

"This isn't the best time to be thinking of big changes like divorce," Fred reminded her.

"It's not my decision," she replied angrily. "Jeff is already having papers drawn up." Joanna started breathing quickly and began to feel dizzy. "Jeff's the only family I have left. No one from my family even returned my phone calls when I came here to Fellowship. Jeff's my safety net." She began to gulp for air. "He's all I've got left."

"Joanna, you are not alone," Fred reminded her in a quiet, calm voice.

"I know, I know, Fred," said Joanna. "You are wonderful, and so are my friends." Again she gulped for air. "But I can't take you all home with me. I'll be living in an apartment by myself."

"Take some deep breaths and get yourself collected," Fred instructed. Joanna sat down in the chair across from Fred's desk and closed her eyes. She took three deep breaths, inhaling to a count of five, holding for five, and slowly releasing the breath. She went on in a slower voice, "When I wake up in the morning, I'll be alone. And when I'm scared in the middle of the night, I'll be alone."

"No, Joanna, you won't be. That's what this program is all about. You're never alone. You have a Higher Power with you, a Higher Power who keeps you sober."

Yes, she thought, *right this minute, I can turn over this problem, this day, to my Higher Power. It's a decision I can make.* That night in bed, Joanna prayed. "Dear Great and Holy Mother and Father, guide my decisions, and give me courage, please."

Over the next week, Joanna had a great deal of trouble turning the divorce over to her Higher Power. It was hardest at night. She generally went to bed about 11:30 P.M., and inevitably, as she closed her eyes, her mind would lock on the same thoughts. *Where will I live? How much money will I need? What kind of job can I get? Where will the children be for Christmas?* The thoughts kept circling each other. *What if Jeff wants to take the kids to his parents for Christmas? How will I see them? Can we share them for Christmas Eve and Christmas morning? But,* she thought, *I want Christmas morning.*

She'd get up out of bed and walk down to Fellowship's kitchen for a drink of water, come back to her room, and stand by the window, looking out at the leaning palms. *If only Phoebe was still here,* she'd think, *it would be so comforting to talk to her.* Finally, she'd get back into bed, close her eyes again, and see Molly's pudgy little fingers tugging at the tape on the Christmas wrap. *I want the Santa part,* she'd think, her thoughts spiraling until they formed a coil in which sleep had no space.

Finally, frantic with anxiety, she said to Fred, "I can't do it, Fred. I can't stop thinking about the divorce. It rattles around in my head all the time."

Fred leaned across his desk toward her and quoted Step Three, "Made a decision to turn our will and our lives over to the care of God *as we understood Him.*" Then he said, "Joanna, I have an idea. Use a God box for the divorce." All the Hazelden treatment facilities made use of God boxes. The idea was to write worries on a piece of paper and drop them into the box as a way of symbolically reinforcing the idea of turning problems over to a Higher Power, of letting go. It was a way to make literal the message of Step Three.

After work the next afternoon, Joanna drove to a gift shop. She found a little box, about five inches wide, in the shape of a heart. It was quilted, covered in an ivory tapestry with small red and yellow roses. She paid for it and took the box back to Fellowship with her. In her room, just before supper, she wrote, "Don't worry about Christmas," on a piece of paper. She lifted the lid, edged in lace, and dropped the paper inside. Before she went to bed, she added, "Don't worry about the money. If you get divorced, the money will work out." In the morning, she added, "Don't worry about a job. If you need a job, it will work out."

She showed the box to Fred later that afternoon, and he teased her. "You think that itty-bitty thing's big enough to hold all your worries?"

"Perhaps not, but my Higher Power is big enough," she shot back.

The Soothing Arms of AA

Prayer helped. The God box helped. Talking to Fred and to Fellowship friends helped. Still the divorce haunted Joanna, but it paled beside her pain over the children.

Almost every morning upon wakening, Joanna felt disoriented. Her first thought was of Molly. The knowledge that Molly was two thousand miles away fell over her like a dark blanket. She talked to Molly at least twice a week, sometimes daily, but it was unsatisfying. She wanted to press her lips against the softness of Molly's cheek. And Stacey. Her body remembered Stacey fiercely, and the emptiness felt like an amputation. Joanna sometimes had trouble remembering the color of Stacey's eyes, and it terrified her. She began to go to bed at night thinking, *There went another twenty-four hours in which Stacey has thought of the nanny as her mother.*

"Let go and let God," she would mouth silently to herself. She would remind herself of what her Jellinek counselor, Vivian, used to tell her. "Your children have their own Higher Power to look after them. Try to visualize them in the hands of God."

Slowly but surely, AA meetings began to help too.

When she was still at Jellinek, it had been easy for Joanna to go to outside AA meetings in the little town of Lindstrom. Almost everyone in the meeting had been from Jellinek. But here, as in Chicago after primary treatment, there were many strangers, and Joanna's self-consciousness was acute. Crowds of strangers were hard for her. But as time went on, Joanna learned to cherish her AA meetings.

Her favorite meetings were those on the beach, both the evening meeting on Wednesdays and the morning meetings on Saturdays and Sundays. She first attended the Wednesday-night beach meeting about three weeks after arriving in West Palm Beach. Phoebe had still been at Fellowship then, and had ridden with Joanna. The moon was bright enough that night to cast shadows, and Joanna could see about forty people, most of them her age, but few of whom she recognized. Joanna and Phoebe took off their sandals and waded across the waves of sand. The chairs had all been claimed, so the women spread out beach towels. Sometimes, Joanna had to strain to hear the speaker over the crash of the waves, but she didn't mind. She felt soothed by the surf.

She never missed the Wednesday-night meeting. After two or three weeks, she was expected. She recognized people from other places, from the beach on the weekday afternoons, and they recognized her. *This,* she thought to herself, *is the famous fellowship of* AA, *which I have heard about all through treatment. This is how I will stay sober.* She wore a light jacket, because even in the heat of Florida, the ocean winds were cool. She sat down, lay her head back, and closed her eyes. Slowly, the salt air dissolved the armor of her self-consciousness.

Two months into her stay, late in April, she spoke at a meeting. Jeff had sent her new photos of the girls, and she had put them on her dresser that afternoon. The changes in them, Molly's long hair, Stacey's new plumpness, pounded like crashing breakers against her heart. She had carried the pain with her all day under the oppressive heat. She had prayed and had talked to her counselor about the pain. She had been tempted to put the photos into the God box. It was Wednesday evening, but she didn't feel like going to the AA meeting. She wanted to go to bed early, hide her head under her pillow. But her new roommate, Morgan, pushed her. "Joanna, you need the AA meeting. The meetings help to keep us sane." Joanna had protested, but Morgan said, "Rebecca's coming too. C'mon. We need a ride with you."

As the women walked across the sand, Joanna began to feel comforted. There was no moon tonight and little wind; the sea was unusually calm. It was dark, but the voices were familiar. She had friends here, friends beyond treatment, and she felt part of this world. At this meeting, speaking was entirely voluntary. At others, people went around the circle and each had a turn to speak. Joanna would get so nervous thinking about what she would say that she would miss what other people were saying. But tonight, under cover of darkness and prompted by acute distress, Joanna spoke. The meeting's subject was acceptance.

"I don't know how to accept being away from my children." As soon as Joanna began to speak, tears spilled onto her cheeks. It was dark, and she didn't bother to brush them away. "They say our Higher Power will give us the strength to bear what we must bear, but tonight, I don't know if I can. When I see in the photos how quickly my daughters are changing, I am afraid, not only that they won't know me when I go home, but that I won't know them."

A woman she saw often at these meetings reached over and brushed her hand down Joanna's back. The comfort of closeness steadied her for a moment, long enough to lighten the burden and experience the hand of her Higher Power. From that time on, Joanna was able to speak more frequently and easily at meetings, to connect with the other supplicants of recovery, and to experience ever more steadily the soothing power of AA.

A month later Joanna prepared to drive north, with Rebecca for company. Rebecca would then fly back to Florida, where she planned to settle. During that month, Phoebe, who discovered that Trevor was involved with several women, contacted Joanna and thanked her. Their friendship, which was reestablished over lunches and at AA meetings, would become invaluable to Joanna as she moved to Minnesota and coped with the stress of a divorce and raising children by herself. In the meantime, Jeff had gotten a new job with a toxicology firm in Minnesota. Because Joanna was in Florida during Jeff's move, she asked him to find her an apartment near his new house. It would make joint custody more manageable. She said her good-byes to her many new friends. She hugged Fred and received his good wishes and his confidence in her. She walked to her car, waved, and went to practice her new honesty with herself and others.

11

Almost Home

WHEN ANDY INTERVIEWED at Fellowship Club, the lawn was green, geraniums grew in the flower beds bordering the buildings, and temperatures were in the high eighties. Fellowship Club was halfway between treatment and daily life.

The house itself, on Stewart Avenue in West St. Paul, was an old Victorian mansion with stained glass windows, Edwardian fireplaces, ornately carved dark wood, wainscoting, and oak banisters along the staircases. Ironically, the house was built from the beer profits of a wealthy St. Paul family. The towering Schmidt Brewery sign on West Seventh Street was clearly visible from Fellowship Club, and behind it, a view of cliffs and the Mississippi River waited.

As at Jellinek, Andy had to be interviewed by the director, Wayne Leden, before he was accepted into the program. Only this time Andy didn't want to go to Fellowship Club. He was interested in Howard Frieze, a one-quarter house for men in Duluth, a city near Lake Superior, about three hours north of the Twin Cities. Hazelden sent many of its male patients who needed a more protective environment to work on gender issues to Howard Frieze. A similar house existed for women, called Marty Mann, in Duluth.

Andy didn't want to go to the all-men's unit because of gender issues, but rather because of his concerns about work. Patients at Fellowship Club were required to develop social skills and work forty hours a week. Not so at Howard Frieze, and Andy didn't want to work. He still believed that what you do is who you are, and the kind of work you did determined your status. What would others think of him if he did menial work, as most patients in Fellowship Club did, like painting houses, waiting on tables, typing, something unspeakably below his station in life? He had heard that even doctors and lawyers temporarily worked outside of their careers while at Fellowship. In Duluth, Andy wouldn't have to face his attitudes about work. Besides, working would put money in his pockets, a regular paycheck on Fridays, and this had been a reason in the past for celebrating, scoring crack, and staying in Harlem with Sal for the weekend.

During his interview at Fellowship Club, when the director asked Andy if he thought he'd have trouble housing with women, Andy implied that he would. If he pressed too hard for Frieze, he wouldn't stand a chance. So, Andy tried to be subtle. He told Wayne that he had continuous problems relating to women—though his chart showed the contrary—and that he believed that his recovery might be made more difficult if he were around women. He wasn't sure he could stay out of relationships with women at Fellowship. "Yes," he answered, when the director asked if he would at least try.

Wayne found Andy honest. Most of the patients at Fellowship Club were unsure of their relationships with the opposite sex, so it wasn't unusual to hear Andy express reservations. Wayne had read Andy's medical records and the recommendations of Thomas Novak, the Jellinek supervisor, who believed Fellowship Club to be the best place for Andy.

Life Work

Fellowship Club wasn't as sheltered an environment as Jellinek, and the first weeks there made Andy anxious. With fifty-five men and women living at the Club, with more outside opportunities to use drugs or alcohol, it wasn't unusual for people to lapse and be kicked out. In Andy's support group, there were fifteen patients who met once a week on Tuesdays and ate every meal together. Any patient who was caught using drugs, drinking, gambling, or having sex with another patient was kicked out, and the news of it spread like wildfire throughout the house, leaving everyone ashen and anxious.

Andy no longer criticized those who used, nor did he call them names or become judgmental. He felt sad for them and afraid for himself. Over time, he saw people return to using, people he knew were committed to recovery, people he had thought would never use drugs again. If there were no guarantee that would keep others or himself from using again, from wasting the money and time spent in rehab, how could he ever feel confident and self-assured? "How can I protect my own sobriety?" he asked his group. It felt as if sobriety were a magical state that could be blown away like a leaf by a strong wind.

As powerless as Andy felt over drugs and alcohol, he felt powerless over his own recovery, too, as if it were in the hands of someone else. The group always helped Andy refocus on living one day at a time as the solution. He remembered his counselor on Shoemaker, Steve Eastman, who had spoken about how the past held his regrets and the future his fears. This helped Andy stay in the present. His transition to the less sheltered environment of Fellowship Club, after the protective comfort of the Jellinek environment, was made easier by the Jellinek friends who had moved on to Fellowship with him. Danny arrived two weeks after Andy and had gotten a job at the Mall of America, a huge shopping mall that had recently opened. Jay had already been there and was working in construction.

Andy immediately began his job search. Perhaps, Andy mused, it was time for him to get back into journalism, to reestablish himself as a talented, aspiring writer. Andy spent hours on Sunday morning pouring through the want ads for writers, editors, and journalists. Randall, his counselor, suggested work outside of his career, at a place called Shoppers, which hired many Fellowship Club patients. It was a phone and computer center for mail-order catalog companies, and they needed people to work the phones, take orders, and forward requests to the warehouse. It sounded dreadful. Andy couldn't imagine sitting for eight hours at a desk in a large room and answering telephones in a syrupy, sweet voice.

Still, Andy did as he was told by his counselor and interviewed for a job at Shoppers. At the same time, he interviewed for a news desk position at the *Star Tribune*, one of the Twin Cities' daily newspapers, and for a position at Minnesota Public Radio. He was immediately offered a job at Shoppers and at the public radio station, where he could intern as an assistant producer of a radio show at the Minnesota State Fair, one of the largest fairs in the country. When he told his support group members, they and the others at Fellowship Club, even his counselor, reacted positively to the news.

Andy began getting the reactions from his peers he had always craved, even when using drugs. They were impressed and congratulated him for securing such a fine position when so many others at Fellowship Club had less glamorous jobs. Many expressed envy. Once again,

Andy was getting attention from his peers for what he did—or was about to do—but not for who he was. For Andy, it was a kind of drug, a way to escape himself. He could focus on being successful, on securing a great job. It was easy for Andy to turn his attention from his interior to his exterior. However, there was a problem: the job wasn't full time. It required only twenty-four hours a week. Patients had to work full time, Randall told him.

"I'll do volunteer work or get a second job," Andy argued.

"No, Andy," Randall asserted. "I'm thinking differently about this job."

"Can't you see how much better producing a radio show would be for my career than answering telephones?" Andy was getting more angry.

"Right now, Andy, I think you should be working on your recovery, not your career. Shoppers will teach you more about yourself than will the job at Minnesota Public Radio. The job itself isn't what's important, Andy. Much of your progress in recovery will happen on the periphery—on the way to work, in the lounges, in the hallways—not at work. Stop focusing on the spotlight and get busy at the edges. It's not about which job you have, how much money you earn, or the advancement you make. It's about how you manage getting to the job, how you manage with co-workers at lunch and at meetings. For now, recovery is not about résumés, appraisals, bonuses, glamorous travel, opportunities, or promotions. You are focused on the prize at the center, but I want you to look away from the center. Look at the little things, like the way you greet the driver, who else is on the bus. There's magic on the number 16 bus," his counselor said.

"I hate the bus," Andy said. "It's slow and clunky."

"That's not the point," Randall reminded Andy, adding that recovery was his life's work, and it didn't happen only between the hours of eight and five. He already had two jobs: one at Shoppers and the one he took to work, brought home again, and shared at dinner with his peers.

"Besides," the counselor told Andy, "you can always go back and reapply with the radio station." Andy didn't agree, but he knew not to fight the counselors. He said he would try working at Shoppers for a while. His willingness to take risks, to "act as if" his counselor might know better right now, showed how much faith Andy had not only in himself but in others too.

Friday After-Hours

Andy's week was busy. Besides working a full-time job and meeting the "expectations," or rules, of Fellowship Club, he attended three Alcoholics Anonymous meetings a week, as well as other groups. On Monday at 8:00 P.M., Andy attended an AA Step meeting at Uptown, a house on Summit Avenue, a few miles from Fellowship Club. On Tuesday, he met with his support group of fifteen peers, men and women. The house was divided into five support groups, and after their Tuesday group, everyone, all fifty-five patients, gathered in the dining room for a community meeting. This meeting, depending on the issues that needed to be addressed, could go on past midnight. On Wednesday, Andy attended a second AA meeting, a Big Book meeting at Macalester Plymouth United Church. On Thursday, he had an intimacy group, a group of twelve men who would discuss relationships and sexuality issues.

Friday brought an AA speaker meeting at Fellowship Club, which was open to the public. Many Fellowship Club alumni showed up, those who lived in the Twin Cities and even alumni from out of town who were visiting the area on business. The speakers usually had two or three years of sobriety in the community and told their stories to the audience.

Flash Point

After having worked a month at Shoppers, Andy felt relieved and more centered in his life. "I'm just like everyone else," Andy delighted in saying. He had joined the human race and felt less alienated. He took the same buses as everyone else, made the same arrangements in the evenings, attended the same meetings, asked for help and rides like everyone else. As a drug addict, he had despised people who used drugs or alcohol out of what he imagined was boredom. Now he saw more deeply into their lives, identified with them, joined in their economic struggles, their quest for love and meaning. In his intimacy group, he continued the lessons of Jellinek and connected with the men in ways that were supportive and helpful, not competitive.

Andy had read in the Big Book about spiritual awakenings that were sudden and dramatic, but his awakening was slow and educational. It happened every day, almost without notice.

He was more comfortable than he had ever been.

Every morning, Andy rolled out of bed at five thirty, got dressed for work, and went to the dining hall, where he made his lunch while Ralph made his. Ralph owned a small Nissan, and he drove Andy and three others to work at Shoppers. It was dark when the car pulled out of the parking lot at Fellowship Club and drove down Seventh Street to the freeway. The car was rusted and small, and the men in back had to sit with their knees up to their chins. Some of them smoked, which bothered Andy. Those early mornings weren't hard just for him, but for everyone in the car and in all the other cars pulling out of the lot each morning, and for every drug addict and alcoholic at Fellowship Club for whom acting responsibly and soberly every day was a new experience.

At work, he received orders from people who were calling from all over the country. Shoppers handled calls for eight major mail-order catalogs. Thousands rang the phone center each day, and the amount doubled on holidays. In the main room, there stood more than three hundred desks where workers like Andy answered phones. He might answer 125 calls in one day, and it became the hardest job Andy ever had. It required him to speak courteously to customers no matter how he felt.

"Good afternoon. This is Shoppers. How can I help you?" Andy responded each time the phone rang.

"I want to order a scarf, a silk one. It's green."

"Yes, ma'am. Do you have the catalog number?" Andy asked politely.

"No. Why? Do I need one?" the woman said in a gruff tone of voice.

"Well, we take orders from eight different catalogs."

"I saw it in one of your catalogs. I want to order it for my daughter. She has a beautiful green coat that the scarf would go so well with. I got your toll-free number from the magazine, but I don't have the magazine now. Can't you look it up?"

Andy rolled his eyes. "I can try, ma'am. It's probably in one of two catalogs that feature clothes and accessories." Andy spent twenty minutes on the phone with the woman before tracking down the green silk scarf, the only one listed.

When he hung up the phone and glanced up from his desk, lights flashing on the overhead board signaled hundreds of callers waiting for an operator. He knew there was no relief ahead, and, at times, he thought he could not finish the day.

Fortunately, many people from Fellowship Club were working and answering phones with Andy. Like him, most were trained in other professions. One of the executives of Shoppers was himself a member of Alcoholics Anonymous. Andy made connections with others while at the phone center or in the lunchroom. He felt a part of things. "I am more ordinary now," Andy told the other men in his intimacy group, "but I feel extraordinarily good." When Andy came back to Fellowship Club after work and sat down for dinner in the evening, he could identify with how everyone felt after working eight hours. He felt a part of a group and remembered what author Ring Lardner wrote: "The family you come from isn't as important as the family you're going to have."

One morning, Andy came into the dining room to make his sandwich for work, and Ralph was nowhere in sight. He went out to the parking lot to look for the Nissan, but it was gone. Had Ralph left him? he wondered. How could he do that? Andy was the only person in Fellowship who invited Ralph along to meetings or movies. Andy tried hard to be his friend. How could he do this? Andy went into a rage. He rushed back into the lounge, shouting, "The moron! Why the hell did he leave?" He didn't understand how Ralph could have abandoned him and treated him so unfairly.

Shoppers placed much value on attendance at work. The work was seasonal, and only a few people would keep their jobs after the holidays. Those who were never tardy were the only ones with even a remote chance of being hired for continuous, full-time employment. Andy was fearful his tardiness at work that day might cost him a chance for future employment.

Furious, he picked up a chair and threw it across the room, over the table and couch. Crashing against the wall, the chair tore messages from the bulletin board, gouging it so badly that it would have to be replaced. Others, startled from sleep, rushed out of their rooms to investigate. The arm of the chair was broken. Andy took a bus to work after cleaning up the lounge. At noon, he found Ralph in the cafeteria and angrily confronted him. The conflict in the public place was too intense for Ralph, who left work and returned to Fellowship Club, leaving the others to find their own ways back from work.

A community meeting was held that Tuesday. Andy was glad. The group would hold Ralph accountable for acting irresponsibly.

"Andy, you will have to pay for damages to the chair and replace the bulletin board," the president of Fellowship Club, another patient, said. "Destroying property is not an appropriate way of handling your anger at Ralph."

"I have to pay!" Andy hollered. "Why shouldn't Ralph pay too?"

"For what?" the president asked. "He didn't break anything. Andy, he may have broken an agreement with you, but he didn't lose his temper and damage property that belongs to all of us. You woke up a lot of people, Andy, scared them."

"Yeah, but . . ." Andy interrupted.

"May I say something?" Ralph asked. He was given permission to talk to the group, as well as to Andy. "I think you're right. I broke an agreement with Andy. I shouldn't have. I understand that. He's right. It was my fault that he'd be late for work, and then maybe he wouldn't get a full-time job there after the season is over. You guys all know I'm having a helluva time staying sober. You know, I just can't think straight sometimes. Everything in my head gets all mixed up. I wasn't thinking straight enough to go get Andy before I left. When he came into the cafeteria at work and started yelling at me in front of all those other people, I had to leave. We could have gotten into a fight, and I didn't want that because I'd get fired, and maybe I'd be kicked out of Fellowship Club, and then I'd probably go back to drinking and doing drugs. Sorry, Andy."

When Ralph sat down, the group remained silent. Andy stood and raised his hand. "I'd like to talk." The president nodded.

"I understand what I did. I see that I lost control of myself. Throwing chairs and damaging property isn't the correct way of expressing my anger. I also understand that Ralph didn't really mean to cause me to be late. He had other reasons for his behavior, which, when I think about it, weren't at all out of line. But my behavior was. I need to work the Tenth Step and make amends. I will pay for the things I damaged, the chair and bulletin board. I want to apologize to the president, to all of you at Fellowship Club, and most of all to Ralph, for frightening him in the cafeteria at work. I'm also sorry for blaming him for the trouble I caused."

Andy finished, said thank you to the group, and sat down. Again, everyone remained silent. Ralph looked down at his feet, then glanced up, smiled, and nodded to Andy. The meeting was adjourned.

Learning happened on the periphery, where Andy least expected it. It became clear to Andy that life wasn't going to unfold like a golden road in the land of Oz. The problems he had to face now didn't include only drugs and alcohol. Andy had come a long way from the Jellinek basketball court where he couldn't express his anger directly. Andy had responded impulsively and angrily by throwing the chair, but he had responded. His exterior matched his interior. There was no doubt about what he was feeling, and subsequently, even at the community meeting and in the months that followed, other men and women could still trust Andy. He was honest, and he recognized when his actions harmed himself and others. He could make amends.

Taking the Fifth

Everyone at Fellowship Club was strongly encouraged to find a sponsor, someone in recovery outside the house and attending Alcoholics Anonymous meetings, who could serve as a mentor and model healthy behavior. Andy had called Brian on the recommendation of his Jellinek counselor. From their first meeting at a coffee shop on Grand Avenue in St. Paul, Andy liked Brian. As the months passed, they attended the same Wednesday-night group, golfed on Saturday afternoons, worked together at Shoppers, and occasionally went to movies or ate at Day by Day Cafe, a restaurant where AA members often dined. In the beginning of his stay at Fellowship Club, Andy talked on the phone with his sponsor every other day.

A week before Andy moved from Fellowship Club to an apartment, Brian suggested that Andy take the Fifth Step. Taking the Fifth didn't mean, as it did in a court of law, allowing the guilty to avoid answering questions that might incriminate them. Taking the Fifth meant that Andy would take a fearless inventory of himself in writing and admit "to another human being the exact nature of [his] wrongs." Andy trusted Brian and decided to take the Fifth with him, instead of with a chaplain, as many people did. Both thought the experience would strengthen their friendship.

Andy had been required to take his Fourth and Fifth Steps in order to leave primary treatment. The two steps were always done together. With a female chaplain at Hazelden, he had taken the Fifth Step as part of his discharge process, but he had done it more perfunctorily than wholeheartedly. As a result, Andy told Brian that it wasn't as cleansing and healing as it could have been.

Andy read and studied pages 64 to 71 of *Alcoholics Anonymous*, commonly known as the Big Book, for guidelines on how to do the Fourth Step. He wrote a list of his resentments and fears, and explained how his actions and misdeeds were related to those feelings. It was time for Andy to rid himself of the secrets he had lugged all the way through primary, extended care, and into Fellowship Club.

While waiting for a friend who worked at a diner in the Mall of America, Andy found a coffee shop at Nordstrom. He had a good hour before his friend would finish work, so Andy took up a napkin and began writing his Fourth Step. He opened the napkin and started listing the past experiences of drug use. It didn't take long before he realized he had already listed these things. In his section work at Jellinek, hadn't he written over eighty pages on the consequences of his addiction? He folded the napkin, put it into his pocket, and found a second one. *What am I most afraid of people knowing about me?* he asked himself. *What am I most ashamed about?*

Memories rushed forward and he began writing feverishly. He listed things he had never told anyone: the time he and Sal, while smoking crack, videotaped their sexual activity, and the time he woke a freshman in the dormitory, took his marijuana, and got caught smoking it moments later. Andy told the teacher the marijuana belonged to the freshman, who was eventually suspended from school. Nothing happened to Andy.

He felt ashamed about how unfairly he was treated as a young boy by his mother. He resented her. She often accused him of things he hadn't done. Once, his father, who played chess on a magnetic chessboard and followed the game of Bobby Fisher and Boris Karpov in the newspaper, lost all the chess pieces. They were suddenly gone, disappeared, and no one could find them. Andy was accused. Years later, the chess pieces were found behind the stove. His mother, who had an extreme temper and would throw plates, could be absentminded. She was often angry at his father. Even later, when scissors or tape were missing, she accused Andy. And finally, Andy listed the time his college girlfriend drove eight hours to see him, only to catch him in bed with another woman. Andy had known his girlfriend was on her way to visit.

It was an unlikely place—a department store at the largest mall in the United States—for Andy to write his secrets, to acknowledge for the first time, to himself and his own God, the power that secrets had held in his life. But the real magic happened a day later, when he sat down at the kitchen table with Brian to share the secrets with him.

Brian shared his secrets too, even though he had already done a thorough Fifth Step. Both men opened their souls to each other. Neither was horrified by what he saw; instead, they felt closer to each other. Andy's Fifth Step didn't create a bridge between himself and others. The bridge was already in place. Taking the Step with Brian, however, let him walk more fearlessly across that bridge into the lives of others. Brian was one of the first in his new family.

Days later, while at Fellowship Club, DJ, who Andy had assumed would share an apartment with him when they left Fellowship Club together, told him that he had found a house to rent with another man. Though DJ and Andy had become best friends, had shared seven months of rehab experiences, Andy had mistakenly assumed the two would live together. DJ said he didn't want to risk their friendship and felt he needed to live with someone who was not so much like himself. He would move into a "sober house," one of many houses throughout the St. Paul area that were rented to people in Alcoholics Anonymous.

Andy felt devastated. He was counting on the two of them staying buddies and living together. He talked about his disappointment with his sponsor, Brian, in his AA groups, and in support group. Andy realized he had acquired perspective on his problems and disappointments, a perspective that kept him from magnifying them into larger-than-life ones. He felt hurt, but he felt strangely confident too. Confident that he would find someone else to live with, confident that deep inside him there was a place, a kind of sanctuary, that held his serenity and faith. Confident that no matter what happened, no matter how disappointed or lost he might get, the interior compass would point him north. He had direction now. Or maybe it was faith.

Sweet Snow

Beginning a romantic relationship before completing a year of sobriety was discouraged. There wasn't a rule written down in stone anywhere, but everyone in early sobriety heard the warning: Stay away from relationships until after the first year. Romantic or sexual relationships between patients in Fellowship Club were absolutely forbidden. So when the president, a woman elected by her peers at Fellowship Club, admitted to being sexually involved with another patient, she was asked to leave. Andy was automatically promoted from vice president to president. He felt honored. This time, however, the position did not inflate his ego, as it might have done months earlier at Jellinek. It meant hard work, extra hours of involvement with the house, and more responsibility, but Andy didn't mind. He had only five more days before he was to join his new roommate at an apartment they had leased.

Andy had been sober for nearly nine months, long enough for a woman to give birth, but not long enough, according to guidelines, for Andy to start a relationship. There were no absolute rules; men and women were too complex for any single rule or commandment. Andy had to look inside himself and decide what was right for him. One Saturday night, after midnight, Andy sat in his room alone, weighing the pros and cons of what he was about to do.

He had met Jenny at the Wednesday-night Big Book group at Macalester College in St. Paul. She lived on Marshall Avenue and had completed Fellowship Club three months before Andy had arrived. He enjoyed listening to Jenny talk. She had a deep, spiritual grasp of things, was wonderfully articulate, compassionate, and stunningly beautiful. In August, he went out with her and three other people for coffee after the meeting. They continued to go out after meetings, though never alone, to comedy clubs, coffee shops, movies, and restaurants. He had always informed his support and intimacy groups about his feelings toward Jenny. The support group members could forbid another member from getting involved in a relationship if they thought it was unwise, but the men in Andy's group were happy that he had met a woman as committed to recovery as he was.

That Saturday night, Andy made a critical decision. He quietly unlatched the back door. No one was allowed out after 1:00 A.M. In flagrant violation of the house's curfew, he stepped out the back door, walked across the parking lot, and began jogging. He had run up Stewart Avenue, four miles down Seventh Street, toward Kellogg Boulevard when it began snowing. He was running to Jenny's house. The flakes freckled his sleeves, and as he ran, he felt a delicious exhilaration. It was better than a second wind, and he lengthened his stride.

At Kellogg, Andy turned west and began the steep run up John Ireland Boulevard toward the majestic St. Paul Cathedral. It was lit, and the dome looked like a huge star. Everything seemed sweetened by the risk Andy was taking. The snow looked whiter and more vivid, as if each flake were suspended in midair before being swept along by the wind. He glanced back over his shoulders to see the flickering lights from downtown. Beyond the lights, he could see the dark Mississippi River.

"Thank you," he shouted at no one in particular. But he was grateful for Don at Jellinek for giving him a personal trainer and allowing him to continue running; grateful for his sobriety, which let him run, breathing the cool air deep into his lungs; grateful for the sight of the majestic cathedral, whose verdigris glistened in the domed lights; grateful that he was no longer trying to do things right, but had enough gumption and willingness to take risks; grateful that even if he got into trouble for breaking curfew, he could trust himself to handle it responsibly. And he was grateful for the woman he would soon see as he turned up Marshall Avenue.

12

Just Something I Do Every Day

HOLDING IT IN HER HANDS, Gloria Radcliffe turned over the brass figure of a young man with long arms and muscular legs, a soccer ball attached to his toe. She could remember the day Nate got this trophy. He was twelve years old, a midfielder on the West Los Angeles United Soccer Team, and she hadn't the faintest idea that he was smoking marijuana. The trophy felt cold and hard in her hand. She set it back on Nate's bookshelf next to the picture of his team. Before he'd gone through his growth spurt, he was one of the shortest on the team, so he stood in the front row with his blond hair hanging in a thick line at his eyes. She brushed the dust off his young face, which still had its little boy softness.

She thought of how shy he'd been, how self-conscious he'd always seemed. But when he played soccer, it looked as though he lost all that. He was totally absorbed in the ball and the moves and the running. To her, he looked like a dancer, gracefully moving with the ball down the field. She pulled up the clean sheet on his bed, tucked in the corners, and added Nate's favorite quilt.

"Glory!" Ted, Nate's dad, called from downstairs. "We've got to get to the airport."

She rearranged a tiger lily in the vase of flowers she had set on the table by Nate's bed, then hurried out of his room. Before she went downstairs, she stopped in her room to pick up the medallion she had gotten at the Hazelden parent program in June. As they left the house, she took a last look around. The glass windows that looked out over the pool had been newly washed, and the potted palms on the deck were moving slightly in the breeze. Nate's favorite fruits were on the counter—pineapple, strawberries, and kiwi. "Please get your room picked up while we're gone," she said to their younger son, David, as she and Ted walked out the door.

Once in the car and out of the driveway, Gloria asked, "Are you nervous, Ted?"

He looked over at her and smiled. "What's to be nervous about? Our son is coming home today," he said exuberantly.

Gloria opened her palm and looked at the medallion. "Remember that afternoon?"

Ted's eyes misted up a bit, and she knew he felt it as intensely as she did. They had spent three days at Hazelden's treatment center for young people, three of the most exhausting and enlightening days of their lives, listening to lectures, talking with other parents who felt as lost and frightened as they did, and meeting with the counselors. When Nate joined the group to present their medallions at the graduation ceremony, Gloria was overwhelmed with gratitude. For a time, she had been sure they would lose him.

"Aren't you glad you finally agreed to come?" Gloria asked Ted.

"Yes, sweetheart, yes." Then he winked. "You were right on that one."

"Remember how hot it was when we arrived?" The day they flew in to Minnesota, it had been unseasonably warm, 85° and humid. The heat had been suffocating, but when they got out of their rented Chrysler, Gloria was sure the sweat on Ted's forehead was not only from the heat. "I think you wanted to turn around and leave before we even got inside."

"I was still so mad at the kid," Ted answered. "The lying he did, and finding out he was stealing cash off my dresser."

"Right, but remember, don't start coming down on him as soon as he gets home."

"And don't you get so soft he runs over you," Ted retorted. Gloria took a deep breath. How would she know where to set the limits? What was it the counselor had said? You can't control what your child uses. Kids use Magic Markers; kids lick South American toads; they get euphoric by drinking a lot of water fast. He'd said that even that can kill them. She shuddered. She was trying to remember what he said about limits. "You can control what comes into your house," he'd said, "and as long as someone lives in your house, you have a right to set expectations. No stealing. No lying. No parties without permission. Help with household chores. Make their bed in the morning. They may not like it, but remember, you're in charge."

Gloria leaned forward to turn up the car's air-conditioning. "I know limits are important. But sometimes it's so hard, especially when I feel like it was my fault he was drinking and using drugs."

"C'mon." There was impatience in Ted's voice. "We may not have been perfect parents, but we didn't make him into an addict, Glory." Ted had had a lot of trouble with the idea that it wasn't Nate's fault, that he couldn't just stop drinking or smoking marijuana. Ted had built his own company by hard work and self-discipline. Where would he be without willpower? And why couldn't his son apply a little to himself?

Ted listened, however, to the counselors talk about new research findings regarding a possible gene that makes one vulnerable to alcoholism, and the strong correlation between family history and alcoholism. That was the kind of evidence Ted respected. But their personal stories were what made him understand at a visceral level. They talked about how desperately they tried to stop, how much they had to lose, and how they couldn't stop drinking anyway. "That is the definition of insanity," the first lecturer had said. "Continued use of mood-altering chemicals in spite of consequences. It's primary, permanent, progressive, predictable, and terminal if untreated. Nobody asks to be an addict."

"I know we didn't make him into an addict, but neither did he," Gloria reminded Ted.

"But he is responsible for his own recovery," Ted reminded her in turn. "Actions show that recovery is working. Kids must take responsibility and be part of the community. Remember that, Glory."

"I know, honey, I know. We're on the same side here. I want to set good limits too."

Gloria reminded Ted of one of the situations during the parent program that had spurred rare and joyous laughter.

Ted started to laugh with her. "We can do this, Glory," he said.

The Call of the Smoke Siren

The first thing Nate noticed when the plane landed was the palm trees in the distance. Minnesota maples and poplars were fine, but there was nothing like the elegance of a beautiful palm, he thought. The next thing he noticed was the sweat in the palms of his hands. He stood up, unlatched the overhead compartment above his seat, and pulled out his Nike bag. In it was his Big Book with autographs and messages from his friends, and he intended to guard it carefully. He slung the bag over his right shoulder and joined the long line in the aisle. As he rounded the corner into the terminal, he caught sight of his mom and dad. Their bright smiles riled his imagination. He could see them eating him up with eager questions. As he walked toward them, he diverted his eyes.

His mom spoke first. "How was your flight, honey?"

"Fine."

His dad was next. "Does it feel good to be back home?"

"Fine."

Then they took turns: "Did you eat on the airplane?" "They didn't try to serve you a drink did they?" "I have your favorite fruit waiting at home." "Do you want to rent a movie tonight?" "How was your graduation ceremony?"

He shrugged his dad's hand off his shoulder. "Yes, I ate. Just quit asking me questions for a while, okay?"

His parents protested a little, exchanged looks, and walked quietly with him toward the baggage claim.

Nate stepped out of the terminal, and he breathed in the dry air as deeply as he could. The sky was the same translucent blue he remembered, absolutely cloudless, the perfect canvas for the royal palms. Although he knew it was only his imagination, this far from the beach, he was sure he could smell the sea air. He remembered parties on the beach, darting along the dancing waves, daring the water to splash their feet. "How's David doing?" he asked his parents.

"David's just fine," answered his dad. "Eager to see you."

He did very little the first week. He and David went to movies; he went out to eat with his parents; he walked on the beach, tanned by the pool, and thought about the new friends he'd left behind at HCYF and the new friends who'd gone off before him. After a few days, he grew restless and was glad in some ways that he was going to summer school. Though he loved being home, loved the pineapple on the kitchen counter, the coral-colored hibiscus by the pool, the smell of clean sheets in his room, and even the questions his parents kept asking him, his house felt like a favorite shirt that had grown too tight during his absence.

So he could begin the fall as a senior, he was taking four classes in summer school, trying to make up for all the credits he had lost in the spring. He planned to ace every class and expected it would be pretty easy now that he was sober. When he walked in the first day he found that two people from his old crowd, Steve and Terry, were taking summer school also. He hadn't called anybody to say he was back, and they were both surprised to see him.

"Hey, man!" Steve shouted when he saw him.

"How're ya doing, guys?" he returned. They stood talking awkwardly for a few minutes before the bell rang, discovered they had algebra together fourth hour, and went off to their separate classes.

After four days of classes, Nate's resolve had begun to soften. He hadn't been straight during class for so long, he didn't remember how to do it. The algebra formulas marched across the chalkboard in meaningless symbols. He couldn't make himself pay attention. Nate could feel boredom pressing heavily on his eyelids. The old butterflies began in his stomach. He didn't know how to do school sober. *Oh man, if I don't ace these courses, how am I going to bring my grades up?* he wondered. *What am I going to do?*

Nate went to an AA meeting in a church about three blocks from his parents' house. The staff at HCYF had contacted a man at this meeting to be Nate's temporary sponsor, and Nate liked him well enough. He and the other people were friendly, but Nate didn't know anyone, and most of the people were older than he was. He went home after school and lay around the pool, did homework, watched television, and rented movies in the evening. He'd think about his old friends, knowing they'd party into the night. Nate imagined his buddies on the beach smoking or dropping acid, the moon painting shadows of them on the sand. He would love to be out there with them.

Every day as school ended, he watched Steve and Terry walk out and meet the old crowd of guys who were waiting for them on the corner. Every day they invited him along. "Can't, guys," he'd say. They tried to be supportive, but none of them really understood. On the third week of school, Nate kept walking with them to the end of the corner. The other guys were passing a joint, and Steve took a long toke and passed it to Terry. Terry passed it to Nate. Nate held the joint between his thumb and forefinger, watched the smoke curling upward. The acrid smell traveled through his nostrils to a point directly behind his eyes.

He could imagine his muscles relaxing, his head growing light and easy. "No thanks," he said, and thrust the joint back to Terry.

He began going to a recovery group run by the school's drug counselor. It meant he could skip class three times a week, and he found some guys to hang out with, but he didn't really like them. He'd known some of them before he went through treatment, and he had never gotten along with them all that well. Pretty soon he found himself mired in his old self-consciousness. He'd walk into a class and think everybody was looking at him. *What is going on?* he wondered. *I'm feeling miserable. Maybe in college I'll let myself go nuts with drugs,* he thought, *but I've got to find a way to stay sober through high school.*

Nate hadn't really developed a relationship with his temporary sponsor. When people from the AA meeting invited him to go out for coffee, he declined. It was a lot easier to sit by the pool than to work at building a whole new life. Still, at some level, he knew he needed them. As his doubts about himself grew more intrusive, he picked up the phone and dialed his sponsor. "I'm miserable," he said. "I'm not reading the Big Book, and I'm letting my homework slide. I've even quit making my bed." He sighed. "I think I hear the marijuana siren calling me."

Leaving Home

When Ted walked in the door from work, he saw Gloria at the kitchen sink, cutting onions and crying. He set down his briefcase, walked over to her, and bent over to kiss the back of her neck. "Be glad it's only onions, honey," he said.

She shook her head and didn't answer.

"What is it, Glory?" he asked. "It is only onions, isn't it?"

Again she shook her head and didn't answer. Ted felt the muscles in his back tighten. "Nate?"

This time Gloria nodded. Ted felt panic spread from the pit of his stomach up through his esophagus. "He's not smoking dope again!"

"No," Gloria's voice was choked by her crying, "but he wants to move back to Minnesota. He says it's too tough, Ted. He wants to move back and go to a place called Sobriety High."

"What?" Ted barked. "Who ever heard of a place called Sobriety High? I'll bet Sobriety High carries a lot of weight with Harvard."

Nate walked in on the conversation and interrupted. He thought about the talk with his sponsor, set his chin with determination, and said, "Dad, Harvard is your dream, not mine. Do you know how close I came to smoking a joint after school last week? I can't even think about college right now. All I can think about is how I'm going to stay straight for the rest of the day."

Ted's shoulders sagged. His son was ahead of him in understanding this disease. But back to Minnesota? Ted wasn't ready for his first son to leave home yet.

"I could go live with Uncle Jay, Dad."

Ted knew his brother would welcome Nate. He knew his brother and his wife would do a good job of looking after him. But how could he let him go? He bent his head. Then he turned back to Gloria and took her in his arms.

Coping with Cravings

When Nate walked into Uncle Jay and Aunt Bonnie's house in the Minneapolis suburb of Edina, he felt sad. Jay and Bonnie were giving Nate the guest room. Their two kids were away at college, so he was the only teenager in the house. He had brought along his Grateful Dead posters, a bowl of seashells, and his soccer trophies. It was a nice place, but he missed his home. He felt certain this was the right move, and he felt relief as he thought about seeing kids at Sobriety High whom he knew from treatment. He worried, too, that a diploma from there wouldn't be very convincing at good colleges, but he was struggling every day with a craving for marijuana, or beer, or acid, or anything to get him high. Sometimes when he closed his eyes, the feel of the rolled paper against his lips and the draw of the smoke into his lungs were palpable.

His temporary sponsor in L.A. had told him he needed to start working the program a lot more actively, go to meetings, pray or meditate or do whatever it was that he did to keep in contact with his Higher Power. When he told his sponsor about the private, nonprofit high school for recovering kids in Minnesota, he agreed it sounded good. Nate's counselor had preached at him about hanging out with kids who didn't use, and Carol had said it to him the day he left HCYF. And here he was, prepared to find a safe environment.

He liked the school's small classes, with plenty of one-on-one attention from the teachers. As he began to pay attention, he even liked learning; in fact, algebra became one of his favorite classes. It was so cool to look at the board and understand all those symbols. There was no soccer team, and that was a loss. That Nate was willing to give up soccer had made his dad understand just how important Sobriety High was to him. There were kids there to hang out with too. His first treatment buddy, Jacob, had transferred to Sobriety High, and another guy from treatment, Tony, was there. They drove out together to HCYF for aftercare meetings every Thursday night.

He loved going to the aftercare group, but as a condition of attendance, he also had to go to two AA meetings a week. He remembered enjoying the meeting he went to before finishing treatment, the big, lively, friendly speaker meeting, and decided he'd try to find one like that close to his house. The counselor suggested a few meetings downtown. There was one on Saturday nights, attended by forty or fifty people, and another with a few hundred people on Sunday nights.

He found a new sponsor at the Saturday-night meetings, a guy about forty-five years old, who was just as tough as his old counselor, Carol. He told Nate to pray every morning, and Nate was to report in to him every Friday after school about how his homework was going. To Nate, he felt like a good, solid fence that would keep the wolves out.

As September moved into October, Nate began to feel pretty settled. His sponsor told him to find a job, so he started bagging groceries, and he liked the feeling of making money. It was a symbol of being responsible and competent. It helped him believe what Carol had said in primary: Nate's an okay guy.

It was getting cold in Minnesota, and he was fascinated by the fall colors around him. The bright reds and yellows seemed so foreign. Many days were gray and chilly, and he called home to ask for money for a warmer jacket. Then one day he woke up to find it unseasonably warm. It almost felt like summer, but a summer the color of an exotic rainbow: burnished gold, golden brown, red, yellow, and burgundy. His aunt and uncle were in high spirits at breakfast. "This weather makes me think we're going to have to take you apple picking, Nate," said Bonnie. "There is nothing better than a crisp Haralson straight from the tree."

The kids in school were in high spirits too, and during lunch they played Frisbee. Out of breath from running so hard, they collapsed on their backs in the grass. The breeze was mellow, the sun gentle. Nate slid his arms up over his head, and his hand brushed against Pam's auburn hair. Pam was a senior, too, and shared most of his classes with him. He jerked his hand back. "Sorry," he said. She looked at him and smiled. The warmth and the sunshine and the pleasure of the day reminded him of the blue skies of California, and suddenly he could taste the marijuana smoke again. It blew into his face. "I'm urging," he told Pam. "I want a joint."

"I get it," she said. "The cravings can come out of nowhere."

It was an example of what he loved about the place. At school earlier that summer in California, Nate remembered telling Steve that he was craving a joint. Steve had said he didn't have any dope, but the guys would have beer on them after school. He invited Nate to come along.

He responded to Pam's observation. "The desire gets so strong that it's all I can think about."

"I know, exactly," she said. "That's how it is with me and cocaine. But remember, you've got to follow it all the way to the end. What happens if you smoke a joint, Nate?"

Nate thought about how badly he would want the next joint, and the next. He thought about the keggers, and the acid. He thought about his grades dropping and being separated from his friends at Sobriety High and aftercare. He looked at Pam's hair, luminous in the sun. "Yeah, you're right," he said.

Getting Back on Track

In November Nate started thinking about college; he thought he would try for a small private college in the Midwest, maybe Macalester, or Augsburg, maybe Carleton. They might be long shots with the grades he'd gotten, but he signed up for the SATs with high hopes anyway. He started going out with Pam. On Saturdays they would go together to the meeting and go out for a movie afterward, or to a party. They'd recently gone to a drug- and alcohol-free Halloween party with their sober friends. At the last minute, they'd thrown together mime costumes. Pam found a black dress to put over black stretch pants, and Nate wore an old black sweatshirt and jeans. They painted their faces white, drew black diamonds around their eyes, and colored their lips black. Someone else went as Mickey Mouse, someone as Elvis, and someone as a bunch of grapes. It was there, all the young men and women in outrageous costumes, listening to music and dancing, that he noticed how much fun he was having at parties without beer or dope.

As time went on, his cravings became less intense, and whole days would go by when he wouldn't think about getting high at all. "This is so great, Pam," he'd said. "I think I'm just about home free."

"It's dangerous to start thinking that way," she corrected him.

Christmas came and went, and the temperature dropped to -25°. It seemed impossible, unreal. When it was so cold, he liked to sleep as late as possible. He started sleeping in too late to do his morning meditation, and he skipped a couple of his AA meetings on especially cold nights. He barely passed his first test of the new trimester in algebra.

He started to feel impatient with his aunt and uncle. They had given him a midnight curfew. Pam's folks didn't require her to get in until one in the morning, and it annoyed him that he had to be in earlier than her. It was just as bad as living with his own parents. He began feeling more and more irritable with them, pushed around. He didn't like having to be home for family meals. With aftercare, AA meetings, school, and a girlfriend, he was too busy to be worrying about their schedules.

One Saturday in January, he came home late. He and Pam were at a pre–Super Bowl party, and it was going strong. He decided no one was going to tell him how to run his life.

When he opened the front door at 1:30 A.M., Jay was sitting on the couch in the living room.

"Do you care to explain?" asked Jay in a controlled voice.

"No, as a matter of fact, I don't care to explain."

"Hey, Nathaniel. You're getting too big for your britches. You are living under our roof. We are responsible for you. You follow our rules." Jay's voice was rising.

Nate upped the ante. "Your rules are ridiculous. And besides, didn't you promise me I could take the car last weekend to go skiing at Wild Mountain? And you broke your promise."

"You know I needed it to go to work, Nate. That's not fair. Get up to bed. We'll talk in the morning."

Nate was seething inside. He was too old for this. *Eighteen-year-olds should be able to run their own lives,* he thought. He stomped upstairs to his room, slammed the door shut, and called his sponsor. "Daryl, I gotta talk to you, man."

"Sure, Nate. What's going on?" asked his sponsor in a sleepy voice.

"My aunt and uncle. They're driving me crazy."

"Oh?" said his sponsor.

"Yeah. I can't stand living with them anymore. Jay was yelling at me tonight about me being too big for my britches," he complained. "They want me home an hour before my girlfriend has to be in."

"Are you embarrassed that your girlfriend's curfew is later than yours?"

"I guess. Embarrassed and frustrated."

"How did you deal with it, Nate?"

"I came in late. I'm tired of the tight rein."

"You need to deal with this straightforwardly and maturely," said the sponsor. "Talk to your uncle about how you feel. See if you can negotiate a later curfew, but speak directly and respectfully. None of this backdoor, resentful stuff."

"Okay," said Nate. "You're right."

"You know," added his sponsor, "I didn't see you last Saturday night at the meeting. You going to meetings?"

"Yes, most of the time."

"Most of the time isn't good enough, Nate," said his sponsor. "Get your butt back to meetings. You making your bed?"

Nate's voice quieted. "No." All of a sudden he recalled the lecturer at HCYF saying you could tell if someone had done a Second and Third Step by their actions. "You can blow all the snot you want in group," he'd said, "but if your behavior isn't changing, you aren't changing."

"Okay, Nate. You've got to get back on track. You know this is relapse behavior. Thirty meetings in thirty days. You're living with your aunt and uncle, you have to be respectful of them."

Nate felt the protective fence go up around him again. His sponsor added, "I want you checking in with me every day for a while, Nate. And Nate—make your bed."

Learning to Give Back

A whole winter had passed. Nate had followed his sponsor's directions with gratitude. He got his curfew extended by an hour, he went to meetings regularly, and he felt grateful to his aunt and uncle for giving him a home away from home. By the end of the winter trimester, he had a

3.4 grade point average and had gotten a good SAT score. He was on student council. He talked to his parents on the phone at least once a
week, and on April 2, he called them with very good news. His mom
and dad were going to be so proud of him. "Guess what?" he began the
conversation.

"I hate guessing," said his mom. "Just tell me."

"I did it, Mom. I got into Carleton College!"

She didn't answer him. Instead, he heard her calling his dad. "Ted!
Come here! Nate has something to tell you." He heard her voice speaking into the phone again. "Oh, honey, I am so glad for you and so
proud of you. I wish I were there to give you a hug."

"Me too, Mom," said Nate. This year was turning out to be everything he wanted it to be, and more. He'd done all the Steps with his
sponsor, first reading and then repeating the prayers as he'd been told,
and taking his inventory and reading it to Daryl on a bench in Loring
Park. He'd worked on his character defects, and then, in February,
Daryl had brought him a new challenge.

"You don't say much in the meetings, you know?" Somehow Nate
still felt like a newcomer, and he had always been shy. It was hard to talk
in meetings. This had been around Valentine's Day, and it stood out in
his mind because he had taken Pam out to dinner Friday evening. They
had looked around the restaurant at the other diners, all of whom had
crystal goblets of red or white wine, and he found himself wondering if
he couldn't someday drink again. He understood the First Step about
drugs: he was powerless over marijuana and acid, and he knew that
would transfer to cocaine or heroin. But the alcohol part didn't always
make sense to him.

He didn't mention the thoughts to Pam. She got annoyed with him
when he talked like that. After their meal, they shared a chocolate torte,
and he gave her a valentine he'd made that afternoon. He'd felt a little
silly, but he had a lot of fun cutting out the big red heart and sketching
in the faces of a man and woman, taping little heart candies around the
edge: "Yours Forever," "True Love," "Hot Lips." Pam had pulled off the
"Hot Lips" piece, poised it between her lips, leaned across the table, and
passed it to his mouth.

At Saturday night's meeting, the speaker, an alcoholic, was talking
about Step One. He seemed about thirty years old, was wearing a suit,

and looked very successful. He reminded Nate of the men he'd seen sitting at the restaurant, sipping out of the crystal goblets. This speaker told the people at the meeting that he started drinking in high school, and it took away his shyness. But there was something about the alcohol that grabbed him by the throat and wouldn't let go. Nate recognized the way this sophisticated man described the effects of the alcohol; it was identical to his own experience, and for the first time, it began to really sink in. Carol had talked to them about cross-addiction, how any drug that gave them the pleasures of being high would eventually bring them back to their drug of choice. He thought about keggers. The beer did the same thing for him that marijuana did. The speaker looked like the kind of guy Nate wanted to be when he was thirty, and he knew now, deep in his gut, that alcohol was as dangerous for him as any other drug.

Two weeks later, Nate volunteered to be one of the two people at the meeting who gave short talks before the main speaker. He only had to speak for ten minutes, and he thought that would be manageable. He said to the AA crowd seated before him, "I'm Nate, and I'm an alcoholic." He told them about the various drugs he had used, and he shared with them the fact that he had only recently begun to understand that he was as powerless over alcohol as he was over other drugs.

Then he paused. He had planned to make an analogy between fixing the hubcaps on his car and relying on a Higher Power for help, but as he looked around the crowd, he forgot what he was going to say. "Um," he pressed forward anyway. "I lost one of my hubcaps this week, but my uncle had two old ones in his garage, so I took off the good one on the right side of the car and put the two old ones on that side. You can only tell the hubcaps don't match if you walk all the way around the car." What was the analogy he was going to make? "Um," he started again. He looked out and saw Pam's auburn hair piled on top of her head, looked down at his hands resting on the podium, and shook his head. He said, "I'm not going to recover from this one," and sat down.

A sympathetic chuckle rippled through the room, followed by a hearty round of applause. His sponsor came up to him afterward and hugged him. "Nate, I'm glad you gave it a try. That's Twelfth Step stuff, you know. People need stuff from you too. They need to hear from you." Another man came up to him and punched him lightly in the arm. "I'm gonna walk all the way around your car when I leave the meeting tonight." The woman standing next to him grinned. "You know what Mike talked about the first time he got up at this meeting?" The man groaned. "He talked about mowing the lawn. That's it. Just mowing the lawn. Then he sat down."

As Pam and Nate left the meeting, he said to her, "I really did have an analogy about the hubcaps and understanding in a new way how I'm an alcoholic."

She slipped her arm through his. "Well, tell me now."

"I can't remember it," he said ruefully. "I'm going to feel like a fool when I come back next week."

"You know nobody here will mind, Nate. They're just glad you gave it a try." He loved this meeting. He knew almost every person's name. Same people week after week. And he was one of them. Nobody minded if you screwed up, even the big things. They always took you back, no questions asked.

Soon, Nate began doing more Twelfth Step work. He spoke in the community as a representative of Sobriety High. He spoke at a chemical-free conference; he spoke to churches, school districts, PTAs. He spoke on panels and answered questions from both parents and kids. He never got tired of telling them how drugs could screw up a life. It gave him a chance to give back, and it felt good. By the time he graduated from Sobriety High, he was an accomplished speaker.

The Jumble of Life

When high school ended in June, Nate was promoted to cashier and worked full time. He also began coaching a traveling soccer team of twelve- and thirteen-year-old boys. They practiced and played games every Tuesday and Thursday all summer, and often played tournaments on the weekends. He was surprised to discover that coaching was as much fun as playing had been. On June evenings, he would watch the boys in their navy shorts, blue and white shirts, and long, white soccer socks blasting up and down the field at Lynnhurst Park.

In July they went to the USA Cup in Blaine, a suburb on the northern side of the Twin Cities. It drew teams from all over the world. Nate's boys were hot, but even in the ninety-degree weather, they ran hard and kept their minds on the soccer ball. The heat got so bad the parents brought out a kiddie pool and filled it with water so the boys could dunk their heads periodically. In spite of the searing heat, Nate's team came within one game of winning their age group's championship.

All summer, Nate kept up with his aftercare meetings and his Saturday and Sunday meetings. He and Pam went to movies. They picnicked with friends from their meetings and from school, swam in Cedar Lake after dark, sometimes skinny-dipping at a hidden beach. He was careful to save as much of his money as possible. Carleton was a very expensive college, and though his parents would pay his tuition, he wanted to contribute as much as possible to his room and board.

He was scared of starting college. It was only a forty-five minute drive south of Minneapolis, but Pam would be living in a dorm at the College of St. Catherine in St. Paul. They wouldn't see as much of each other or their other friends as they were used to. He was going to keep up with his meetings. He had gotten special permission to keep a car on campus, which would enable him to drive up to his regular meetings twice a week, and they had an AA group on campus.

His parents were flying in to drive him and his stuff down to college. They arrived on the Saturday of Labor Day weekend. When they drove up to Jay and Bonnie's white colonial on Woodland, Nate was waiting at the front door. His dad got out of the car first, looking tall and fit in a pair of khakis and a short-sleeved shirt. He had a little more gray around his temples. His mom got out next, and he thought she looked younger than the first time he'd seen her in Minnesota, standing across the cafeteria at the Hazelden Center. Her hair was still short and curled around her face. She was wearing a sundress. There was something about her eyes; they were brighter than before.

Nate reached over to pick a purple carnation from the flowers spilling out of the window boxes before he walked to the sidewalk to greet them. "Here, Mom," he said as she reached out to hug him.

"How are you, sweetheart?" she asked.

"Fine," he said.

"How are things going?" echoed his dad.

"Fine," he said.

They took turns asking questions. "Have you started packing for college?" "What time do you want to leave?" "Aren't you too warm with that long-sleeved shirt?"

"I'm fine," Nate said. He laughed, remembering the airport in Los Angeles, the endless questions and his monosyllabic answers. His parents looked puzzled. "Fine," he said. "I am so very fine. How are you guys?"

They spent the weekend at Jay and Bonnie's, and on Tuesday morning they loaded the rented minivan with Nate's boxes of clothing and books, a fan, a floor lamp, and a rug. David sat in the middle seat behind his folks as they drove toward the Cannon River. They passed shorn cornfields and sod farms, apple orchards, and fields of soybeans. After a half hour, they could see spires above the gathering of thick trees in the distance. Nate's heart was in his throat. "See over there," he said. "That's it." Sometimes he could still hardly believe this was real. It seemed only a short time ago that he considered his future completely ruined.

His mom's voice was eager. "Oh, Nate, I am so excited to see Carleton. You know my friend Virginia's nephew went to this college. She said he loved it."

About ten minutes later, they drove onto the campus, and his parents were thrilled. "Oh, it's just lovely," his mother enthused. "Look at the chapel! And the central square!"

"It's called the bald spot, Mom," said Nate. "It's where they play Frisbee. This is the Frisbee capital of the world."

They pulled the minivan up behind a line of cars parked by the long sidewalk that led up to Burton Hall. After going over to administration and picking up a room key, his dad opened the back of the van, and each of them carried a box inside. David ran ahead of his folks, climbing the steps to the second floor just as Ted and Gloria reached the front entrance of the building. Nate's room was three doors to the right of the steps. There was a welcome sign on the door. It read: "Welcome, Nate from California, John from Vermont, Peter from Illinois." There was no answer to their knock, so they opened the door to the empty room.

After they emptied the car, Nate's family helped him unpack. While his dad assembled the floor lamp, he asked, "What classes are you taking this quarter?"

"Well, I know I'm taking a freshman writing seminar," he said. "And I'm going to give Italian a try."

"Really!" exclaimed his dad.

"You going to take Frisbee?" his mom asked.

"I wish."

After unpacking, a campus tour, and dinner together, Nate's parents left for Jay and Bonnie's. His mom hugged him tightly and kissed his cheek. His dad, in turn, did the same, and whispered in his ear, "I'm so proud of you, son. For a while I didn't know if you were going to make it."

"Thanks, Dad. Me neither," he whispered back. He thought to himself, *It wasn't me, it was my Higher Power.* Somehow, it seemed too corny to say it out loud. He hugged his dad and jogged up the sidewalk toward the long, dark building with its forest of turrets and chimneys that would be his home for the next year.

Two months later, Nate was finishing midterms. His schedule had shifted dramatically. He didn't get out of bed until 10:00 A.M. He went to classes, washed dishes in the cafeteria, and went to the library. He and his roommates took Frisbee breaks, and he was playing soccer again. At six o'clock a batch of students would watch *The Simpsons* in the lounge across the hall, and every Thursday night, they would gather to watch *ER*. They'd spend evenings writing papers at computers, reading textbooks and *The New York Times*, and visiting each other's rooms. Around midnight, they'd start playing Nintendo, going through a hundred rounds in two hours before they'd quit and go to bed.

On Thursday evenings he went to a small Big Book meeting on campus, where someone would read a passage and everyone would discuss what it meant to them. One Thursday, he had come into his room and found his roommates drinking beer. Underage drinking was against the rules, of course, but like on any other campus, it happened. For the most part, beer on campus didn't bother him. He knew it was around, and he could leave it alone, but it was too hard to have it this close to home. He'd braced himself for the worst and asked his roommates to drink somewhere else. They weren't angry about taking it somewhere else, but they were curious.

"How long is it since you've had a drink?" asked one of his roommates.

Nate stopped to think. "Ummm," he looked at the ceiling as he calculated. "One year, five months, and twenty-three days."

"Cool. After that much time, I bet you're safe. When are you going to start again?"

"I hope never, but I just don't want to drink today," he answered quickly.

"Really? Why never? That seems a little severe," said the roommate.

"Because," he said, "I believe if I took a drink, I'd lose it, and I sure don't want to find out. Recovery is just something I do every day."

On weekends his roommates and college friends went to their parties while Nate met Pam and went to his AA meetings. He was usually back on campus by about 1:00 A.M., and he would find his roommates and other college buddies at the Magic Chef, where they would eat burgers and drink sodas. The Saturday after midterms, they sat there and joked and chatted until nearly 4:00 A.M. The air was crisp as they went out to Nate's car to drive back to campus. It was the second time he'd seen the exotic autumn rainbow of Minnesota, and it was beginning to feel like home.

As they drove the mile back to campus, they hashed over their midterms. Back on campus, they trudged up to the second floor of Burton and opened the door to their room. It held the full mess of college life: clothes strewn on the only easy chair in the room, a wet towel on the floor, papers littering all three desks, a bike parked to the right of the door, and rumpled bedcovers. As Nate surveyed the jumble of things comprising his new life, he registered satisfaction to see, in the far corner of the room, that his bed was made.

13

The Wisdom to Know the Difference

WHEN LIZ WAS DISCHARGED from primary treatment and finished her two-week outpatient treatment, she and her husband decided to stay another three weeks in West Palm Beach at a hotel on Singer Island before returning to Iowa. March in Iowa was cold and snowy, and Liz loved the seventy-degree temperatures in Florida. The hotel was just a short ride from the treatment center, so it was easy for Liz to return for the Sober Seniors' group on Wednesdays, her aftercare group on Thursdays, and Saturday-morning meetings on the beach just down from their hotel.

Liz was glad they'd made the decision to stay a little longer when she went to her first meeting after discharge. Attending the senior group with alumni at Hanley was so comfortable; she was glad to be able to talk about what she had learned in treatment. It was almost like a review for the test ahead.

"I really didn't want to quit drinking when I came here," she said to the group. "In the back of my mind, I was hoping they would teach me how to control my drinking. I didn't know that I could no more control the effects alcohol had on me than I could control the effects any poison would have on me. It has nothing to do with willpower."

Some of the twenty-five older adults in the group smiled and nodded, knowing perfectly well what Liz meant. None of them had wanted to admit to being alcoholics, not at their age. They wanted, instead, to stop drinking for a while or learn to control their drinking so they wouldn't embarrass their grandchildren, fall and break their hips, or feel so lonely. "But after hearing all your stories about drinking—they sounded so much like mine—I decided I didn't want to drink anymore. I wasn't a bad alcoholic. I never drove drunk and endangered the lives of innocent people like some of the young women in treatment have done. And all those drugs they use, like that new one, cocaine." Liz shook her head in disapproval. "But I wanted to get sober. I was willing to try. So, now I'm nearly two months without drinking, and I want to continue." Many in the group clapped.

"Thank you," Liz continued. "My husband is upstairs in the spouses' group, and I've talked to him about this program, especially about Steps Two and Three." Liz hesitated and looked around at the faces in the group. They all seemed attentive, except Harold, an alumni of Hanley-Hazelden, who had fallen asleep. She had seen him sleeping at other meetings and didn't take it personally, but she still felt anxious.

She hesitated to express her agnosticism to her peers, men and women who believed in a Christian God and had practiced their religions for over fifty years. It was easier for Liz to talk to the younger women in treatment about this subject, since many of them thought like her and had little religious upbringing or belief.

"Doing these two Steps are very hard for me. They talk about God and Higher Power. My counselor said all I had to do was understand that I was 'not God.' Of course, I can see that quite easily. So I "act as if" I can succeed in this program, though I don't believe in that old bearded God sitting in a throne in heaven," Liz said.

Liz's older friends, Vera and Sophie, who were still in primary treatment, were attending the meeting and sat directly across from Liz. Vera had been a Lutheran since she was a child, and Liz was afraid of offending her. "I'm envious of people like Vera," she said, looking directly across to her and smiling. "She is such a kind and good person because of her beliefs. I am envious of those who believe in God. It seems so simple for them."

Liz, brought up in a family with no religious affiliation, was unusual. Her father, a seventeen-year-old from Denmark who immigrated to the States in 1893, was very antireligious. In Denmark, there had been no separation between the Lutheran religion and the state, and he was forced to practice what was taught him in school about God. Though he would never have kept Liz from attending church with her friends, he had nothing good to say about church. Liz walked to a Methodist Sunday school just down the street every Sunday. Although she liked going to church with her friends, she had learned Midwest moral values from her parents, who were ethical humanists. Honesty and respect for elders were essential. To Liz, there seemed to be nothing worse in her family than lying.

Much later, after she returned from New York and her mother had died, she began attending a Unitarian church for about five years, quitting after she moved. It seemed the church was just too long of a drive for her. By then, she was an agnostic. "No one," she used to argue during parties, "could be sure if there was a God." The Sunday mornings after the parties, Liz wasn't found in church praying. She was at home with a hangover.

"Not long ago," Liz continued talking in her AA group at Hanley, "when I first entered primary treatment, I just couldn't say the Our Father or Serenity Prayer after meetings. It rankled me to say them. I talked a lot about it, especially with the younger women on my unit and with my counselor. Now I can say the prayers, not because I believe them like you and my dear friend Vera do, but because they connect me to you, to my sobriety, and to Alcoholics Anonymous. For now, my Higher Power rests in all of you, in this AA group. I trust you all implicitly."

Every morning at the hotel, Jonathan and Liz loved getting up early to watch the dawn and walk along the shore. When they saw the dark begin to lighten on the horizon, they'd stop walking along the white sand and watch the sky become tinged with red as the sun rose above the edge of the ocean. The sky turned a brighter blue as the day arrived. The beach was dotted with shells, many broken, some perfect, and Liz liked to pass the time walking and picking up the best shells: the pinkish-brown scallops; the muscular, gray oyster shells; and once in a while, a perfect conch. Every morning Liz and Jonathan walked, sometimes in silence and sometimes chatting about how lovely the ocean was.

On Saturday mornings, there was a meeting down the beach from their hotel. Jonathan and Liz would set out their lounge chairs and watch as AA members began to arrive and form a circle on the beach.

After ten or so members had arrived, Liz would leave Jonathan relaxing in his lounge chair and walk barefoot over to the group. On this particular Saturday morning, one younger man, who had recognized Liz from AA evening meetings at Hanley-Hazelden, had gotten her a chair and was motioning to her. Liz nodded, thanked the young man, and sat down. She loved looking out at the sea. That morning, the waves were small, but they sounded as they washed onto shore. She felt soothed by the surf, like a child in a rocking chair. Surely the hour ahead would be a good one. She could smell the salt air and hear the wild squawking of the seagulls as they soared and dipped, looking for fish to eat. Down the beach, she spotted her husband with the newspaper in his lap, his head tilted to the side, sleeping. In this setting, Liz couldn't imagine anyone in the meeting with problems.

Two months later, back at home in Ames, Iowa, Liz began a ritual that would last her entire life. One morning, while her husband was still asleep, Liz got up and went downstairs. It was the day before her seventy-first birthday, and she flicked on the switch for the coffeepot and opened the curtains. Normally, she would begin to prepare breakfast for the two of them. But that morning, she stood at the window, looking out at the backyard, beyond the tulips beginning to bloom in the garden, beyond the elm and willow trees and the neighbor's soybean field, to the horizon and the blue sky. If she had been up a half hour earlier, she would have seen the sun rise and color the fields red. Liz opened her arms that morning, as if gesturing, taking in the entire landscape to her chest. She began saying the Serenity Prayer.

Saying the Serenity Prayer in front of the kitchen window would become a spiritual exercise, helping her sort out things for the day. Though the prayer began with "God," she said it aloud, without hesitation, in the kitchen, and she remained an agnostic. When she wrapped her arms around herself, she was connecting with a Higher Power that was nature, the earth, the trees, and sunlight. She decided to connect with the most elemental forces of life: the earth, the sky, and the universe. Her Higher Power was not like a good father or mother who would protect her; Liz still couldn't imagine that. But in speaking to what was outside her window, for a moment, a sacred moment that morning, she felt her consciousness expand into something more global and eternal.

At her AA meeting that evening, she said, "This morning, I felt like a willing participant in my destiny. It is something I embrace, including those things I'd rather not have in my life. In my own way, I prayed. I stood at my kitchen window and said the Serenity Prayer. I prayed for my alcoholic stepson, that someday he might know peace. I said, 'Higher Power, help me to let go of his life, and help him to find his way.'"

For Liz, the next morning would begin much like the one before it.

It began with the sun rising over the field she had seen but barely noticed for the past thirty years in her alcoholic fog. Once again, she opened her arms and took the view into her heart, where she now held her stepson. Later that day, Liz would attend her first Al-Anon meeting, which became as important to her as her AA meetings. She admitted to a number of things at her first Al-Anon meeting, and one of them concerned her husband's failing memory.

A Different Window

Liz had been sober for over two years, attending an AA and an Al-Anon meeting each week, when she visited her family doctor for a physical. It was the first of July, and the Iowa sun seemed especially hot. Nearly all the grass in front of her house had browned from the lack of rain. Liz had heard on the television that local farmers were worried for their crops. Jonathan usually watered the lawn in the evenings, but he hadn't that summer. A week later she returned for her annual mammogram. The exam was routine, but she felt anxious. A neighbor, a sixty-three-year-old woman she had known for the last fifteen years, had died from breast cancer. She changed into a gown for the X ray. The technician reminded Liz that she would feel uncomfortable as her breast was squeezed, but it would only last a few seconds and would not damage her breast. "You may feel tenderness for a few days," she said. Liz was relieved to hear the last whir and click of the machine. She waited for the technician to develop the X ray and make sure the picture was a good one.

Two days later, her phone rang. "Mrs. Toggen, this is Dr. Anderson. I have the result of your mammogram in front of me, and I'm terribly sorry, but it looks like you have tumors in both breasts. We need to have you in the clinic as soon as possible for a biopsy."

Liz didn't know what to say.

"Mrs. Toggen," the doctor repeated. "Do you think you could come in tomorrow for a biopsy? It won't take long."

"Sure," Liz said. She stared at the floor. "How serious is it?"

"Well, we won't know until we have a biopsy. Can you come in tomorrow morning at eight?" the doctor asked.

"Yes, tomorrow at eight. That will be fine." Liz hung up the phone and walked directly downstairs where her husband was using the power saw to make a shelf for their bedroom. She stood at the top of the stairs, waiting for the noise of the saw to stop. "Jonathan," she hollered. "Will you please come up here? I need to talk to you."

Liz arrived early for the biopsy, which the doctor performed in the clinic with a local anesthetic. The very next day Liz talked with a few women in her Tuesday-morning Al-Anon group. "I'm scared," she told her best friend in the group. "Jonathan is too. We've hardly said a word to each other since the biopsy. We're walking on eggshells waiting to hear from the doctor." Liz tried to reassure herself. "But you know, I've known my doctor for nearly thirty years, and he couldn't find the slightest lump in my breast when he examined me. He's never been wrong before."

That afternoon, the doctor called. Jonathan answered the phone and called his wife over. "I'm sorry," said Dr. Anderson. "The tumor is malignant. We need to have you come in to discuss treatment alternatives with the surgeon."

Liz hung up the phone and turned to her husband, who had been standing beside her. The furrowed brows, tight mouth, and watery eyes said everything. Jonathan held her.

For the next two nights, around three in the morning, Liz would wake and stare into the dark room. It was easy at that hour to convince herself that the news wasn't true, that she didn't have cancer, and that, in fact, the doctor had called to tell her the results of the biopsy were negative. While Jonathan lay asleep next to her, she was convinced that she was all right and some terrible mistake, a mix-up in the X-ray department, had been made. Sure, her neighbor, as well as her friend Ella from the university, had died months earlier from breast cancer, but Liz wouldn't. Her sister-in-law was diagnosed with breast cancer and had been doing fine since her surgery. In fact, she reasoned to herself as she turned in bed, if she had cancer it would probably require only a simple cut, a lumpectomy, and not the removal of the entire breast. Only then, after she had reassured herself that she would be okay, could she fall back to sleep.

In the morning, she awoke happier than the night before. Even so, she felt strangely disconnected from things, as if she didn't entirely exist or belong anywhere, not even in the kitchen pouring coffee that morning.

It was the Fourth of July. Liz was returning from Des Moines on Interstate 35 when she recalled a lecture in treatment about denial and about opening herself to what was true. Maybe she was denying her cancer as she had denied her alcoholism. Maybe she needed to admit her powerlessness over cancer too. She saw the highway, the road stretching out ahead of her, as a metaphor for her predicament. She could not just exit the freeway anywhere and expect to get home. She had to stay on the road and continue. She had no choice but to drive on, to accept things as they were, in order to reach home. Having cancer was another road that required all her attention, and from which she couldn't exit.

While driving and looking out across the fields, she felt the force of the First Step, the relief in admitting to what she was seeking to deny. She had cancer, and her life was once again unmanageable. But she had her Higher Power, whether it was God or destiny or nature. She could continue on, despite the fear and depression caused by the diagnosis. She had friends, family, a good husband, Al-Anon and AA, and her sobriety. She turned off the air-conditioning in her car, opened the window, and felt the fresh, hot wind on her face.

That night, she wouldn't wake up at three o'clock and try to deny what was happening.

When the day of her surgery arrived, Jonathan drove Liz to the hospital. It had been decided at an earlier meeting that she would most likely lose one breast. If the other breast contained cancer too, she would lose both. Whether her lymph nodes would be removed depended on how far the cancer had spread. "We need to be aggressive and remove all the cancerous cells," the surgeon said when she saw him in his office.

At seventy-nine years old, Jonathan's reflexes were slow, and he failed to see a car pulling down a drive. The car never stopped, backing right out into the street. When Jonathan finally saw him, he hit his horn, slammed on his brakes, and careened into the other lane. A near collision was avoided, but Liz's anxiety skyrocketed. She started crying. Jonathan pulled over to the curb and parked.

It was only six in the morning, and they still hadn't arrived at the hospital. "I don't see how I'm going to get through the rest of this day," Liz cried.

Four hours later, after a mastectomy was performed on one breast and lymph nodes were removed, Liz awoke in the hospital room. Jonathan was sitting alongside her. "Just rest," he reassured her, as he held her hand.

Liz winced and moaned from the pain that throbbed in her chest. Even her legs seemed to ache.

"Everything went fine. They removed all the cancer and saved one breast," he said.

At that moment, the nurse walked in. "Hi, Liz," she said cheerfully.

"Hi," Liz mumbled, surprised. It was Cheri from her Al-Anon group. Liz had forgotten that she was a nurse at the hospital and was relieved that one of her Al-Anon friends would take care of her.

Cheri would have liked to pull up a chair and explain to Liz as much as she could, but she had other patients who required attention. "I wish I could stay with you all morning," she said to Liz. Cheri reassured her that the surgery went well and that she would soon be on her way to recovery. "All of us at the meeting will be thinking about you," she said.

Bandages were laid over Liz's chest, and she couldn't see anything until the doctor arrived the next day to inspect the wound. Liz lay back and looked up at the ceiling when they removed the bandages.

She considered not looking but then glanced down to her chest when the doctor said, "The wound will heal nicely."

"Did you get all the cancer?" Liz asked.

"Everything," the doctor said to reassure her. "The surgeons did an excellent job, and we believe all the cancer was removed."

"But are you sure you got all the cancer?" Liz asked again. "All of it?"

Cheri touched Liz's hand. "You're going to be just fine, Liz. Really."

When Liz glanced down at her chest, it didn't strike her that she was missing a breast. The gouge across the one breast and the smaller incision in the other looked tidy and simple, nothing like she had imagined. She had pictured a gaping hole in her chest, but noticed only a small incision, about three or four inches long. Surely, it would only leave a simple, thick scar.

She looked up at the doctor and felt odd, as if nothing really terrible had happened. She wasn't really missing a breast, but had simply acquired a wound, to which bandages were being applied by the doctor.

"You'll do well," he said, reassuring her. Cheri was still standing next to the doctor. She smiled.

Cheri said nothing about working the Steps or praying, but her brief presence in the hospital room reminded Liz of the Serenity Prayer, which she said after the doctor and Cheri had left her room. She looked outside the window, so different from the one in her kitchen. The medications made her groggy, and she repeated lines in the prayer. "Grant me the serenity to accept . . ." she said twice before whispering more of the prayer.

For the next three days, old friends, relatives, and members from her Al-Anon and AA groups came to visit. She liked chatting with everyone, but by early evening, she was ready for sleep. Her husband never left the room except to have lunch or supper in the cafeteria or to give Liz some privacy with her women friends. If he did leave when she was asleep, he would tape notes to her bed rail explaining where he had gone and when he would get back. Get-well cards were opened and made steeples on the windowsill. Three of them were from women she had met in primary treatment in West Palm Beach. They had continued to write each other over the years.

Before the surgery, Liz was terribly worried and upset with the prospect of losing a breast. It struck at her very identity as a woman and threatened to make her feel less attractive and feminine. But after the surgery, she felt less concerned about the mastectomy and more concerned about losing her life if the cancer reoccurred or metastasized. She would willingly have her other breast removed to stay alive. It troubled her to feel this vulnerable. Her life seemed like a plum hanging from a thin stem on a tree.

That September, three months after her surgery, she began attending an exercise group for survivors of breast cancer. It met once a week at a nearby YWCA. The first hour of the group was set aside for discussion, which was easier for Liz than for others who weren't used to small-group discussion. They discussed practical things, like wigs for those who were losing hair from chemotherapy. And they discussed more difficult matters: loss and the deaths of group members. Liz had invited her own sister-in-law, who had a mastectomy three months before Liz's, to the cancer group.

After group discussion, the women changed clothes and began water exercises in the pool: rolling their shoulders, lifting their arms, stretching the upper torso, strengthening their muscles with water weights.

In the months that followed, two members of the group died. One of the women was Jonathan's sister.

After the funeral, Liz stopped going to her AA and Al-Anon meetings for a couple of weeks. She felt such a sense of anxiety that she began to isolate herself. She also felt ashamed that she wasn't more supportive of Jonathan, but his sister's death made her feel at risk of dying too. She couldn't talk to him, she decided. He was grieving, and she didn't want him to worry about her now. "Nobody understands," she said quietly one afternoon. The sound of her voice, what she had said, startled her. She remembered a grief group discussion about self-pity, and how important it was to reach out to others for understanding and help. Liz stood up from her chair and dialed an Al-Anon friend.

"I've been feeling real sorry for myself," Liz said on the phone to her friend. "I've been afraid of dying, but I have today, this minute, and I need to live one day at a time, as corny as that may sound. All I have is this moment to appreciate the universe."

The next morning, she was at her meeting. Liz talked about her cancer group in her Al-Anon meeting. "They are such great women to be with," she said. "I don't want to stop going to that group, or this one, for that matter. It seems to me that when people in AA or Al-Anon become very vulnerable and begin to despair, as I've been, some of them stop coming to meetings. They disappear, go back to using. They think no one understands, and they feel lonely. Sometimes I think no one understands me, and I feel lonely. But I've come to this meeting, and you remind me how many people do care."

Jonathan certainly cared for and loved Liz most. When she came home from the hospital, he was always there to help, to cut the gauzes for her dressings, to run the bathwater, and to help her in and out of the tub. He had never winced at the sight of her scar or her missing breast. Liz knew that a mastectomy impacted some women's sexual or intimate relationships, but Liz, after fifty years of marriage, never felt repulsive in Jonathan's eyes. She was grateful for him. As the months passed, however, Jonathan was becoming more and more absent-minded, as if someone or something was beginning to occupy him.

Which Way Is Home?

Jonathan pulled up to the stop sign two blocks from their home. It was late November, and the air was cool. Leaves had begun to fall. Liz looked out the car window at the one elm that still held its leaves. She loved fall best of all the seasons, and she loved the color of the sky as much as the color of the leaves. The blue had a darker tone than the summer sky.

"There's no car coming," Liz said to her husband, after realizing how long they had been stopped. She looked right and left again to be sure.

"I know," he said, annoyed at her comment. He gripped the steering wheel and began turning left at the stop sign.

"Where are you going?" Liz asked. He was turning in the opposite direction from home.

"Which way?" he yelled, and shot another look at Liz. Suddenly, she guessed what was wrong. Liz felt her heart fall like a rock over a cliff. She had suspected it for some time, but now it seemed too dangerous to ignore any longer

"Well," Jonathan said again. "Which way is home?"

"Right," Liz said impatiently. "Take a right."

Jonathan was diagnosed with Alzheimer's disease, and he had other health conditions that caused a variety of problems. He had a muscle disease, called polymyalgia rheumatica (PMR), that made it difficult at times for him even to raise his arms. He also experienced syncope, a brief loss of consciousness caused by insufficient blood flow to the brain. He and Liz might be watching the evening news together, when she would glance over at him, see his head leaning to the side, and realize he had gone unconscious. Until medication began to control the spells, she had to call the paramedics, who, in one year, came seven times. His arthritis required him to walk with a cane most of the time.

One afternoon, after they had finished eating dinner, Liz watched Jonathan reach into his shirt pocket and pull out a pack of cigarettes. He held them in his palm, looked puzzled for a moment, and, after remembering that he smoked, lit it. Fortunately, he soon stopped smoking altogether, but not because smoking was bad for his health. He simply couldn't remember to buy cigarettes.

Liz thought it strange. All the years she had been drinking, she had been dependent on him. When she would get angry and throw a dinner plate, he would clean up after her. He did nearly all the driving. It was too dangerous to let Liz drive when she had been drinking. Though she did most of the cooking, Jonathan did all the dishes, cleaned the kitchen, swept the floor, and even vacuumed. Liz would take the sheets off the bed, but it was Jonathan who always made it. Now it was up to Liz to do all the chores.

She locked the doors at night, made breakfast, picked up the mail, did grocery shopping, and washed clothes.

"I'm going downstairs for a cup of coffee," he'd say to Liz while they were upstairs in their bedroom. She would walk down with him, prepare a pot of coffee, and pour him a cup. After finishing, he'd say again, "I'm going upstairs for a cup of coffee." Each day Jonathan became more and more unlike himself.

When Liz was diagnosed with cancer, she thought her ability to accept her life had been tested thoroughly. She didn't think she could endure yet another challenge. Her Al-Anon group was supportive, but when she tried to apply its principles to Jonathan, they didn't work. She couldn't let Jonathan make his own mistakes, as you might with an alcoholic. If she did that, Jonathan would die: he would forget to take his medicine or to eat. She had to care for him, become a "caretaker," a term used to imply codependency. But now she was learning to understand the term "caregiver." It meant a kind of love that required devotion, patience, and energy.

At her AA and Al-Anon meetings, she heard other women talk about how important it was for Liz to take care of herself too. So, after Liz went grocery shopping, she would stop at Coffee Chat, a local coffeehouse that served pastries. Liz might bring a book and spend an hour reading before going home to Jonathan.

Some mornings after waking, she'd look at Jonathan asleep next to her and think about the work ahead: organizing the pills he needed to take for the day, making breakfast, selecting his clothes, and getting him dressed. She tried to remember him when he was well and younger. She would cry, quietly, as he slept.

It was always on those mornings that Jonathan's brother would show up unexpectedly and help Liz with chores; a neighbor down the street would bring over a loaf of homemade bread; an Al-Anon friend would call to ask how she was doing; a letter from Vera would arrive in her mailbox; or Liz would look out the window as she prepared breakfast and see the son of one of Jonathan's friends shoveling the drive.

She felt so grateful to be sober and free of her addiction. She couldn't imagine drinking, having a hangover, and carrying up a tray of food to Jonathan.

One Sunday morning in early October, when the autumn leaves were at their brightest, she returned home from her walk and found Jonathan still in bed. The night before he had left on the TV and forgotten a towel on the dining room floor—things he had never done before. It was strange behavior. Usually he was awake when she got back from her walks, waiting for her. Liz wondered if he had forgotten to take his pills, so she brought up a breakfast tray with medications to give him. He awoke, rolled to the side of the bed, and stood. He stumbled and fell to the floor. "Take my hand," Liz said, and when he reached away from her hand, as if it were floating somewhere else, Liz suddenly realized the seriousness of his condition. She called the paramedics, and Jonathan was rushed to the hospital. It was determined that he had suffered a stroke and would probably suffer a fatal one soon.

Two days later, on a Tuesday morning at her Al-Anon meeting, while listening to a young woman talk about her grief over ending a relationship, Liz cried.

She would cry the entire week.

Finally, Liz signed papers not to resuscitate Jonathan. While he was in a coma, she stood at his bedside and thanked him for their life together. She leaned over and kissed him.

The Picture

Weeks after the funeral, Liz was in the grocery store when an old friend of Jonathan's asked about him. "How's Jonathan?" she said. Liz realized immediately that the woman didn't know. "Oh, Liz," the woman said after Liz told her about his death. "We all loved him. He was such a good man."

"I just found this picture of him," Liz said, opening her purse. In the middle of the aisle, the two women examined the picture Liz had found in some of Jonathan's papers. Taken thirty years earlier, the photograph showed a younger Jonathan wearing his police uniform. He was sweeping a floor, smiling. The photographer must have made a wisecrack to evoke such a grin. "That smile of his! It was wonderful!" the woman said to Liz. It was true. When he smiled, it was as if his whole body showed joy.

"Look at his hand on the broom," Liz remarked. "It seems so real I could almost touch him."

Liz felt as if she were visiting him at the police station. He was so handsome then, so happy.

"You know," Liz said, putting away the picture, "Jonathan loved AA and the Twelve Steps. He was so happy for me. He had never known anyone to sober up from alcoholism. His first wife, his brother, his son, his brother's wife—they were all alcoholics and died from it, except his son. Jonathan was my main support. I was lucky. I know a lot of women whose husbands never supported them when they got sober."

The two women hugged. "He is still alive in our hearts," the woman said to Liz. "We will keep our memories of him."

Liz left the grocery store, got back in the car, and cried.

The Wisdom to Know the Difference

Less than a year after Jonathan's death, Liz began seeing a counselor for her grief. During their first session, Liz said, "I can't tell whether I'm grieving Jonathan, my lost breast and sexuality, my life as a married woman, being old, being an alcoholic, or whether it's the depression I've always lived with.

"I can't afford to mope around the house. I'm not getting anything done, and there's so much to do. I think I should sell the house, but I've lived there so long I can't imagine living anywhere else. If I move, I'm afraid I'd feel as if I was abandoning Jonathan. I know that sounds strange, but being in the house now keeps me close to him. I guess I really don't want to leave, but I think I should move into something smaller, easier to take care of, and more sensible. Our house, I mean my house, is so big.

"I'm tired of feeling sad. I don't want to feel this grief, loneliness, and depression. I don't want to feel anything anymore."

It was hard for Liz to accept the grief and loneliness of losing a thirty-year marriage with a man whom she regarded as her best friend. With her counselor's help, though, she was beginning to understand that she had no more control of what she felt than she did over the weather.

"I know," she said to her counselor, who pointed out to Liz that feelings came and went, like winds that can't be controlled.

"At any moment," the counselor said, "we can be hit emotionally or suddenly feel happy. We are responsible for what we do with our feelings and how we act," the counselor told Liz, "but you aren't responsible for this grief. It's a natural response to all your losses these last few years.

"Can you apply what you've learned in AA and Al-Anon to your grief?" she asked.

Yes, Liz thought to herself. Simple phrases rushed into her mind: *Accept the things we cannot change . . . one day at a time . . . courage to change the things we can . . . surrender, not compliance . . . act as if.*

"I've been fighting my own feelings as if they were the enemy," she told her counselor. "That's what I've been doing. I've been trying not to feel. I think I need to quit fighting and let things be, and that means I unlock the door and let my feelings back into my house."

Liz knew that wouldn't be easy, but now she knew the difference between what she couldn't change and what she could.

A few months later, Liz signed up for a women's literature class. She made plans for an elder hostel trip to Minneapolis for a week during the summer at the University of Minnesota. It wasn't easy for her to locate the catalogs and select the classes she wanted. Sometimes Liz wondered why she bothered, but she would "act as if" and trust that she would change for the better.

She also planned a trip to California to visit her brother, whom she hadn't seen since Jonathan's funeral, and began discussing with friends a second trip to Denmark, her father's birthplace. She still thought of Jonathan, but slowly the sting of loneliness lessened. There were things she could do now that she hadn't thought of before. She called other widows in the neighborhood, and together they might play cards in the evening, or Liz would encourage them to attend her book club. Many called and invited her out, something she was more willing to do now.

Liz was becoming more active in her AA groups; she sponsored two younger women and planned to attend the upcoming International Women's AA Conference in Minneapolis, a three-hour drive north of Ames. Vera and Sophie promised they would try to come to the conference and be with Liz. She had already attended other international women's conferences in Reno, Phoenix, and Atlanta. She regretted that Jonathan wouldn't drive her to the airport, wish her well, and call her every night at her hotel.

She was also asked to speak to a women's lawyers group and to sit on a panel about the history of women in law. She felt honored, and talked about the event to Jonathan in her mind. Sometimes she missed him so much. She would happily tie his shoelaces every day if she could have him back.

"I am handling my depression better," Liz later told the counselor. "I know that drinking wouldn't solve anything. Some people go their whole life without sharing anything of themselves with anyone in a very meaningful way. But I've been fortunate, ever since I got sober, to have many people I can talk to. I have friends in AA and Al-Anon, and other family members and lifelong friends. I can go to a meeting anytime and talk about what troubles me, even though I don't like burdening people with my problems. Still, if I need to talk, I will. It doesn't matter that I'm fifty years older than some people in my groups. It doesn't matter that I've been drinking longer than some people have been alive. I still find ways to connect with them, and when I leave a meeting, we may not have solved all our problems, but I leave feeling more hopeful, more certain of myself.

"Hope is what the Second Step is about to me. The Step says, We 'came to believe that a Power greater than ourselves could restore us to sanity.' A lot of people hate the word sanity. But I don't. To me, being restored to sanity means that I am being restored to a wholeness that I once knew as a child. I like to think of that wholeness as home. So I am coming home, you see."

Liz paused. Her eyes watered. "One time, about a year before he died," she said to the counselor, "Jonathan asked me, only two blocks from our house, 'Which way is home?' It made me sad. And I felt impatient with him too. 'Right,' I said. 'Take a right!' But you know, if I could answer that question now, I would say something different. I would say, 'Jonathan, I love you. We are home. It doesn't matter which way you turn.'"

14

So Angels Came and We Weren't Alone

JOANNA AND REBECCA, friends from their days at Jellinek and Fellowship, pulled onto the Hazelden campus in Center City about 2:00 P.M. on May 28, 1996. They had driven straight through from Florida, taking turns napping and driving and drinking coffee, and now they were tousled and tired. Still, the rolling campus, brightened by the occasional yellow forsythia and purple spirea, felt like a field of flowers to Joanna. She was reminded of her childhood in Illinois, the green of spring that was still soft and inviting, that hadn't hardened into the heat of summer, and as they walked into Jellinek, Joanna felt the joy of coming home spread over her weary body.

She and Rebecca visited Vivian and the other counselors, and they went for a walk on the campus. Afterward, they headed south to see the apartment Joanna's husband had found for her in White Bear Lake, a suburb northeast of St. Paul. It was further from the city than she had wanted to be, but Jeff had bought a house on White Bear Lake, and he wanted them to be within easy driving distance of each other. They had decided they would share custody of their daughters, although Joanna would have primary physical custody. Jeff would have the girls every other weekend, but he expected to be busy with his job, and Joanna was eager to be a full-time mom again.

Joanna and Rebecca turned into the drive leading to the complex of two-story brick buildings around a central courtyard. Her three-bedroom apartment was on the second floor of the first building. They stopped to get a key from the caretaker. As Joanna climbed the flight of stairs, her heart fell. She thought about the large house they had owned in Chicago. When Joanna opened the apartment door, the first thing she noticed was the emptiness. She walked into a square room of plain white walls and beige carpeting. The living room window was large, but it faced north and left only a flat square of light on the carpet, nothing compared to the extravagant splashes of sunshine that flooded her Chicago home. The kitchen was to her right, tiny and dark. "Oh, God," Joanna cried. "Is this my new life?" She sank to the carpet, sliding her back against the white wall, put her hands over her face, and sobbed.

Rebecca sat down next to her, put an arm over her shoulders, and waited silently. When Joanna's crying had spent itself, Rebecca reassured her that she and the other Fellowship women were with her in spirit and by phone, and that they would hold her in their thoughts and prayers every day. They talked about finding meetings in Minnesota and staying in touch with Hazelden. They looked into the bedrooms and talked about decorating, about how Joanna could use curtains and colors to re-create for Molly the sense of her old room.

They went back to the hotel for an hour before going on to a meeting in St. Paul. The house was called Uptown, a kind of club where meetings were held mornings, afternoons, and evenings. Joanna met a couple of people who had been at Jellinek with her. They were excited to see her and glad to hear she was moving to Minnesota. *This is the irony of being an alcoholic,* she thought. *If I didn't have this disease, I wouldn't have a group of wonderful people waiting for me, accepting me fully, even though I'm a stranger.*

Wednesday morning, Joanna took Rebecca to the airport for a 7:00 A.M. flight back to Florida. Driving away, Joanna kept thinking, *I am so alone. I'll never find friends like I had at Fellowship.* She couldn't face going back to the apartment yet, so she stopped at Mickey's Diner for breakfast and read the paper over coffee and eggs. After more than an hour, she folded the newspaper and prepared to make the drive back to the apartment. She had to pull herself together for her children. Some of the furniture from the house was arriving that afternoon, and Jeff was bringing the girls to see the apartment the next day. It would be the first time they'd seen their mother in four months.

She got back on the freeway and drove north. It was about 9:30 A.M. and the freeways were relatively empty. As she passed the majestic dome of the St. Paul Cathedral, she wished that she lived in the city itself instead of a suburb. She wished she was closer to the Saint Paul Fellowship Club, where so many Hazelden alumni attend AA meetings. An intense sense of loneliness washed over her, and she found herself thinking, for the thousandth time in her life, *I can't do this*. She veered to the left, following 35E as it wound through downtown, and corrected herself. "I can do this," she said aloud in the car.

The next afternoon, she stood, very nervous, looking at Jeff climbing out of the car, lifting Stacey out of her car seat, and unbuckling Molly. Jeff walked toward her with Stacey in his arms and Molly hurrying beside him, and Joanna was stunned by how much Molly had grown. Molly was almost to the door when she spied Joanna. She came to a complete halt, started to laugh, and then looked shyly at the sidewalk. Joanna opened the front door and beckoned to Molly, who ran into her arms. "Mommy, I had pancakes for breakfast this morning," she said breathlessly. "I helped to put Stacey's dress on her, Mommy, and Daddy said we can stay for three hours. Can I have orange juice? Do you have any cookies?"

After taking some time with Molly, Joanna turned her attention to Stacey. She found herself putting the moment off not only for Molly's sake, but for her own. Jeff had been telling her that Stacey was very shy and wouldn't let anyone she didn't know well touch her. Joanna was afraid Stacey would scream when she tried to pick her up. She had bought a pop-up book about a farm for Stacey, which she'd left on the coffee table. Jeff set Stacey on the floor and gave her the book. Stacey began slapping her pudgy arm against the white fur of a lamb. Joanna sat down next to her on the floor, holding her breath. Stacey tilted her head to look at Joanna and smiled, almost coyly. Joanna tilted her own head in imitation and smiled. "Hello, my little girl." Within two minutes, Stacey had crawled into Joanna's lap.

"I don't know how she could have a memory of you after four months, Jo, but I swear she does," said Jeff. "She never goes to anyone like that."

For three hours, Joanna did nothing but play with the girls, and during the moments when they were beyond her reach, she longed to touch them. And then they were gone, with the promise they could sleep there in four days. Joanna was relieved. *I can do this,* she thought. *I do remember how to take care of my children.*

So Angels Came to the Party and We Weren't Alone

Jeff brought the children and full suitcases on Sunday morning. He stayed for a few hours to help with the transition, and then he was off. Joanna kept her promise to Molly that they would have their long-anticipated Valentine's party when they saw each other again. She had decorated the living room with red paper hearts, and lace napkins rested on the coffee table. When Stacey went down for her nap, Joanna said to Molly, "Shall we have our party now?"

They got out red paper plates and the tiny porcelain cups from Molly's tea set. On the plates Joanna set cupcakes, and into the cups she poured 7-Up. Molly directed the action. "Mommy, put a napkin there for Stacey," she said.

"Honey, Stacey is napping."

Molly frowned and puffed out her cheeks. The pitch of her voice moved to a whine. "Who will we have at our party?"

Joanna was stricken. Here was Molly, away from all her old friends, in a small apartment that must have felt as alien to her as it did to Joanna. Did Molly feel as alone as she did? Suddenly, she had an inspiration. "I know, Molly. Let's invite the angels," she said.

Molly responded eagerly. "Okay, Mommy. Put the napkin there for the angel."

"Shall we invite another angel for that end of the table?"

"Yes!" exclaimed Molly. She danced in place as she directed her mother. "Put another napkin there for the other angel."

Inviting angels to the party made Joanna think of the Christmas movie with Jimmy Stewart, *It's a Wonderful Life*, and how an angel earned its wings every time a bell rang. She went into her bedroom to get a tiny bell, the one she'd gotten because it reminded her of graduation from Hazelden. She put candles on the table and lit them, and then rang the bell to summon the angels. She and Molly folded their legs under the coffee table and ate the cupcakes and drank their 7-Up. Molly continued a stream of conversation, making solemn observations about her room at Dad's house, about how she would swim in the lake this summer, and how she would take good care of Stacey. "Will the angels come whenever we ring the bell, Mommy?"

Joanna's eyes drifted toward the window, but she wasn't looking out. "Mmmm," she murmured, thinking to herself, *Isn't that what AA is all about? You have a need, you ring a bell, and there is a sponsor, or a friend, or a meeting, or a serendipitous event. Always an angel is waiting.*

Finding a Home Meeting

Through June and into July, Joanna went to at least three meetings a week, often more, at Uptown. Although the group was large and diverse, she didn't find many young mothers at the meetings, and the sheer size of them exacerbated her shyness. In early July, she heard about a women's meeting that was beginning at the Day by Day Cafe near downtown St. Paul.

She arrived a little after 6:00 P.M., walking into the restaurant's entryway, which was filled with large green plants, a disheveled wall of notices, and homemade advertisements. As she walked into the main room of the restaurant, she felt transported to what she imagined the late 1960s and early 1970s must have been like.

There were old, high-backed wooden booths against the far wall, the wood as dark as molasses. Assorted tables made a long row down the center of the room and were surrounded by old kitchen chairs. The floor was planking, darkened by many years of footprints. Painted black pipes crossed the ceiling. Best of all was the art on the walls. Brightly painted chairs sprouted at various angles near the ceiling. A yellow one said "Crabby Chair" in turquoise letters across the seat. Another stated "Girls Rule." The cafe smelled of hamburgers and chili and was filled with people in casual dress.

Joanna smiled, delighted by the messy creativity and the informality of the cafe. She continued into the back room where the meeting was to be held. A few women were sitting in the booths nestled against huge, plate-glass windows. Candles were lit, and coffee, tea, and cookies waited on a table against the wall. She sat down quietly in one of the booths, and women continued to drift in over the next ten minutes, until fourteen had arrived. As they entered, they greeted each other warmly. The meeting was a guided topic meeting; they discussed issues such as powerlessness, spirituality, sexuality, relationships, anger, and grief, but there was the flexibility to talk about whatever was on one's mind.

Joanna loved it. Although she knew immediately that she wanted to come back, her shyness kept her from joining in easily. After a couple weeks, one of the women mentioned they came early for coffee and suggested she join them. Not long after, she walked in early, and one of the women turned and said loudly, "It's Jo!" Everyone turned to chorus with her, "Joanna!" She felt herself blush with the attention and with pleasure. *This is truly beginning to feel like home,* she thought.

Several weeks earlier, Joanna had asked a woman she felt drawn to at the Uptown meeting to be her sponsor. She told her sponsor, Nicole, about this meeting and Nicole joined her. The women talked enthusiastically about a Tuesday evening Step meeting, where a different Step was discussed each week, and Joanna began attending that meeting as well. Slowly, with effort and determination, Joanna built a network of people, a community in her new home. Over the next few months, the community would prove critical to her recovery, especially the Wednesday-night meeting at Day by Day Cafe, which she now claimed as her home meeting.

One Day at a Time

"Why did you have to get a lawyer, anyway?" Jeff nagged Joanna on the telephone. "I had everything worked out. I'll take good care of you."

Joanna's voice was querulous. "Maybe it seems that way to you, Jeff, but I don't want to be dependent on you and always asking for money. I want a division of the stock, the retirement fund, and the house sale."

"I have worked so hard for all that, and I did it in spite of you. I'm not going to be one of those husbands who gets taken to the cleaners," he shot back.

"That's the attitude that made me get a lawyer," she said acerbically.

"No lawyer in the world will get a judge to give you joint custody of the kids if I don't agree, not after the kind of mother you've been."

Joanna's cheeks burned. When she hung up the phone, she walked back into her bedroom, wringing her hands. *He's right,* she thought. *I have damaged my children for life.* Whenever Molly awakened before Joanna, Molly would come to her room and stand beside the bed, shaking Joanna's shoulders as hard as she could. "Mommy, wake up," she'd beg, with a note of hysteria in her voice. *She must be remembering the day the police came, the day she couldn't awaken me,* worried Joanna.

When Joanna caught a nasty cold in August, Molly was forever covering her up, keeping her from getting a chill. *A three-year-old shouldn't feel like she has to protect her mom from getting sick,* grieved Joanna. She sank back into the shame that she had struggled out of over the long months of treatment. *Oh yes, Jeff is right,* she thought, *I don't deserve these children, and I don't deserve anything more in the divorce settlement, not after the drinking and the way I behaved. He's right, he put up with horrible things from me. I have been bad, and I don't deserve anything more.*

She could feel the pressure building in her chest, and she began to pace. In the past, she would have relieved the pressure with vodka. *Thank God for the program,* she thought. She could hear Vivian saying to her, "Just do it one day at a time, Joanna. And if you can't do that, do it one hour at a time." But Jeff's words came back at her again. "No judge will give you the kids." She began to pace the room and wring her hands again. She heard Molly in her bedroom, whining, "Mommy, I'm hungry."

"You just ate," she snapped. She paced back and forth, her fear increasing with each step. Back in Florida, Fred had helped coach her through her anxiety. She repeated to herself his instructions. *Slow down. Take a deep breath. Hold it. Let it out slowly.* She forced herself to sit down in the easy chair in the corner of her bedroom. Quietly she mouthed the Serenity Prayer. *I'll call my sponsor,* she thought.

She went to the kitchen, made Molly a peanut butter sandwich, and got on the phone. "Nicole, what should I do?" she asked.

"Remember, you have a Higher Power, Jo."

"Yes, yes," she said impatiently. "I know I have a Higher Power." She paused and shut her eyes. "Yes," she added, "Thanks for reminding me. I know I have a Higher Power." She felt herself relax a bit.

"So what do you think you should do?" Nicole asked.

"I don't want to get rid of my lawyer. I need her," Joanna asserted.

They talked on the phone for a half hour, and Joanna remembered what it was like to be honest with herself in Fellowship. It had been hard to stand up for what she knew was right when she had reported on Phoebe and Trevor. Phoebe had been angry with her, and so had others, but it had worked out well in the end. She had stood up for herself and survived. "I'm just going to tell Jeff I'm keeping the lawyer," she said, "and that I want a fairer distribution of property."

Jeff called a few days later. His voice was muted. "Sorry about that thing I said about the kids."

"You're not angry anymore?" asked Joanna.

"I'm still pissed you've got a lawyer. It's a total waste of money. But what I said about the kids, about a judge not letting you have them, that was out of line. I get carried away by my anger sometimes, and awful things pop out of my mouth before I know what I'm saying."

During the family program, Jeff had come to recognize that some of his behavior was similar to Joanna's alcoholic behavior. He tried to control events and the people around him, including Joanna, and when he couldn't, his temper would swallow him and he'd say cruel things. Like Joanna after a drinking binge, he'd be overcome with remorse the next day. *At least he had the guts to own up to it and come back with an apology,* Joanna thought.

"It's okay," she said to Jeff. "This is really hard on both of us."

Jeff's a good man, Joanna thought to herself. She knew holding on to resentments was deadly to recovery. *I don't want to let myself forget the good parts in the middle of this haggling over money and property,* she thought. She reminded herself of what a soft touch Jeff was when people came to the door fundraising for environmental causes or cancer research, of the volunteer work he did once a month at the food shelf, of his generosity with his parents when they needed money, and of the soft crinkles around his eyes when he laughed with Molly. *Yes, he is a good man and a good father,* she thought, *and he gets caught by this mess just like I do.*

That afternoon, she got a phone call from her mother. Her family continued to be difficult for her. Both her dad and her oldest sister continued to drink a lot, and there was no way to fit in with her family unless she was drinking. Her father had refused to give her financial help at the beginning of the divorce, and her sisters simply didn't call her. It was as if she were no longer a member of the family. And her mother . . . Her mom tried, she really did. But her mother loved a good crisis. She had decided to hate Jeff, and whenever she called, she would launch into haranguing criticism of him. Joanna didn't need her own resentments fed.

As soon as she would hear her mother's voice on the phone, Joanna's head would begin to spin. A multitude of thoughts overwhelmed her, and she couldn't focus. It was exactly the way she would feel before she'd take a drink; in fact, planned visits to her parents had often precipitated drinking binges. On the phone, her mother was saying that Jeff was cheap. "You know, he could afford to buy you a new car. Yours has sixty thousand miles on it. Who knows when it could break down, and with you living in that awful climate, hauling those two little girls around. Jeff's always been tight with his money."

Joanna knew better. On the contrary, Jeff had always been generous with his money, even toward her parents. She didn't want a new car. Hers ran perfectly well. She knew she should stand up for Jeff, but then she'd have to face her mother's hostility and listen to more bitterness. She felt tears building behind her eyes, and she said, "I know, Mom, I know, but the kids are fussing and I gotta go now."

"That's another thing," started her mom. "Why doesn't he give you more baby-sitting money?"

"I don't know, Mom, but I've really got to go now. Good-bye, Mom." Joanna hung up. She hated herself. *Why do I go along with her like this? Why do I let her get to me?* Her head continued to spin. Molly walked into the kitchen, whining, "I'm hungry." Joanna turned to the refrigerator and pulled out milk and butter.

"You want to help me make macaroni and cheese?" Joanna asked.

"No, dumbhead," Molly pouted.

"Tell you what. You sit here at the table and smear peanut butter on these crackers while I make dinner. Okay?"

Molly smeared peanut butter on the crackers, on her fingers, and on the table.

Joanna reached into the cupboard to pull out a bottle of olive oil, and it knocked against the vinegar bottle. The sound of the clanging bottles triggered the sound of her father mixing a drink after work, the sound that meant she would soon have a happy dad. Almost like music. It sent a shock wave through her, a minor chord forming under the harmony.

Stacey began to tug at the sides of the playpen, and her fussing grew to a full-fledged wail. Joanna lifted her out and brought her to the kitchen. She set Stacey on the floor with some wooden spoons to keep her occupied. Stacey beat the spoons on the floor and against the table legs. One of the spoons missed the table leg and hit Molly. Molly wailed and kicked Stacey, who wailed in turn. Joanna stood at the counter looking at the peanut butter smeared on the table and the two little girls with tears and snot mixing on their faces. What should she do? She couldn't hold them both at the same time.

Her head already spinning, she felt the pressure begin to build in her chest. *How dare I feel so frustrated by the one thing I wanted all those months I was gone? What's wrong with me?* Her body began to feel like an electric current, and all she could think was, *I've got to get out of here.* For the first time since she'd been out of treatment, she called Jeff to take care of her.

"I need a break, Jeff. I can't do this right now. I have to get out of here." Her voice was frantic.

"Joanna," he protested, "I can't drop everything and come over there and get the kids. I've got dinner plans with friends."

Joanna's voice broke and she began to cry. "I can't . . . " she started to say.

"Damn it, Jo. I can't come rescue you every time you feel tired." He paused, and there was silence on the other end of the line. Jeff sighed. "Okay, okay, I'll call my friends." Within a half hour, Jeff was at the door. Joanna was afraid he would take her car keys or her money, afraid he would assume she was starting to drink, but when he arrived, all he said was, "Are the girls okay?"

She met her sponsor and went for a long walk. The next morning, after twenty minutes of meditation, and after the kids had had breakfast and were watching *Sesame Street*, Joanna got out a list of relapse triggers she had made two years earlier while in primary treatment on the Lilly unit. At that time, she had thought she would use it to manage her drinking, cut back to a glass or two of wine. Now, she pulled them out to remind herself how to be on guard against the first drink. Her list read: "Sleeping too much or too little; eating too much or too little; not having the energy to do my hair; letting the house go; isolating myself; not caring; not feeling anything at all." Then she looked at the list of coping skills: "Talking to friends; calling sponsor; going to meetings; taking time out for myself; meditation and prayer." She tacked the lists up on the refrigerator.

On Wednesday, at her home meeting, she talked about how frantic she had felt. She told the women that if her house got to be a chronic mess, dishes piled in the sink, piles of dirty laundry scattered around, if she showed up for meetings looking scraggly and not caring, it meant the beginning of relapse for her, and she wanted them to intervene. "I told Jeff that after my first treatment," she said to them. "And he tried, but I didn't want to be stopped. I'd just get mad and fight with him if he said anything."

The women nodded in recognition.

"But now I want to be stopped," she implored.

During the month of September, the women were very attentive, calling her between meetings, inviting her to breakfast or lunch, and she was grateful. But her serenity ebbed and flowed as she struggled with loneliness, with being the primary, single caretaker of two precious, energetic young children, and with the process of divorce. Though she and Jeff worked hard at being respectful of one another, the task was difficult, and she often felt like their conversations were sandpaper on her skin.

It was a hard month anyway. Fall was approaching, the time of the year during which she had been raped. The slow-down, swim weather of summer was gone. The leaves had yet to turn and brighten the bland days of September with colors that looked like inner illumination to her. Near the end of the month, her serenity dipped low.

Joanna missed both a Tuesday and Wednesday meeting, and Nicole stopped by her place the following Saturday morning. She saw the dishes and laundry piled up in the apartment, and she saw Joanna still in pajamas at 11:00 A.M. Joanna met Nicole with a mixture of relief and annoyance. She felt caught in the act, but cared for too. "Come to a meeting with me this afternoon, will you?" asked Nicole. "It's a meeting with day care, so you don't even have to get a baby-sitter."

Reluctantly, Joanna agreed to go. She fed the kids lunch, got dressed, and when Nicole came back at 1:30 P.M., she grabbed her Big Book to bring along. During the discussion, she remained silent for a long time. It was a Step meeting, and they were discussing Step One today. She used her Big Book to read along during the opening reading. In the margins she had written, almost three years ago now, "Denial: One of the things that stands in the way of my recovery is believing that things will be different this time, that I can have just one drink." As she read it, she realized that she had made enormous progress, but denial still crept up on her. She decided to speak.

"Though I have felt the anxiety and pressure that used to precede my drinking, I thank God that I haven't experienced that deep, physical craving since I got out of treatment." She looked around the room and continued. "But still, the thought that I can drink sneaks up on me sometimes. It's real tricky. When I realize that I haven't given alcohol a second thought for a long time, I think, 'Maybe that means I'm not an alcoholic anymore.' That's how it works. So I imagine myself with that first drink, and I can feel the obsession take hold. I can feel myself wanting more, more, more, and more." Her voice rose. "I feel like I'm going to go crazy. I need more, more. I'm going to get more."

"Don't stop with the drink," interrupted her sponsor. "You have to walk yourself all the way through. Remember the consequences."

"Right," said Joanna. "The key is to put myself back in that place." She grimaced. "I've got to make myself remember the hangovers, the nausea, the blackouts, the kids being scared to death." Yes. This is what she had learned to do in treatment when the mental obsession threatened.

She turned to Nicole. "Thanks for bringing me," she said.

One Year Sober

As time went on, Joanna felt blessed by the support around her. She went to a Second Sunday at Hazelden, which was held in the Cork Center on the campus. It began with candles, coffee, and doughnuts. It was a time to attend a lecture, participate in a discussion group, and have lunch with other people in recovery. She attended at least three AA meetings a week, and she talked on the phone regularly with Phoebe and Rebecca, calling frequently at night, when the children were asleep and darkness pressed against her. She began to realize that part of her isolation was due to the fact that she had no friends who were stay-at-home moms. So she pushed herself to make contact at one of her meetings with a young woman who was home with her children. Together they decided to start a young moms gathering on Saturday mornings, where they would bring the children to play together.

Joanna's job was being a full-time mother, and with primary custody of the girls, she faced the problems of exhaustion and loneliness that single parents often feel. Jeff had the girls on Wednesday evenings and every other weekend, but with the pressures of his job, he often dropped them at his parents on his weekends or left them with Joanna. Despite the pressure of never-ending child care, she felt lucky to have her children. Phoebe had lost custody of her boys to their father.

Joanna spent many mornings with her girls at the playground. She brought them back to the apartment in the afternoon, and she would do dishes, laundry, and cleaning while they napped. After dinner, they might go for a walk, or she would push them on the swings in the apartment courtyard.

She enrolled Molly in a preschool program, which left two hours for concentrating on Stacey or doing the grocery shopping with only one child along. Some afternoons between naptime and dinner, she would take the girls to the Children's Museum or Camp Snoopy at the Mall of America. As the days got cooler, they spent more evenings inside, watching television, coloring, or baking cookies. When she would finally tuck the girls into bed at about 8:00 P.M., she'd put her feet up and make phone calls. As much as she treasured this time with her children, she knew she needed more balance in her life. Perhaps, she thought, she would sign up for ballet lessons. She had loved ballet as a child. She would get entirely caught up in the music and the movement, the triumph of the well-executed maneuver and the joy of the crowning leap. Perhaps it was time to look for a part-time job, and when she felt a little more settled, after a little more time in recovery, she wanted to go back to school and finish her bachelor's degree.

The one-year anniversary of her sobriety arrived. It was a time of jubilation and disappointment, of hope and dread. Phoebe and Rebecca were flying in from Florida to celebrate with her, to honor the importance of this milestone. They were staying with her for five days. On the weekend, they were going to drive with her to Madison, where Sam had moved. Since leaving St. Paul's Fellowship Club last March, he had gotten a job teaching at a university. He and Joanna had kept in touch, and though the romantic overtones of the relationship had dissipated, they remained friends. He was having a party, and the three women decided a weekend away would be an adventure. They could rent a hotel room and talk late into the night as they had at Fellowship. Joanna decided to invite Nicole along as well. Jeff would take Molly and Stacey.

As they approached the Wisconsin Dells area on Interstate 94, Joanna noticed the hills increasing in size and the rock cliffs she had loved to visit when she was in college. The leaves were in full fall glory, and she was thinking how much more beautiful they looked to her this year than they did last year, when she was entering treatment for the fourth time.

"What a glorious day for your anniversary," said Phoebe. The sky was white with sunlight, a welcome relief after so much grayness.

"Isn't it?" agreed Joanna. But something inside her felt dishonest as she said it. She shouldn't feel this way, she thought, but she was disappointed. She had expected to feel exultant: a year sober, on a weekend adventure with three very close friends.

"You don't sound like you mean it," observed Rebecca.

Nicole, who was driving, reached over to turn down the volume on the tape of Beethoven's *Ninth Symphony*.

"Come on, Joanna," said Phoebe. "What's going on?"

"I don't know what's wrong with me," she answered.

"I do," said Phoebe. "You're spoiled rotten. Nothing's ever enough for you."

Joanna laughed.

Phoebe continued. "It's okay, sweetheart. You don't have to feel glorious today. You have a right to feel some other things too."

"It's just that . . . I don't know . . . just . . . um," she struggled. "I thought things would be easier after a whole year. I thought they'd be better."

"In what way?" asked Nicole.

"Oh, everything," she answered impatiently. She sighed. "I guess the biggest thing is the economic security. The divorce is driving me crazy. I just want it over. And I do feel spoiled, but the fact is, I used to live a cushier life. I'll probably never have the kind of house I used to live in. I can't count on someone else to take care of me, and it still scares me."

Phoebe, who was sitting in the backseat with Joanna, leaned over and took Joanna's face between her hands. She planted a kiss on her cheek. "Cinderella," she said, "we'll take care of you."

"Oh, Phoebe, I know you will, but you know what I mean."

"I wasn't making fun of you. I do know what you mean, exactly. I'm divorced. Remember? I'm an alcoholic. Remember?"

"It's a slow process," Nicole reminded her from the front seat. "Patience, honey. Even though it's your anniversary, it's just one more day in your recovery. One day at a time.

"It's not an unusual feeling to have, you know," Nicole continued. "I remember feeling the same way on my first anniversary. You think,

'Shouldn't it be easier by now?' But remember, you're just a year out of a long history of drinking. You're doing beautifully." Nicole's voice sounded very sure, and Joanna felt some of her strength restored.

The party was a pleasure. Several friends who had been at Jellinek with Sam and Joanna were there. Sam baked fresh bread for the party, and he greeted Joanna with an embrace. "Remember those fish we painted?" he reminisced.

"I'll never forget them," answered Joanna. "You helped me so much that night."

Yes, she had come a long way this year, she thought. She felt like a whole different person. If it wasn't always easy, at least it was manageable.

On the way to their hotel, several hours later, they drove by the neighborhood where Joanna had lived in college. As they neared the duplex she had lived in, she spied the bar. For a moment she felt her stomach tighten, but as they continued on the street she had walked the night she was raped, she saw that the shrubs were much taller now. She was relieved to see how much everything had changed. Already her stomach was relaxing. *I'm not going to let this get to me,* she thought. She didn't remind her friends.

"Oh look, there's my old house," she told her friends in the car. Laughing, she said, "I'll bet the landlord still hasn't fixed the crack in the kitchen window." As they came closer to it, her eyes fell on the mailbox. She saw its rain-streaked metal and was transported. His breath was on her neck. His dirty fingernails were digging into her skin. She began to shake.

"Are you okay?" asked Rebecca. "You look pale as a ghost."

"Y-y-y-yesss," stuttered Joanna. "N-n-n-no, I don't feel so good."

"What's the matter?"

"I just don't feel too well. That's all."

They drove quietly for a few minutes, and Joanna felt certain she was being watched. They stopped at a convenience store so Nicole and Rebecca could run in for some aspirin. As soon as Phoebe and Joanna were alone in the car, Joanna started sobbing. She gasped for breath. "It's the rape, Phoebe. This is where the rape happened."

"Oh," said Phoebe, understanding Joanna's state. "We're going to get you out of here."

When the other women returned, they drove directly out of the neighborhood. But Joanna felt sicker and sicker. She became dizzy, and sharp lights seemed to flash in her eyes. They had to stop and let Joanna out of the car, where she threw up on the pavement. When they arrived back at the hotel, she was exhausted. She took a hot shower, crawled into bed without drying her hair, and immediately fell to sleep. She awakened from nightmares and was comforted by Phoebe, who was sleeping next to her.

She felt better the next morning. The women breakfasted together, talked about the incident, discussed the possibility of Joanna seeing a therapist, and slowly the nightmare let go of its hold. The rest of the morning she felt normal. They went for a walk along the lake by the university, did a bit of shopping, and, that afternoon, drove home. Phoebe and Rebecca returned to Florida. Jeff brought the girls home, and Joanna tucked them into bed about eight o'clock. Nicole called to make sure she was all right. "Do you want me to come stay with you tonight?" she asked.

"No," Joanna reassured her. "I'm really okay. I feel much better now." But as the silence of the night continued, Joanna felt the dark pressing against her again. She decided to go to bed early and wrapped herself tightly in her covers. About three in the morning she awakened with his breath on her neck. She gasped, stunned. She kept very still, her eyes searching the dark room, until she realized where she was. She turned on her light and called Nicole. After a few minutes, she felt grounded and went back to sleep.

In the morning, she put in a call to Vivian. "My guess is that this is a sign you're ready to deal with the rape at a deeper level," said Vivian. "You may be far enough along in your recovery, and your psyche may feel safe enough, that you can reopen that chapter and do some more healing."

Another Healing

The next day, Joanna called the Center for Ongoing Recovery on the Hazelden campus and set up an appointment with Donna O'Brian, the psychotherapist she had seen when she was in treatment. The center specialized in helping people who were recovering from chemical dependency and who had other mental health issues as well. She made the half-hour drive up to Center City a few days later. Near the end of her session, Donna told her that she agreed with Vivian. It would be a good idea for her to begin more intensive therapeutic work. Her depression seemed stabilized, and Donna believed Joanna could handle facing the effects of the rape.

"There's a high potential for relapse with post-traumatic stress disorder," she explained. She suggested Joanna begin individual therapy on a weekly basis and move into a PTSD therapy group soon. "We also have intensive weekend-long psychoeducational programs here," said Donna. "They're on various topics—depression, anxiety, eating disorders, sexual compulsivity—all the mental health issues that can block progress in recovery. Next weekend, we're having a program on PTSD. You may want to think about attending."

And so Joanna began another journey of healing. She arrived Friday, before 9:00 A.M., for the program and heard a presentation first. She felt a rush of relief, an understanding, as they described some of the symptoms: the recurring nightmares; the dulled feelings or lack of feeling, that utter emptiness she sometimes felt; the difficulty sleeping and concentrating; and, worst of all, the flashbacks. She learned from one of the chemical dependency counselors how PTSD can be a relapse trigger, how as the anxiety grows, people turn to chemicals to assuage the pain and terror.

Joanna had another individual session with Donna as well as a group therapy session, where she heard the experiences of others who were feeling the confusing effects of flashbacks. The recreation therapist taught them relaxation exercises to help them cope with stress and disrupt anxiety attacks. The chaplain, the same one who heard her Fifth Step when she was on Jellinek, led a session on nurturing spiritual growth. She explained that abuse seriously damages people's spiritual life, especially if it continues for a long time. *At least the rape was mercifully short-lived,* thought Joanna, *even if the effects aren't.* A counselor from the family program and a psychiatrist were also in attendance.

There was a discussion of coping mechanisms. Joanna's favorite was the "emergency kit"— a box, basket, or drawer with a rainy-day letter in it to yourself about the progress you've made; your strengths and accomplishments; your hopes for the future; names of supportive people to call and their phone numbers; and handouts to read. She decided she would make a kit the moment she got home. She visited the gym, went swimming in the pool in the Cork Center, and went over to Bigelow Auditorium to attend a lecture and reconnect with old counselors. Before the weekend was over, she had a continuing care plan in place, including weekly visits to a therapist, which she would follow for many months. Slowly, she gained confidence and peace, and her body gradually integrated the memories, so that they didn't ambush her anymore.

As Christmas approached, Joanna was feeling more and more settled. Her Wednesday-night meeting at Day by Day Cafe continued to be her favorite. One particular Wednesday night, with Christmas cookies adorning the table, they talked about acceptance. A young woman spoke about doing Twelfth Step work by going up to Hazelden once a month and talking with the women in primary treatment. She made it a point to walk through Ignatia, she said, and remember how awful she'd felt the day she first arrived, how panicky and empty and physically ill she'd been. "That helps me appreciate what I have now," she said. "I never want to go back to that place."

Another woman, a little older than Joanna, said she struggled a lot with trying to control people, and that it was a setup; it only made her lose her serenity. If she thought someone didn't like her, she'd slap a label on them, she said, like "bitch" or "user." But she'd asked her Higher Power to help her practice acceptance of people, and as she did, a richer world had opened up to her. She'd begun to see the variety of color tones in people, instead of the simple blacks and whites. The thought Joanna enjoyed the most was spoken by another woman, who said she'd discovered that the more she practiced acceptance, the more she was able to feel gratitude. Joanna practiced gratitude every day, thanking her Higher Power before she went to bed for the blessings of that day, and she was discovering that she really did feel the gratitude. She didn't have to "act as if" so often anymore.

She woke up on Christmas morning to a light snow, big, wet flakes that made her imagine she could hear them as they hit the ground. The apartment was quiet; Jeff had taken the girls to his parents' for Christmas. She stretched slowly and reached over to pet the new calico cat, an early gift. She and Stacey and Molly had celebrated two days ago.

Molly's favorite present was the crystal angel that Joanna gave her to hang on the tree. To Stacey she gave a miniature lamb.

She couldn't help but think of Christmas three years ago, the day she entered Hazelden for the first time. It had been frigid, and she had lain sick and terrified in the backseat of the car from her in-laws' house to Center City. She felt a shiver go through her body, a sensation of nausea. Quickly, her mind jumped to Christmas morning of last year, surrounded by the warmth of her friends on the Jellinek unit, but far from her own children. This year, she still could feel the warmth of those friends, and her children were close.

She got up and fixed herself some coffee and went back to her bedroom to meditate. She picked up the two meditation books she relied on most, *The Language of Letting Go* and *A Woman's Spirit*. Today she chose *A Woman's Spirit* and read the entry for December 25. Afterward, she called Jeff and chatted for a while with him, his parents, and her daughters. "I love you, Molly," she said before hanging up. "See you tomorrow."

"I love you too," said Molly.

She got dressed and went to a Christmas Mass, and then she drove home for a luxurious afternoon of reading. She put Pavarotti's *Ave Maria* on the CD player, fixed herself some peppermint tea, and lay down on the couch. On the coffee table next to her was a pot of paper-whites she had gotten for herself. She used to wait for Jeff to buy her flowers when they'd had a fight, a signal she needed from him before she could feel any measure of peace. Now, she thought with pleasure, she could buy flowers for herself, with no strings attached. She noticed the little bell she'd used for the Valentine's party on the day, six months ago, when Molly and Stacey had moved into her apartment. The bell was lying next to Stacey's teddy bear.

Joanna sat up and put her book on the coffee table. She went to her sewing kit and pulled out black thread and scissors. She returned to the living room, picked up the bell, pulled the thread through its little handle, and tied a knot. Pavarotti's voice was soaring into a long, mellow "Maria," and the snow had lessened to light dust in the air. She hung the bell on a branch of the balsam tree, picturing Molly's face bright with excitement during their private, June Valentine's party. "There are so many angels in our lives," she murmured.

15

The Promises

ANDY SAT at the kitchen table in Jenny's apartment. They had just finished eating dinner. In a few weeks, it would be Christmas. Outside the window, snow had piled up and covered the roof and hood of Jenny's car. Tree branches sagged with snow. The snow was falling, too, that day he snuck out of Fellowship Club after midnight. Though he disapproved of that behavior, of not being entirely honest, he was more willing now to accept himself and his shortcomings.

"Get ready! Fifteen inches of that white stuff by the time you wake up tomorrow morning," the broadcaster on WCCO radio announced.

"Did you hear that?" Andy shouted to Jenny in the other room. He felt excited. Surely that much snow would give him the day off from work.

When Jenny came back into the kitchen, she had the Big Book with her. She and Andy had been discussing finances, and their prospects looked gloomy. "This will cheer us up," she said, as she sat back down and opened it to page 83. "Here they are. The promises. I'll read them. Would you mind? It's my favorite passage."

"Sure, it's been a long time since I've heard them. Go ahead, read them," Andy said, leaning back in his chair and glancing once more at the falling snow. The storm had gotten worse. Jenny took a sip of her coffee before reading.

"We are going to know a new freedom and a new happiness," Jenny read. "We will not regret the past nor wish to shut the door on it. . . . We will intuitively know how to handle situations which used to baffle us. We will suddenly realize that God is doing for us what we could not do for ourselves."

"Yeah!" Andy said when Jenny finished and looked up across the table at him. "Since I left Fellowship Club a year ago, a lot of those things have already come true. I don't feel the kind of self-pity I used to about working as a telephone service representative instead of being some prize-winning journalist. Things have happened for me that I couldn't have made happen for myself." Andy walked over to the window and looked out at the snow again. He kept his back to Jenny. "That one about the fear of people and economic insecurity will leave us—that fear still has me," Andy said.

"Me too," Jenny said. Though she was making plans for a new career as a travel agent, she still worked as a waitress at a Mall of America restaurant. She wished they had enough money to afford better things, and perhaps they could move into a nice, large apartment—together. Andy wanted that, too, but he was afraid they couldn't afford anything better.

"We can hardly make it now," he said, reminding her. Andy's entire trust fund, left to him by his father, had been spent on paying for primary and extended treatment at Jellinek. His mother also contributed and helped pay the bills. Hazelden had waived half the cost of Fellowship and loaned him the balance. Andy was still making payments.

"Let's make a wish list," Jenny said. "We'll list all the things we want as a couple, then we'll put the list away and bring it out later." Andy hesitated. "Come on. It'll be fun. At least we'll find out what we want. They'll be the things we promise each other. I would really like a potted plant. Something large, like a Boston fern or a spider plant, to hang from a hook on the ceiling, so it will drape like a green curtain in front of the window. Wouldn't that be nice, especially in the winter?"

"Okay," Andy agreed. "Let's write down everything we need, and it will give us something to work for. Let's pretend it's Christmas and list whatever we want, as if there were a Santa Claus. We'll list the plants first." Andy felt excited; he took out a pen and some scratch paper and wrote, "Plants: ferns and spiders."

Before they had gone to bed that evening, they had listed over twenty items. Each item had a box to check, and the list was posted under a magnet on Jenny's refrigerator: queen-size bed, sneakers, armchair, end table, basketball, lacrosse equipment, a dog, dresser, bikes, desk chair, stereo, compact discs, tapes, computer, VCR, pool table. The prices were listed, except for the expensive items, like a car, an apartment together, and a trip south during the winter. They put asterisks by these items. Andy wanted the computer, since he started freelancing and writing magazine articles. They both wanted a vcr for snow-laden nights. And Andy had added the pool table. He had learned to shoot pool in treatment and had become an avid fan of the game.

The total price was $2,875 and it could have been ten times that amount for all that Andy could afford. He didn't even own a credit card. No bank would issue him a card. The time he fraudulently used an American Express card to finance his crack habit had sabotaged his credit rating. Andy couldn't even open a checking or savings account in any of the Twin Cities banks.

Before going to bed that night, Andy went back into the kitchen for a glass of milk. As he opened the refrigerator, he glanced at the list. It felt discouraging; there were so many things they wanted with so little money to pay for them.

He looked outside and noticed what seemed like another six inches of snow on top of Jenny's car. He loved how white and fresh everything looked. The snow swirling under the streetlights reminded him again of the early morning he ran from Fellowship Club to Jenny's apartment. It seemed like a million years ago. He drank the milk, set it on the counter, then glanced again at the list. "Tomorrow," he said out loud, after deciding he would take some money from his savings, walk to the florist, and buy a fern for Jenny. It would be a present for no other reason but that he loved her.

Continuing Care

Andy swung open the back door to Fellowship Club and stomped the snow off his shoes in the lounge area. He had arrived for the weekly transition group meeting. A small group of ten men and women who had been patients at Fellowship Club met each Thursday evening in the dining hall to discuss their living situations, jobs, relationships, room-mates, or the relapses of friends. Andy could attend the meeting for as long as he wanted, and it seemed like a good place for him to discuss practical issues and get guidance.

"Hey, Andy," one of his friends called out. "How are ya? What's new?"

"Fine. But I'm glad I'm not washing those dishes anymore," Andy said, motioning to a patient who was taking out dishes from the washer. The patient reminded Andy of himself, of the days he worked hard to be part of the recovering group. That was another reason he liked returning on Thursdays for continuing care. It reminded him of how far he had come, how much he had grown.

The meetings always started with a Serenity Prayer, as they did in the Alcoholics Anonymous meetings that Andy attended on Mondays and Wednesdays. Billy was the moderator of the group. He had been sober for three years, and he facilitated the group as a volunteer in order to be of service to others, as he was encouraged to do in the Twelfth Step.

"Andy, how did you do on your commitments?" he asked. Commitments were promises people in the group made to each other to do something concrete about a particular problem or concern. Andy had agreed to contact two additional banks to see if he could get a checking account started.

"Well, I visited two banks, First Bank and Norwest, and both turned me down."

"Try Cherokee Bank up the street," Betty said. She was a patient who had left Fellowship Club a couple of months before Andy. "I know one of the managers there. Mention my name. If you explain your situation, he might let you open an account."

Andy made another commitment and said he would try the bank that week. He was glad the group focused on situations, not on feelings like anger and shame, resentment and despair, as he did when he was in treatment. Andy wasn't struggling with his feelings anymore, but more with practical things, and he appreciated the help and focus from the group.

The following Monday, just an hour before Andy left his apartment to visit Betty's friend at Cherokee Bank, the phone rang.

"Is Andy there?" the voice asked when Andy picked up the phone.

"Speaking."

"Andy, this is Janet Chesterton from Hazelden. I'm the clinical case manager in charge of your file. We talked last week about our new study."

"Sure, how are you?" Andy said. He had agreed to be a part of a pilot study for a clinical case management system that would be implemented the following year at Hazelden. It would involve case managers who called patients, with their permission, after they had left Hazelden. They would be called during the first and second week after treatment, then once during the first, second, and third month, and afterward, intermittently until two years had passed. The case manager was to ask patients about their recovery and sobriety, give encouragement and contacts, if any were needed. As part of the pilot study, Andy had been called just weeks after he left Fellowship Club.

"Are you still going to AA meetings?" Janet asked.

"Absolutely. I have two meetings a week that I go to. I wouldn't miss them. I attend a Friday-night open meeting at Fellowship Club too."

"I assume you're still sober?"

"For sure. If I weren't, I wouldn't be answering the phone now. Without sobriety, I would probably be dead or robbing homes to get money to support my habit."

Janet asked Andy a number of questions concerning his attendance at AA, if he had a sponsor and was seeing him, about his continuing care meeting at Fellowship Club, if he was at all worried about his bill from treatment, and even how his mother was doing. She recorded all his replies into a computerized program, which would signal her when she needed to call Andy next.

"Andy," she said, "it says here that you have some interest in computers and the Internet. Did you know that they now have online AA meetings? Hazelden will probably have their own, or a kind of chat room for alumni, in the near future."

"Really, that sounds interesting. I'm hoping that someday I'll be able to afford my own computer, and I'll be sure to check out those Internet sites. Thanks." Andy liked Janet; she was one of the first people he met at Hazelden. He was glad to have her for his clinical case manager.

After hanging up, Andy left his apartment for the bank. After talking with the manager, he was allowed to open up a savings account, but not a checking account. "However, if within a year," the manager told him, "you maintain this account without any trouble, you can have a checking account with us." It would be his first since he left New York City.

The people in transition group were elated to hear the news. Opening a savings account didn't mean much to most people, but to Andy it signaled another step in his recovery. Five months later, in May, when temperatures began more regularly to reach the seventies and tulips bloomed in the flower beds bordering Fellowship Club, Andy attended his last transition group meeting.

"I won't be coming back," he told the group. "I'll miss all of you, but league softball starts at Shoppers. I'm going to play on their coed, slow-pitch team at Battle Creek Park, and all our games and practices are scheduled on Thursday evenings. When I can, I'll stop back to visit."

Play Ball!

Their first game was scheduled for the end of May. Andy played center field for the team. He was no longer working at entry level as a telephone service representative, or TSR. He had received a promotion and was working as a seasonal team leader. He monitored a group of TSRs who took customer calls as he once had. Andy was hopeful of another promotion. Not long after the holidays were over, he was offered a permanent position as day-shift assistant. Now that he had turned his seasonal position into a regular position, Andy felt more job security.

Three-fourths of the softball team were TSRs. It seemed to Andy that everyone was overqualified and underpaid. All were going through some important transition in their lives and were working temporarily at Shoppers. Some were from Fellowship Club and were in recovery. Johnny, who was playing second base, was from Fellowship Club. He had asked Andy to sponsor him, and Andy looked after him as he would a younger brother. Others on the team included stockbrokers who had gotten laid off, students working their way through graduate school, mothers whose children had left home. They were all going through an intense career renewal, and it seemed to bond and energize the players.

"Play ball!" the umpire hollered. Andy and Johnny ran out onto the field together. As the game went on, players drank pop, mineral water, or beer they had brought in a cooler. No one got drunk. When the team came in to bat, Andy sat on the bench next to one of the TSRs, a man named Harry, who sipped from a beer can. Andy liked him, and he appreciated the extra effort Harry always made at work. He congratulated Harry for making a leaping catch of a line drive that would have gone for a double if he hadn't caught it. "What a catch," Andy said, slapping him on the back.

Andy stretched out his legs. The sky was darkening, and the stadium lights had gone on. He loved the smell of fresh grass and dust and the sound of hands smacking leather gloves, the crack of the bat. Even the smell of the beer. Strangely, it didn't trouble him.

Andy was still amazed that people could drink a beer or two during or after the game, and that drinking wasn't the primary focus of what they were doing. He wondered how anyone could sip from one can of beer for hours.

Andy and the team won their first game of the season. He was glad, but it didn't really matter to him whether they won or lost. Sober, he was playing more than just a game, and loving every minute of it.

Throughout his life, recreational sports had always been important for Andy's sense of self-esteem and well-being. When he began drinking and using drugs, he had lost all interest in sports. The activities eventually got in the way of using drugs. Now, in his thirties, Andy was returning to sports, and after having played coed softball, he was moving in the direction of more competitive men's sports.

The following year, Andy would join the 3M soccer team, playing outdoors in the summer and indoors in the winter. Andy fit in well with the soccer group, many of whom were older than he. However, the Minneapolis lacrosse team was different. A game of Native American origin with ten players on each team, they used a long-handled stick with a webbed pouch to pitch a ball into the opposing team's goal. As the oldest member of the team, Andy found himself struggling to prove himself among the younger athletes.

Andy hadn't been playing for the team for more than a few weeks when one of his teammates, Ron, bumped him hard during a practice. Andy raced at him. It seemed that Andy had not moved one inch from the spot where he had stood, nose to nose, with Billy on the basketball court in Jellinek. This time, Andy leaped at Ron, and they wrestled on the ground and swung at each other until teammates pulled them apart. The coach was furious, sending both of them home immediately.

From his apartment, Andy called his sponsor, Brian, and the two men met for coffee. "I've got a long way to go, don't I?" he said sadly to Brian.

Brian smiled. "You've come a long way, Andy. Remember that. And remember the Tenth Step: '[We] continued to take personal inventory and when we were wrong promptly admitted it.' So tomorrow at practice an apology might be in order."

The next evening, before the entire team left the locker room to begin practice, Andy stood in the middle of the room and announced, "I have something to say to Ron and the whole team. . . . "

"Made a Decision . . ."

It was June 1993 when, with the help of numerous friends, Andy and Jenny moved in together. The apartment was a small one-bedroom, not far from Macalester College and the Uptown house, where Andy went to AA. A friend from one of his meetings had told him about the apartment with affordable rent. Andy set up his computer on the small dining room table, and Jenny hung her Boston fern from a hook above the kitchen window, which allowed the plant's stems to arch and color the window green. The bedroom was so small that a bed and dresser could barely fit. The kitchen area barely allowed for two people to cook and wash dishes at the same time. Still, it was theirs, and they were both happy to have a place of their own, where they could keep the puppy they found at the animal shelter.

Months later, when Christmas arrived, they discovered they couldn't fit a tree into the apartment. Instead, they had to hang wreaths and string lights throughout the small apartment. By then, Jenny had quit her job waitressing and was being trained as a travel agent for a large travel agency. She had met the owner at an AA meeting, demonstrating once again how the network of fellowship worked for them in recovery.

Andy continued working at Shoppers. Though he supervised a number of men and women who worked in the call center, he now had a life after work that was just as important as his work life. He had begun to do more service work for Alcoholics Anonymous, socialized more with his lacrosse team, and most important, there was Jenny. By now, Andy had been away from treatment for a while, and new patients at Fellowship Club who worked at Shoppers saw him as a role model, someone who held the promise of serenity and success in recovery.

"I got it! I got an interview for the job!" Andy hollered from the kitchen one evening. Jenny was in the living room reading. Andy was sorting out the mail and had opened a letter. It was from a small, bimonthly community newspaper in southwest St. Paul. "Look," he said, waving the letter as he walked into the living room. "They want to interview me."

While working at Shoppers, Andy had continued applying for editing and writing jobs with different newspapers. He still wanted to get back into journalism. Now, he was a finalist for a full-time editor's position at the newspaper. "I'm so happy," he said that night.

The next day he called to arrange for an interview with the publisher, and though he would later discover that he wasn't picked for the job, they still wanted him to freelance articles for the paper. In less than two months, Andy was writing two or three articles a month while he still worked at Shoppers. At their apartment, weeklies and publications that featured his articles were piled on the floor alongside the computer desk.

One month later, Andy cut back to twenty-five hours at Shoppers and gave up his supervisor position for a more regular customer service job. Though the pay was less, without benefits or health insurance, it gave him flexible hours, which enabled him to venture further on the road to freelance writing. It was risky, but everything about recovery was a risk, and he had learned to measure and carefully consider each choice he was presented with. The only thing he wouldn't risk was his sobriety. His busy schedule only allowed him two AA meetings a week, but he was still able to sponsor Fellowship Club patients at Shoppers.

One afternoon, Andy met with the Shoppers director of public relations. "I have a great idea, one which will provide the continuity and community that you are always striving to create here at Shoppers. What if I agreed to lay out, write, typeset, and take photos for an eight-page employee newsletter. It would come out once a month and feature articles on employees of the month, connecting all the workers in the call center and warehouse."

The director thought it was a great idea, and days later talked with him again. "We've discussed this idea of yours and like it. But we want one issue every other month, instead of every month as you proposed. If you coupled that work with additional work we'd assign you in public relations, then we might be able to swing a deal." Andy agreed. Soon he was writing the newsletter and working on new ways to use the media to advertise Shopper's mail-order catalogs.

Two months later, Andy was offered a full-time position as a media relations coordinator. When Andy balked, after considering all the freelance work he was doing for other publications, Shoppers sweetened the offer. They would promote him to public relations manager for the catalog's marketing division, which included a 60 percent pay increase.

Andy could hardly believe the offer. "The job is yours if you want it," the manager said to him.

Andy was overwhelmed. It was a whirlwind, and he felt pulled in many directions. "This is a wonderful offer. I can't resist. But let me think about it over the weekend, and I'll give you my decision on Monday."

He met Brian twice that weekend at a coffee shop to discuss the offer. "I just don't know what to do," he said. "If I take the job, I will have to give up all the freelance writing I've been doing. I'm right at that point of getting a better, more reliable position, perhaps an editorial position.

Brian took a sip of his coffee. "And what does Shoppers offer that freelance writing doesn't?" Brian asked.

"Shoppers gives me guaranteed job security, good weekly pay, health insurance, and vacation pay. That kind of stability would let me think more realistically about marriage and maybe a family someday." Andy and Jenny had begun talking about marriage and how much they would like to have children.

"I have to admit," Andy said, "some of my old using behavior has come up. I feel a little arrogant at times, as if being successful makes me better than others. I hate that feeling, but it's there sometimes. I might be walking out the door at Shoppers, headed for my car in the parking lot, and I see a young man walking in for the second shift at the call center. 'I'm glad I'm not him,' I say to myself, as if I were better.

"I sometimes feel like I've wasted my life. And this problem now, this having to decide between two jobs or directions, between writing as a freelancer or settling down for an eight-to-five job, is a consequence of my addiction. If I hadn't been using all those years, if I had worked more conscientiously all my life like most people do, I wouldn't be in this jam. I might have come to it long ago and have resolved the matter. But here I am, stuck."

Andy had always wanted to write, to be his own boss, to compose articles and essays that would challenge the status quo. Freelancing gave him the opportunity to write passionately about the people and places he cared about. If he took the job at Shoppers, he wouldn't have much time to write anything but corporate copy.

Brian ordered refills and a blueberry muffin. "Andy," he said, "you are facing what many people have to come to terms with in their careers. You can no longer afford to be the darling rebel who drank and drugged whenever he wanted. That kind of freedom will take you straight to hell. The other road, which gets narrower and narrower as you go, is far more difficult. Whatever you decide, it will require hard work, long hours, and sobriety. Trust yourself. You can go anywhere you want and take risks, because with sobriety and the Twelve Steps of AA you can always correct what has gone wrong and make amends. Your compass will always point you back, even if it feels like you're spinning in circles and have lost your direction."

It was uncanny how similar the two men's lives had been. Brian, too, had left his career in Atlanta and had come to work at Shoppers from Fellowship Club. Brian, like Andy, had found ways to improve Shoppers by linking their three hundred computers into a network, and eventually, he was promoted to vice president of information systems.

"I have to decide," Andy said, finishing his coffee.

"Maybe you don't."

"What do you mean?" Andy said, puzzled.

"Well, maybe you've already decided, and all you have to do is realize that decision."

"Sounds kind of Freudian to me."

"No, not really. You know what is best here. Trust yourself. When you walk into the Shoppers office Monday, what you should decide will be perfectly clear. Remember: '[We] made a decision to turn our will and lives over to the care of God *as we understood [God]*.' Your most important decision has already been made. The rest will fall into place."

Andy smiled. "Come on," he said, feeling relieved. "Let's go for a walk."

That Saturday night, Andy and Jenny stayed at home. They talked about finding another place, a larger one to rent, getting a second dog, Andy taking a new job, about writing and reading, about marriage.

He had heard many times at meetings that you don't always get what you want, but you will get what you need. He felt certain now that whatever he decided, it would work out. Before going to bed that night, he felt a confidence in himself and in others, in people like Brian and Jenny, whom he had come to love. No matter what he decided, whether he would return to work full time in public relations or continue developing his career as a freelance writer, it would be the right thing. His friends and Jenny would help him through, either way. It wasn't really a question of right versus wrong, good versus bad. His sobriety and relationships would sustain him, no matter what. *Brian was right*, he thought to himself as he kissed Jenny goodnight. *I'll know Monday what to do.*

Birth

By March 1994, AA had become less about Andy's urges to use and more about his daily life, the simple and sometimes complicated decisions everyone makes each day of his or her life. Whether he would go to the grocery after work, whether he or Jenny was cooking supper that evening, what movie they would go to on the weekend, simple things like these occupied his daily thoughts. Andy didn't take simple things for granted, nor did he forget where he had been not long ago. His eight o'clock AA meeting kept him connected to his past, and now he did not "wish to shut the door on it." AA helped him remember that he was an alcoholic and drug addict. No matter how well or how poorly things went, he didn't want to forget that sobriety was his priority, without which he could have nothing else. He knew the equation. Drink + Drugs = Death.

On November 5, 1994, Andy and Jenny were married. Three of the six bride attendants, as well as the groom attendants, were recovering people from St. Paul. Brian, his sponsor and best friend all these years, was his best man.

Less than two years later, Jenny and Andy moved into a house near an elementary school and park in south Minneapolis. Andy got a loan for the down payment from a local bank. The lacrosse team helped move them into their new house. Two days after they moved in, their first child was born, Robert Andrew Monroe.

"Hi, my name is Andy, and I'm chemically dependent," Andy said, starting his presentation at Bigelow Auditorium at Hazelden. He glanced up at the projection room where he once sat as a patient, producing videos for the closed-circuit television. "I used to tap the screen, making the video jiggle for the patients in Ignatia Hall, who, I imagine, got woozy from watching it shake." The crowd of men and women, many from Shoemaker, where Andy had spent his first four weeks in treatment, laughed.

This wasn't Andy's first return home. He was now leading transition groups as a facilitator for Fellowship Club, and he had occasionally talked at Friday open meetings. He had also spoken at Ramsey County detox. He felt obligated to return the generosity he had received from AA members in the community. Soon, Andy's responsibilities as a father and his duties at work wouldn't allow him the extra time he needed to do volunteer work. But, while he had the time, he would give it.

"When I first got sober," Andy said, starting his presentation as the evening outside AA lecturer, "I couldn't imagine what was in store for me. . . ."

That evening, when he returned home from the long ride, nearly an hour from Hazelden, Jenny greeted him at the door. "You wouldn't believe what I found," she said.

"First, tell me how Bobby is," Andy said anxiously.

"Oh, he's fast asleep. Come here. Look at this."

While unpacking boxes from the move, Jenny had found the wish list they had written in her old apartment.

"Oh, my gosh," Andy exclaimed. Together they went over the list again. They had everything they had dreamed of, and even more. They had two dogs. Andy had long ago gotten lacrosse equipment, and they had a queen-size bed and a bedroom with plenty of space for it. The only things they didn't have were the pool table and a trip to the Caribbean. But Andy did have a finished basement and room for a table if he wanted one. He had taken one trip to the Caribbean in his life, and that was enough for him.

When they went to bed that night, Andy stood a moment at the crib, watching Bobby sleep. He seemed so fragile. "If we were to make a wish list now, what would you put on it?" he asked Jenny, who was already in bed.

"Oh, I don't know," she said.

"Come on, really, what would you put on it?"

"Hmmm. Let me think. I guess we could use a new bedspread."

"Do you know what I'd put on the list?" he said.

"What?" she asked.

"Nothing, absolutely nothing. At this moment I have everything I'll ever need."

Alive and Free

ON A FRIDAY AFTERNOON in the first days of May, the clouds scurry across the sun, making the day alternately chilly and balmy. At Center City, the Hazelden campus is teeming with activity. Three hundred alumni are expected over the weekend for the annual "Alive and Free" celebration of recovery. People come from across the Upper Midwest, and from as far away as New York, Texas, Florida, California, Oregon, even Sweden and India.

Pots of geraniums, red, pink, white, and salmon, ordered for the spring planting, have been placed generously throughout the buildings on campus, securing a sense of abundance. Registration tables are set up in the Renewal Center, the sprawling retreat center on the south reaches of the grounds. Schedules printed on royal blue paper announce the keynote speakers, the workshops, the banquet, and the dance.

At three in the afternoon, Andy Monroe and his wife pull into the parking lot. He is excited. This is the second time he has attended the celebratory event. He leans over and pats his wife's knee and says, "Jenny, you're going to love this." When he climbs out of the car, his eyes scan the campus, taking in the Cork Center, where he once learned a difficult lesson in moderation; the dining room, where he rang the brass bell that signaled the beginning of his recovery; and in the far distance, Jellinek, where he had finally come to understand that he was truly loved and would always have company and comfort on this journey.

"Andy," says Jenny, "shall we register before we go visit our old treatment units?"

"Sure. Yeah. Let's." He is suddenly preoccupied with how he will feel when he walks onto the Shoemaker unit. When Andy finally winds his way through the long hallways between the dining room and Shoemaker, he sees a new patient, his skin sallow and his movements jittery. It reminds Andy of the night he moved into his room on the unit, feeling sick and utterly alone. "Thank God," he says under his breath. The sight of his old counselor, sitting at the desk in his office, gives Andy quick reassurance.

"Steve," says Andy, sticking his head around the corner.

"Hey, how are you, man?" Steve welcomes Andy with an outstretched hand.

"You back for the big weekend?"

Andy smiles and nods.

"It's so good to see you. How are you doing? You look great!" exclaims Steve.

"Good," Andy grins. "Good. I'm really good."

After dinner, Andy and Jenny go over to the vaulted atrium in the Cork Center for the welcoming ceremony. The mood in the expansive room is bright. There are probably 150 people already sitting in folding chairs. A master of ceremonies is at the microphone, and laughter ripples through the room. After the welcome and introductions and housekeeping remarks, the MC announces that they will break into groups for AA. "We'll count off by fourteen," he instructs, "but first, we're going to observe a long tradition here. Everyone please stand up." Andy looks at Jenny, motions for her to stand with him.

"Now, everyone who has thirty days of sobriety, please sit down." A handful of people sit, and the room erupts in applause for them. About twenty more people sit down for the ninety-day mark, and another twenty or so for the six-month mark. When the MC calls out to anyone between one and two years, a thirtysomething woman with shoulder-length dark hair sits. Satisfaction stirs in Joanna Thomsen's chest when she hears the thundering applause. It says to her that she has a place in this family now.

The applause continues through the two-year mark, the three-year mark, and Andy notices Jack Carlson, who graduated from Shoemaker with him. *Why only three years?* he wonders. *He must have relapsed.* The mounting euphoria of the evening is briefly punctured for Andy. After the four-year mark, almost a third of the room is seated. When the MC announces five years, Andy smiles at Jenny, squeezes her hand, and sits down. Jenny sits at six years. The applause ebbs and flows as the MC intones, "seven years, eight . . . seventeen years, eighteen," and the room is left with two people still standing.

Saturday morning, as Andy and Jenny are rising in their room at the Renewal Center, Nate Radcliffe is waking up in Northfield, almost two hours south of Center City. He groans as he thinks about the paper that is due Monday, the paper he only started yesterday. Midterms are beginning next week. In a little over a month, he will have finished his freshman year in good academic standing. He had been running scared during the first term, even the second, but by the end of winter, he knew he could make the grades.

He is taking a computer graphics class this term. He loves it and thinks it might make a good major. But he is excited for a break. He is looking forward to moving back in with his aunt and uncle in Edina for the summer. The supermarket said he could have his old job back, and he is going to coach soccer again and also spend more time with Pam. But first he is going to California for a couple weeks. He thinks about the summer he went home right after treatment, how shocking it had been to discover school was more difficult straight than stoned, and how he'd felt a general agitation morning, noon, and night, cravings for marijuana when he watched his old buddies on the corner after school.

He looks around his crowded room, at the books piled on his desk. He begins to hum "California Dreamin' " to himself. He climbs out of bed, pulls on a pair of pants and a sweatshirt, and walks down the hall to the bathroom.

In Ames, Iowa, Elizabeth Toggen stands at her kitchen window contemplating the day. Spring comes a few weeks earlier to Ames than to Center City, and she delights in the showy tulips growing under the greening aspen in her backyard. She added a new color last fall, digging the Dutch bulbs into the rich, dark loam in September. The velvet red brings depth and counterpoint to the silvery lavenders and yellows that she put in a couple of years ago. And now they are swelling open, almost bursting, some of their petals lost already, gracing the ground like summer's version of snow.

"Thank you for this glorious morning," she says going through her morning ritual, opening her arms to let in the universe. "Thank you for tulips, both blooming and spent. Thank you for the fragile scent of lilac coming in my window. Thank you for friends, and thank you for another day of sobriety."

Liz's hip aches this morning, and she is acutely aware of how much she misses Jonathan. She is startled when the phone rings. She walks across the kitchen to answer.

"Liz, it's Vera."

"Oh, Vera, how lovely to hear from you."

"I hope it's not too early to call. I went to the sunrise AA meeting on the beach this morning, and I just kept thinking about you. The gulls were calling, and I was remembering how you and Jonathan would feed them chunks of bread after our meetings and how you'd delight in the shapes of their wings. So . . ."

"It's not a bit too early, Vera. I can't sleep late these days, no matter how late I've been up the night before. Except for a little arthritis, I'm doing very well."

"Well, I wanted to tell you that I'm going to be able to come up for the International Women's AA Conference in Minneapolis."

"That's wonderful!" Liz's voice is energized. "Thank God for old friends."

"Did you say 'thank God'?" Vera asks.

Liz chuckles at her teasing. "A figure of speech, Vera."

At 7:30 A.M. Joanna is driving from her apartment toward Center City for her second day at the annual celebration of recovery. Rebecca, an old friend from both Jellinek and Fellowship, has flown in from Florida for the party and is staying with Joanna. Joanna glances over to see Rebecca's head tilted back against the seat, her eyes closed against the morning sun.

"Can it really be less than a year since we left Fellowship?" Joanna asks after taking a sip of coffee from her thermos. When they turn onto the familiar winding road that will open onto the vista of lake and lawn, she adds, "Every time I drive on this road, I remember that first time I came here, lying in the backseat, terrified, humiliated, and sick."

"Amazing how much has happened in such a short time," says Rebecca. "You really like your new job, don't you?" Joanna had gotten a part-time job in February as a library assistant.

"I love it. I love how quiet and orderly it is," she muses.

In the evening the banquet is opulent, the dining hall transformed with multicolored linens and geraniums everywhere. Bouquets of tulips brighten the hors d'oeuvres table.

About seven o'clock, the two women drift over to the Cork Center atrium. The band is set up on the far side of the arching room, playing ragtime. Joanna is feeling unsettled. She's always felt self-conscious dancing, but at least she no longer needs alcohol to fuel her arms and legs. She looks around nervously, her arms feeling awkward at her sides, and she wonders if the old craving will hit her. A well-known AA speaker from New York walks to the microphone, and the band hushes.

"Welcome, everyone, to 'Alive and Free.' How're you feeling tonight?"

Clapping echoes through the room. When it calms down, the speaker continues. "I went through treatment on the Cronin unit twelve years ago, and it's great to be back. It's been a good twelve years, and it's been a good day. We've done some pretty important sharing in the workshops, learned some new things, remembered some old things. But you know, the real point of this weekend is what's coming up. Having fun."

Again the atrium erupts in applause. Enthusiastic whoops are called out from the other side of the room. Joanna finds herself smiling in spite of her nervousness. "Dancing sober has a lot of meaning for us," he continues. "How many of us used to feel uncomfortable in our own skins, so uncomfortable that we couldn't be at a party without getting oiled with alcohol? Or cocaine? Or something else? This, folks, this is a real mark of recovery. Knowing how to just plain have fun without the help of chemicals. So go for it."

Joanna can still taste the chocolate dessert on her tongue. She turns to Rebecca. "So? Are you going to go for it, or do you feel as awkward as I do?" But as the evening wears on and the band plays "The Maple Leaf Rag" and "The Sunflower Slow Drag," and they learn the Charleston with a group of other novices; as the helium balloons slowly lose their buoyancy and hover lower over the crowd; as her body becomes buoyant with the elation of fun and she does the kicks and twirls, Joanna feels as luminous as the round moon hanging like a medallion in the western sky.

INDEX

Minnesota Multiphasic Personality Inventory test, 51, 91
moderation, 122–23
Monroe, Andy, 1, 5
  beginning treatment, 6
  extended care, 117–30
  halfway house, 167–80
  relapse of, 7–8, 11–17
  sobriety, 235–47, 249–50
  telling his story, 75–76
  treatment plans, 80–81, 119, 122
  work issues, 167–70, 172–73,
    235–36, 240, 244

N

Novak, Thomas, 117, 119–20, 126–27,
  168

O

O'Brian, Donna, 91–92, 100, 138,
  230–31
One Day at a Time, 44, 87
outpatient treatments, 103, 115, 199

P

perfectionism, 52, 64
Peterson, Marilyn, 148–49
phenobarbital, 25, 86, 88
post-traumatic stress disorder, 92, 138,
  231
powerlessness
  admitting, 80, 85, 95, 97, 99, 132,
    138, 152, 168, 193
prayers
  agnostics and, 104–8, 114, 201–2,
    207, 251
  Lord's Prayer, 53, 104–8
  Serenity Prayer, 44, 63, 70, 87, 98,
    107, 114, 221, 238
  treatment plan and, 80–81, 83, 188,
    192
Prohibition, 36, 38
psilocybin mushrooms, 45

R

Radcliffe, David, 181, 184, 196
Radcliffe, Gloria, 181–84, 186, 192,
  195–97
Radcliffe, Nathaniel (Nate), 1
  entering treatment, 40–44
  primary treatment, 51–70
  sobriety, 181–98, 251
  telling his story, 58–61

Radcliffe, Theodore (Ted), 41–44, 46,
  181–84, 186–87, 192, 195–97
rape, 18–19, 90–94, 100, 229–31
recovery
  AA meetings, 100, 156, 163–64, 171,
    185–88, 190–98, 219, 225–26,
    232, 238–39, 246
  family members, xi
  groups, 186
  responsibility for, 183, 198
  work and, 170
relapse trigger, 93, 98, 111, 224, 231
relapses, 168, 250
  controlled use, 68, 110–11
  halfway house, 168
  post-traumatic stress disorder, 231
  signs of, 186, 190–91, 224–25
  stories of, 7–17, 20–22, 131–34, 152,
    228
religion
  treatment and, 104–10
  See also agnosticism; Higher Power;
    prayers; spirituality
Renewal Center, 249, 251

S

Second Sunday, 226
seizures, 11, 25, 82
Senior Peer, 72
Serenity Prayer
  agnostics and, 107, 201, 202, 207
  calming power of, 162, 221
  in group meetings, 44, 63, 70, 87,
    98, 107, 114, 238
sexual abuse, 18–19, 57, 90–94, 100,
  229–31
shame, 60, 85, 146, 220–21
Shoemaker Hall, 32, 71, 74, 77, 82, 117,
  145, 247, 249
Shoemaker, Samuel, 71
Shoppers, 169–73, 240, 242–44
Significant Event Sheets, 91
Singer, Ruth, 121, 125
sober houses, 177
Sober Seniors' meetings, 104, 199
sobriety anniversaries, 227–28, 250
Sobriety High, 186–89, 194
social drinking, 18, 19
Spiritual Odyssey, 130
spirituality
  Alcoholics Anonymous and, 107–10,
    201
  awakening, 148–49, 171